# Structuralism

*Other Titles*

**DIALECTIC AND DIFFERENCE** by Jacques Taminiaux, translated by James
Decker and Robert  Crease
**THE QUESTION OF LANGUAGE IN HEIDEGGER'S HISTORY OF BEING**
by Robert Bernasconi
**UTOPICS: SPATIAL PLAY** by Louis Marin translated by Robert Vollrath
**SEEING AND READING** by Graeme Nicholson
**BEYOND METAPHYSICS?** by John Llewelyn
**THE LANGUAGE OF DIFFERENCE** by Charles Scott
**MARTIN HEIDEGGER'S PATH OF THINKING** by Otto Poggeler translated
by Dan Magurshak and Sigmund Barber
**IN THE PRESENCE OF THE SENSUOUS: Essays in Aesthetics** by Mikel
Dufrenne translated by Mark S. Roberts and Dennis Gallagher

*Forthcoming*

**THE DECONSTRUCTION OF TIME** by David Wood

# Structuralism

## The Art of the Intelligible

PETER CAWS

Humanities Press International, Inc.
Atlantic Highlands, NJ

First published in 1988 in the United States of America by
HUMANITIES PRESS INTERNATIONAL, INC., Atlantic Highlands,
NJ 07716

©Humanities Press International, Inc., 1988

**Library of Congress Cataloging-in-Publication Data**

Caws, Peter.
  Structuralism : the art of the intelligible / Peter Caws.
    p.  cm. — (Contemporary Studies in philosophy and the human
sciences)
  Bibliography: p.
  Includes index.
  ISBN 0–391–02740–9 : $39.95 (est.)
  1. Structuralism.  I. Title.  II. Series.
B841.4.C39 1988
149'.96—dc19                                          87–24407
                                                         CIP

Printed in the United States of America

*N. A. B., M.D.*
*principium felicitatis*

# Contents

*Preface*                                              xiii

**Introduction**                                          1

   1. What structuralism is                1

   2. Situation and plan of the work       2

   3. The concept of structure             4

   4. Structure and intelligibility        6

PART IA—ASPECTS OF THE STRUCTURALIST MOVEMENT

**1  Convergence**                             11

   5. Beginnings                           11

   6. System and structure                 12

   7. Bourbaki and group structure         14

   8. Cassirer and the "symbolic forms"    16

**2  Structuralism in France**                 21

   9. Paris fashions                       21

   10. Mind in its natural state           23

   11. Structural transformations          26

   12. Stability and subjectivity          28

   13. The word of the patient             30

   14. The end of man                      32

15. Critical work                                            34

16. Complexity and humanity                                  36


**3   Structuralism in America                              41**

17. The New World and the postwar period                    41

18. Morgan and Peirce                                        43

19. Structural linguistics                                  45

20. Structural anthropology                                 49

21. Structure and violence                                  51

22. Criticism, new and even newer                           53


PART IB—LANGUAGE AND THE HUMAN SCIENCES


**4   The Linguistic Base I: The Cours de linguistique générale   59**

23. The natural history of language                          59

24. Language as system                                       62

25. *Langue* and *parole*                                   66

26. The doctrine of the sign                                70

27. Interpretation and linguistic value                     76

28. A Saussurean aberration: the anagrams                   80


**5   The Linguistic Base II: After Saussure                83**

29. The structure of the system                             83

30. Oppositions                                             86

31. Double articulation                                     89

32. From distinctive features to free discourse             92

33. Distributive and mathematical structure                 95

34. Diachrony and the acquisition of language              100

35. Formalism and complexity                           105

6  The Social Superstructure                          109

36. Semiotics, linguistics, structuralism             109
37. Signs without language                            114
38. The mythical structure of the world               116
39. Relations in society                              121
40. Individuals and idiosyncrasies                    124
41. The human family                                  127
42. The exchange of gifts                             130
43. The prohibition of incest                         133
44. Structure and sentiment                           137
45. The reality of social structure                   141

7  Humanistic Structures and Deconstructions          145

46. The humanities and the human sciences             145
47. History as archaeology                            149
48. Varieties of religious belief                     155
49. The practice of writing                           159
50. A short course in deconstruction                  161

PART II—STRUCTURALISM AS PHILOSOPHY

8  Structure as a Necessary and Sufficient Condition of
   Intelligibility                                    169

51. Structuralism and philosophy                      169
52. Russell and the structure of relations            171
53. Carnap and structural descriptions                175
54. Wittgenstein on form and structure                177

## 9 Meaning in Life, Language, and Philosophy — 183

55. Meaning and the signiferous — 183

56. The delusion of global meaning — 185

57. The life of meaning — 186

58. Meaning in thought and language — 189

59. The language of philosophy — 194

## 10 Mind, Structure, and System — 197

60. System building — 197

61. Local and global systems — 200

62. Necessitation and accommodation — 204

63. The multiplicity of mind — 208

64. Apposition and mental structure — 212

65. Instruction and optimum complexity — 215

## 11 Human Nature and Society — 219

66. The distribution of structures — 219

67. Operational and representational models — 220

68. Explanatory models and social structures — 226

69. Models and mind-dependence — 230

## 12 Structuralism, Materialism, and Phenomenology — 237

70. Singularity and incompleteness in systematic description — 237

71. The persistence of the subject — 239

72. The stuff of the world — 241

73. The insistence of materialism — 242

74. The world of relations                                    246

75. Subjectivity and structural materialism                   250

**Postscript on Poststructuralism**                           **253**

76. Macaulay's anchor                                         253

77. Synchronicity                                            256

78. The poststructuralist scene                              257

**List of Works Cited**                                       **261**

**Index**                                                     **271**

# Preface

THE PHILOSOPHICAL INTERESTS that have led, in their roundabout way, to this book have occupied my attention intermittently over some twenty years. Twenty years is a long time in the life of contemporary culture, but a very short time in the life of philosophy. According to the calendar of cultural trends, structuralism has come and gone; poststructuralism, for that matter, seems by now to have come and gone. But according to the calendar of philosophy, as I read it, structuralism has only just arrived. It has been a serious possibility, as a mode (among others) of understanding some aspects of the world, since the early years of this century, but has begun to achieve focus and formulation only in the last few decades.

In the work presented here (some of it previously published in the form of essays and occasional pieces, rewritten for the present purpose, but much of it new or previously communicated only in the form of lectures) I have been concerned to understand this emerging philosophical position and to use its insights in connection with some old problems. I have not approached it from an ideological point of view or tried to defend its hegemonic claims, nor have I been too much concerned to assess its status in relation to other contemporary trends. I have treated it, in other words, for the most part positively, as offering a way of looking at the intelligibility of the human sciences that I at least have found stimulating and useful.

There have been many works on structuralism since my first contribution to the subject in the *Partisan Review* in 1968. This book is still in the spirit of that article: it wishes not only to make the phenomenon intelligible, but also to acknowledge its challenge and its usefulness, neither of which, it seems to me, has lessened in the intervening years, in spite of so much exposition and argument. I am grateful to William Phillips for commissioning that early piece, to Hugh Silverman for his persistence in encouraging me to make it and a dozen or so succeeding pieces the basis for a book (and for his patience in waiting for it), and to the American Council of Learned Societies for a fellowship to work on structuralism in 1972–73. I have contracted the usual debt to colleagues, fellow symposiasts, and lecture audiences, as well as to my students at the City University of New York and at the George Washington University.

In the 1968 *Partisan Review* article was reproduced, with the permission of the *Quinzaine Littéraire*, a now familiar cartoon of the four most notorious structuralists of the 1960s (Lévi-Strauss, Barthes, Lacan, and Foucault) in grass skirts under a palm tree, looking benign and exotic. Of the four Foucault was perhaps the least benign (and the least amused at being called a structuralist), but they were all approachable, and I have been indebted to each of them not only for enlightenment but also for personal courtesy and in some cases for kindness and encouragement. Three of them are now dead, and the fourth has undergone an apotheosis available only to Frenchmen; but what they briefly held in common in those days was less exotic than it appeared and has still, I think, unrealized and central philosophical significance. It was more fundamental and more important than perhaps even they themselves knew, more so certainly than most of their epigones knew, since otherwise they would not have given it up so readily. I would be happy to think (though it may be unrealistic to hope) that this book will help to preserve and consolidate the insights of that time.

In addition to the *Partisan Review* the sources of various parts of what follows include the *Philosophische Rundschau, Gradiva, The New Republic, Idealist Studies, Philosophers in Their Own Work, Diacritics, Via, Dialogues in Phenomenology*, and the *American Anthropologist*. Most of this material is cut and interwoven in such a way as to make specific identification troublesome, but I acknowledge with thanks the indulgence of my editors in allowing me to use it.

# Introduction

## 1. What structuralism is

STRUCTURALISM IS A philosophical view according to which the reality of the objects of the human or social sciences is relational rather than substantial. It generates a critical method that consists of inquiring into and specifying the sets of relations (or structures) that constitute these objects or into which they enter, and of identifying and analyzing groups of such objects whose members are structural transformations of one another. These groups jointly constitute the domains of the respective sciences.

Since the objects in question may be linguistic, psychological, anthropological, mythological, social, economic, political, literary, historical, philosophical, and so on, many "structuralisms" have developed independently in the corresponding domains. Some of them have made claims that go beyond the defining features set forth in my first paragraph. However these need not constrain the rest.

It is useful to distinguish between the objects of the social sciences and those of the natural sciences by noting that the causal determinants of the former always include human intentions, while those of the latter do not. (Objects whose causal antecedents do include intentions continue to be governed by natural laws: social objects are embodied in physical objects. But for natural scientific purposes their intentional origins can be ignored.) Since human intentions always involve an element of significance it is not surprising to find that the structures dealt with by the social sciences are *signiferous*, or "meaning-bearing," and that structuralism therefore generates also a theory of significance and of meaning. It is equally unsurprising that along with the structuralist activity of specifying those structures often goes a hermeneutic activity of interpreting them.

Since structuralism is willing to grant the structures in question the status of intentional objects, it clearly rejects the methodological and antimetaphysical cautions of positivism and behaviorism. But since it does not grant them the status of substantial entries in an ontology independent of human intentions it is just as clearly not an essentialist position.

Structuralism therefore does not require (although it does not exclude) the view that there exists some objective or deep generating structure of which the structures it studies are transformations. Nor does it require

1

(although it is compatible with) the view that the carrier of those structures, up to and including the structure of subjectivity itself (or the structure that subjectivity is), might be neurophysiological. The relations that carried the structures would on this view not be abstract but concretely embodied in the individual who intended them.

## 2. Situation and plan of the work

THE FOREGOING SUMMARY definition makes a working point of departure for this book but gives no hint of the controversies that have been stirred up by structuralism in the past decades. "Structuralism, I do not renounce the word, but it has become uncertain." This understatement is due to the late Roland Barthes (1971a:4). The career of the structuralist movement, at any rate at the level of popular enthusiasm in France, where—at that level—it originated, was meteoric: a brilliant streak followed by relative extinction. It managed to pass from novelty to fashion to cliché in a very few years, with hardly any interval of mature reflection, and ceased to be of topical interest some time ago. But on the other hand this very fact may permit its philosophical development in a more measured way, now that the agitation of popularity has subsided. Not every idea that comes to general attention deserves such development; that structuralism does so, quite apart from its notoriety (or its status as passé) in the public eye, is one of the conclusions I hope to establish.

This book falls into two parts. The first deals with structuralism historically and critically, as a movement; the second deals with it systematically, as philosophy. The first part is subdivided in its turn, dealing first with the more popular, and then with the more technical aspects of the movement. The same domain is therefore traversed, in effect, three times, but in different orders and by different methods. The relationship between the movement and the philosophy is complex: there is some genetic determination, which however goes in both directions; there is some overlapping; there is some incompatibility. For this reason the distinction between the two parts is not sharp or rigorous and there is a certain amount of redundancy, although I have tried to keep this to a minimum. In general, however, the material of the first part has its sources in the writings of linguists, anthropologists, and others who at one time or another were admitted by themselves, or alleged by their critics, to belong to the structuralist movement, or who can reasonably be said to be its precursors, while the material in the second part derives from my own reflections or from the reflections of other philosophers belonging to that movement neither by admission nor allegation, but indeed for the most part ignoring its existence.

In one sense it is stretching things somewhat to speak of structuralism as a "movement" at all, since it never had the combination of doctrinal and social unity that that term implies. But it was, in its period of popular dominance, a recognizable cluster or writers and ideas with a geographical and temporal focus, namely Paris in the 1960s. This period came to a rather abrupt end in May 1968, but by then the idea of structuralism had become entrenched among the intellectual commonplaces in France. By 1966 it already had this status, as was made clear to me by a conversation I fell into at about that time with an inquisitive French intellectual. Discovering my origins and profession, she wanted to know at once if I was a positivist. No, I said. A Marxist, then? she asked, having exhausted her acquaintance with Anglo-American philosophy in the first question. No, I said again. "Donc vous êtes structuraliste," she said with finality and obvious relief.

In fact I was not then, nor have I since become, a structuralist, if that means anything like an exclusive commitment to a doctrine. As formulated in the second part of this book I believe structuralism to constitute a viable and valuable, even an essential, subdiscipline of philosophy, but I take it to be neither comprehensive nor final. As expounded in the first part, however, I hold no particular brief for it, although I have been greatly stimulated by the work of those I name there as its creators and representatives. It is because in their work I found it philosophically suggestive, but in each particular case incompletely developed and admixed with other prejudices and commitments, and because they and their followers impatiently twitched their mantles and, following the call of fashion, hurried on to fresher woods and newer pastures without stopping long enough to understand or work out what they had stumbled upon, that it has seemed to me worthwhile to attempt the double task of disengaging it from those sources and articulating it in my own terms.

In spite of the deficiencies of structuralist theory, however, my main concern in the first part has been to make it as lucid and coherent as possible, rather than to show it up *as* deficient, a task that some commentators have felt obliged to perform, sometimes rather testily, even while expounding its principles (cf. Clarke 1981, Seung 1982). At the same time I have for the most part limited myself to those aspects of the various disciplines involved in the exposition that are specifically structuralist or particularly relevant to structuralism, so that in discussing linguistics, for example, the attention paid to Saussure (to take the most obvious case) is out of all proportion to his importance in the history of linguistics as a discipline. On the other hand his importance, like that of some of the other figures dealt with here, has been underestimated, thanks largely to the habitual xenophobia of Anglo-American scholarship, so that a redressing of the balance is not out of order.

I take this opportunity to acknowledge, and try to dissociate myself from, the xenophilia, or more specifically the Francophilia, of some epigones, that leads to a countervailing tendency to *over*estimate the importance of certain writers. This is often accompanied by excitement about the new or the exotic, and the writing it produces tends to have the breathless urgency of sports commentary: revolutions occur, paradigms succeed one another, movements rise and fall, at a dizzying rate. I discuss this rather French malady in chapter 2, but wish to make a point here about the historical setting of structuralism. It just is not the case, it seems to me, that we are at the mercy of wild paradigm shifts or even that we need to think very much about what paradigm we are working under (though my obvious discontent with this way of talking is not meant to belittle Kuhn's original study, which in its own domain was seminal). The last serious revolutionary in philosophy I take to have been Kant, the implications of whose work we are far from having exhausted. He concluded that we were subjects in a closed world of appearances, and nobody has yet found a way out—not Hegel, not Nietzsche, not Dewey, not Heidegger, not Wittgenstein, not even Husserl. They have shown us different ways of living in that world; structuralism, I think, helps to make it more intelligible.

Philosophical history is long and slow, and remembering this helps keep momentary events in perspective. In reading accounts of the current intellectual scene I am sometimes reminded of Macaulay's remark about the American Constitution, that it was "all sail and no anchor"; only such a vessel is likely to worry about what one of the more excitable commentators has called "the new maelstrom" of poststructuralist modernity (Fekete 1984). These upheavals belong, it seems to me, to microclimates of intellectual opinion. What corresponds to the anchor is the accumulation of empirical work that has continued since Kant: we really do know more than was known two centuries ago about logic and theory construction and languages and social customs and brains, and this knowledge helps in our understanding of the ways we structure experience and the artifacts and institutions we create from it and for it, which form the problematic domain of structuralism.

## 3. The concept of structure

A WORD ABOUT the name "structuralism" itself. The trouble with the formation of such terms from ordinary roots is that their meanings seem straightforward but in practice become confused for that very reason. For the meanings of the ordinary roots themselves, at any rate of those that designate relatively abstract categories, are various and multiple, and require a good deal of supplementary clarification before two people can be sure they are interpreting one in similar senses. "Structure" is from the past participle form (*structum*) of the Latin verb *struere*, "to put together, put in order," which has the special senses of piling up, building, and arranging; it is from an Indo-European root meaning to lay out, extend, and so on, from which we also get "strew" and other cognates. The ordinary-language meaning of the word is now either the way in which some more or less organized and stable entity is built or put together, or alternatively the entity itself seen as organized in this way. But the entity can be anything from a molecule to a skyscraper, from a word to a novel, a game, a tradition, a constitution; by applying to almost everything, "structural" runs the risk that it will not be enlightening when used of any particular thing. Adding the suffix "-ism," a standard Greek device for turning events or processes into objects (*baptizein* into *baptismos*, "baptize" into "baptism," is the paradigmatic example), lends an air of definiteness without necessarily bringing any clarification.

When, as in the present case, many people seize enthusiastically upon such an expression at the same time, semantic chaos ensues. Prudence suggests avoiding the term altogether. But this is unrealistic: structuralism as a movement is too recent, and its methodological legacy, at least in certain domains, too pervasive; since I shall be discussing the movement and the methodology, as well as their philosophical setting and implications, it has seemed wise to embrace the name of "structuralism," stipulate a definition of "structure," and proceed (adopting one of Descartes's provisional maxims) to "follow no less constantly the most doubtful opinions, once determined upon them, than if they had been most assured" (Descartes 1953:142). The enterprise as a whole thus remains open to criticism but aims at least for sufficient clarity and distinctness to make this possible without further redefinition.

In fact this strategy is not as desperate as it sounds; like materialism and existentialism, structuralism does lend itself to an interpretation based on a plausible definition of its ordinary root. (The definition I adopt—of structure as a set of relations—is given implicitly in my opening paragraph and will be elaborated upon as the book proceeds.) This association with existentialism and materialism goes further, for human existence, matter, and structure have a complementary relation to one another in a sense to be explained at length in chapter 12. Structuralism therefore has, at least potentially, an important role to play in contemporary Western philosophy. The limitation on the sense of the term that is imposed by the cluster of recent ideas to be studied in this book has been admirably expressed by Leach:

> Empirical structures can be recognized in every aspect of the universe. . . . but in linguistics and social anthropology we are only

concerned with the special class of structures which are generated by human brains. They have the peculiarity that the surface manifestations of these structures tend to be non-repetitive. New forms are being created all the time. (Robey 1973:41)

It is this surface proliferation of structures and classes of structures—for the products of human brains are not limited to language and social behavior—that has made structuralism as diverse and hence as unmanageable as it has been. (And yet its underlying coherence is such that it remains a point of reference even in eclipse; the best name that has been found for the mixture of attitudes and techniques that is taken to have succeeded it—and on which I will have more to say later—is precisely "poststructuralism.")

## 4. Structure and intelligibility

LONG INVOLVEMENT WITH structuralism induces a certain sympathy with the *dénicheur d'oiseaux* or bird's-nester whose exploits are recounted in the "reference myth" with which Lévi-Strauss opens his four-volume study of the mythology of North and South America (1964:43). The hero of this myth, which occurs in many different variants and transformations, climbs a high tree or rocky cliff in order to get to nests in which are to be found birds or eggs prized for their feathers or culinary value or whatever. While he is climbing, the pole or ladder is snatched away, or the rock or tree grows magically higher and higher, so that it is impossible for him to get down again. What is worse, the nests when he reaches them are empty, or contain rotten eggs or the wrong sort of bird. The result is that he starves. Not to death—but to bring in his motivations for the climb, or all of his subsequent adventures, would strain the analogy. Many people who have worked on structuralism in recent years must at any rate be familiar with the feeling that what they were trying to get to the top (or bottom) of was all the while growing uncontrollably, and have experienced doubts as to the value of what they found when they got there.

One version of the myth, however, has what may be a relevant sequel. At the top of the cliff or tree the hero discovers, somewhat after the fashion of our own Jack and the Beanstalk, another country in which he goes exploring. It is a sparse and unrewarding country, but he thinks he recognizes there some varieties of edible root habitually gathered by his tribe, and he pulls them up to eat them. It turns out that he is walking on the sky, and that pulling up the roots has made holes in it. These are the stars. Now the stars give light: not perhaps of the kind that illuminates, but of the kind that orients. And the orientation that it offers seems to me the chief virtue of structuralism in philosophy, a virtue of which, in spite of doubts about its avatars in other domains, I remain firmly convinced. It is, as my subtitle suggests, a matter of lending intelligibility to the world, not so much introducing new methods of explanation or analysis as providing a new perspective from which apparently unrelated features of individual or collective experience are seen as congruent.

I speak of the "art of the intelligible" to indicate that the activity of creating and recognizing intelligibility is a matter not only of theory but also of praxis, that no formal program or effective procedure will generate it automatically but that it arises out of acquaintance with cases and consequent insight into problems. And the subtitle is meant also as an illustration of something about structuralism. It is a case of structural transformation (from Bismarck's "art of the possible" via Medawar's "art of the soluble"), or alternatively of *bricolage*, the making of new cultural artifacts out of fragments of old ones. If it sounds in the least familiar and seems in consequence to mean anything at all, then to that small degree the reader has already experienced what it is referring to: all understanding of no matter what variety, however rigorous, is, I maintain, from the point of view of the subject who understands, somewhere along the same continuum.

As to the concept of the intelligible itself, this might seem redundant in a book on structuralism were it not for the fact that it has a familiar currency, which structuralism lacks, through the use of the term in ordinary language. It is perhaps not too fanciful to read the "-lig-" in "intelligible," which shifted at some point from "-leg-" (as in *legere* "to choose, discriminate, read" etc., and still in "intellect," so that intelligibility would be as it were availability to understanding), as connected like the parallel form in "religion" with *ligare* "to bind"; for something to be intelligible, then, would be for it to lend itself to "interbinding," that is, to understanding in terms of connecting links that hold things in place with respect to one another. The term shares with "structure" a fruitful ambiguity (to which I shall revert later), in that the binding may be among the parts of what is to be understood, so that its own structure is revealed, or it may be between what is to be understood and some other thing, so that it is bound into a more inclusive structure. To see how an object or event "fits together," and see how it "fits into" some larger complex of objects or events, are alternative modes of intelligibility. Either will do as an outcome of inquiry; to have both is to have located the object in question in the hierarchy of parts and wholes that composes our world—not yet to have explained it, perhaps (though that work too will have begun) but to have seen it for what it is. Structuralism does this for its proper objects. In this book I have tried to do it for structuralism.

# Part IA

## Aspects of the Structuralist Movement

# 1

# Convergence

## 5. Beginnings

STRUCTURALISM AS A recognizable trend dates from 1916, or 1928–29, or 1944–45, or 1949, depending on one's taste in historiography and one's bias in the human sciences. Nineteen sixteen was the year of the posthumous publication of Ferdinand de Saussure's *Cours de linguistique générale*, a work that said almost nothing about structure but expounded the basic concepts on which structuralism was to be built. Nineteen twenty-eight was the year of the first International Congress of Linguists at The Hague, to which Roman Jakobson, S. Karcewski, and Prince Nicholas Troubetzkoy submitted a set of propositions for the first time explicitly structuralist (Troubetzkoy 1933:230), and 1929 that of the Congress of Slavists where Jakobson put forward "modes of analysis . . . . tentatively christened STRUCTURAL METHOD" (Jakobson 1962:633). Nineteen forty-four was the *annus mirabilis* of the refugee community in New York, where the linguist Jakobson and the anthropologist Claude Lévi-Strauss discussed the structuralist ideas later popularized by Lévi-Strauss, who (as yet far from popularization) published in 1945 the crucial article "L'Analyse structurale en linguistique et en anthropologie" and in 1949 the first major treatise of his anthropological structuralism, *Les Structures élémentaires de la parenté*.

But in fact the notion of structure was a pervasive one in intellectual circles between the two world wars. "The epoch in which we live," wrote Troubetzkoy in 1932, "is characterized by the tendency of all scientific disciplines to replace atomism with structuralism . . . " (1933:246). Thirteen years later, in one of the last lectures he gave before his death, Cassirer made a similar point: "Structuralism," he said, "is no isolated phenomenon; it is, rather, the expression of a general tendency of thought that, in these last decades, has become more and more prominent in almost all fields of scientific research" (1945:120). The context of both these remarks was the discipline of linguistics; Troubetzkoy was writing about phonology, and Cassirer was addressing the Linguistic Circle of New York. But both took for granted the extension of the concept of structuralism into other fields, as

11

though it were something perfectly familiar to a professional audience. And indeed the views to which structuralism was seen as a corrective in linguistics—atomism, behaviorism, positivism, or the psychologism of which the neogrammarians were thought to have been guilty—were present in many other domains as well. There was widespread dissatisfaction with the worldview of reductive mechanism, although this view was not always fully understood. "A mechanical agglomeration due to the play of chance or of heterogeneous factors," said Jakobson, "—such is the favorite image of the European ideology prevalent in the second half of the 19th century." But that was changing: "The contemporary ideology, in its diverse manifestations, genetically independent from one another, throws into relief, with growing clarity, instead of mechanical addition a functional system, instead of a thoroughly bureaucratic reference to similar cases immanent structural laws, and instead of blind chance an evolution moving towards an end" (1962:110).

The teleological claim introduced into this remark is not, of course, implied by the functional and structural ones, and it is uncomfortably reminiscent of the antimechanism of Bergson or of Teilhard de Chardin. But even if its rejection of teleology was justified, the mechanistic view certainly lacked discrimination when it came to questions of value, to contexts of *concern*; as Geschiere has put it, "People realized the necessity of integrating the numerous facts observed by sciences of positivist inspiration into a grouping capable of demonstrating more adequately their exact value. Hence the extraordinary increase in the use of the terms *structure, system, function*" (Dresden 1961:110). The interrelation of these terms is important and a preliminary stipulative distinction among the corresponding concepts may be helpful.

## 6. System and structure

BY A *SYSTEM* I shall understand a set of entities (called the *elements* of the system) mutually related in such a way that the state of each element determines and/or is determined by the state of some other element or elements, and every element is connected to every other by a chain of such determinations, that is, the system has no isolated elements. Depending on what counts as an admissible determination, the same element may turn out to belong to more than one system; in the limit, when every conceivable form of determination is admitted, the universe as a whole forms a single system in the above sense. In general, however, some restricted form of causal or logical determination will be specified, and this will have the effect of locating propositions or entities in different systems. By its *function* I shall understand the contribution of an element of the system to some process or end that the system undergoes or effects. A system as a whole has a function only if it is an element in a more inclusive system, that is, only if it affects something other than itself. (Self-perpetuation does not count as a function in this sense.) By a *structure*, finally, I shall understand a set of *relations* among entities that form the elements of a system; the structure will be said to be *concrete* if the relations are actually embodied in some system, *abstract* if they are merely specified but not so embodied. For the time being I leave aside the question whether relations are eventually to be defined intensionally or extensionally. Also I do not insist on completeness or consistency in order to grant systematic status to some set of interrelated elements. The set may be partially connected by one kind of relation and partially by another, and the relations themselves may be specified more or less exactly. An organism is a system, but so is an organization, or a family, or a game, or a language.

It is clear at once that the notion of structure is ambiguous, in that for any entity $X$ a structural analysis may wish to specify the systematic structure of $X$, or it may wish to specify the structure of the system to which $X$ belongs. I will call these respectively the internal and the external structures of $X$. In fact, an open-ended hierarchy of structures and functions is implied by these definitions. Functionalism, which defines the elements of a system in terms of the specific parts they play in it, is by itself therefore unsatisfactory, even though a great improvement on mechanism, and this was already seen in the case of linguistics by the Prague structuralists. "The application of a functional method," says Horalek, "soon led to the conclusion that the isolated analysis of partial functions was not enough, and that attention had to be concentrated on the interplay of the ensemble of functions" (Vachek 1964:421)—in other words on a "structure of functions." But the remarkable thing about such developments was that gradually the material identity of the elements of the systems under discussion became less and less important as the network of their structures and functions came to carry more and more the burden of systematic reality.

This tendency accorded well with the dissolution or at any rate the attenuation of material substance that seemed to be implied by discoveries in physics. What had before been solid entities proved to be systems of dynamic relations among smaller elements, which might well in their turn prove to be systems on a reduced scale, and so on indefinitely. By the time one had got down a couple of layers in a progression like this the inclination to fall back, after the manner of Locke, on a "something I know not what," seemed less pressing. People had become accustomed to living on a planet freely suspended in space, and they might become accustomed in turn to regarding matter as a hierarchy of relational structures having no lowest term. This theme will recur repeatedly, in the most diverse contexts, but it could hardly be summed up better than in the words of Braque, quoted approvingly by Jakobson: "I do not believe in things, I believe only in their relationship" (Jakobson 1962:632).

There were of course other, independent sources for the concern with structure—the Formalists and New Critics, the Gestalt psychologists, Freud, the conjectures of nineteenth-century thinkers like Peirce and Morgan and Marx, to which more detailed attention will be paid in what follows. Indeed the structuralist convergence had such diverse points of departure that it is hardly surprising if it did not quite come to a single focus. Thus François Wahl, speaking of the situation in 1968, wrote: "Today one might enumerate two positivist structuralisms (the second accusing the first of empiricism), one straightforwardly rationalist structuralism, two structuralisms at least announcing the overthrow of the subject (the second accusing the first of reductionism); there is a philosophy in the classical sense that makes use of structuralism, and several structuralisms that claim to refute all philosophy on its own grounds, etc." (Ducrot et al. 1968:9). In the eyes of many people the Marxist origins of some elements of the movement polluted the whole. Aron, for example, in an essay on Althusser, takes it to share this flaw with later existentialism: "the so-called structuralist school, now in fashion, differs from the phenomenologico-existentialist school which has reigned for a dozen years, it succeeds it and borrows from it its style, its pretension and its ignorances" (1969:72). At the same time new lines of inquiry came into being, outside linguistics and anthropology, which had affinities with structuralism and shared some of its sources: in developmental psychology, for example, the genetic epistemology of Piaget, in biology and cybernetics the General Systems Theory of von Bertalanffy.


## 7. Bourbaki and group structure

IN ALL THE contexts so far mentioned the idea of structure is relatively informal, and emphasis falls upon its conceptual import rather than on any exactness of definition. There occurred independently, during the nineteenth and the early twentieth centuries, an evolution in mathematics centered on a more rigorous idea of structure, in which a similar liberation from the intrinsic nature of systematic objects took place. In this case, however, it was a matter not only of replacing the elements of systems by their interrelations, but also of freeing the structures from the specificity of the systems themselves. Mathematical objects are automatically systems, with internal and external structures, according to the definitions given above; changing the dimensions or the values of one element in a figure or formula necessarily entails changes in other elements, and the whole is recognizable as an entity (a hyperbola, a partial differential equation, and so on) belonging to a higher-order system (geometry, algebra, and so on). It was formerly supposed that the relations linking the elements of a given mathematical object were specific to that kind of object, that is, that each family of objects had its proper structure. But mathematicians came to realize not only that structures are not "given" with the objects (Bourbaki 1969:34) but also that the same object can enter into different structures:

> The axiomatic method allows us, in the case of complex mathematical entities, to dissociate their properties and regroup them around a small number of notions, that is . . . to class them according to the *structures* to which they belong (a single structure being able of course to come into play with respect to diverse mathematical entities); in this way, among the properties of a sphere, some are topological, others are algebraic, still others can be considered as referring to differential geometry or the theory of Lie groups. (Bourbaki 1966a:3).

This realization followed the axiomatic development of the theory of groups, in effect a theory of pure structure in the sense given above.

A mathematical group consists of a set of elements and a binary operation on ordered pairs of these elements, such that carrying out the operation on any two elements yields a new element of the group. That is of course just the beginning: group theory is an extended and ramified branch of mathematics. But it is enough to convey the essentials of the metaphor that group theory contributed to structuralism, namely the tendency of the objects of the human sciences to come in groups whose members can be generated out of or transformed into one another by operations of displacement, inversion, substitution, and so on. The internal structure of such an object is the set of relations that, if they held among different elements, would realize a different member of the same group; its external structure is the set of transformation relations that effect the substitution of elements and produce the other members of the group.

A graphic illustration of transformational principles in action is provided by D'Arcy Wentworth Thompson's studies of animal morphology in *On Growth and Form*, where he shows how the shape of a particular fish, say, projected on to standard rectangular coordinates, will yield the shape of a different fish if the coordinate system is distorted (1961:299–301). Not every distortion yields an actual or even a biologically possible fish; in a similar way, not every transformation of a cultural object yields an actual or a psychologically or socially possible object. What the permissible transformations are is a matter of empirical inquiry. In this respect the borrowed or metaphorical group-theoretical features of structuralism are sharply restricted in comparison to their mathematical originals, and it is questionable how far it is worth insisting on the metaphor.

## 8. Cassirer and the "symbolic forms"

THERE WAS ONE philosopher in whose work these strands already came together before the Second World War. Had it not been, in fact, for an unfortunate terminological choice, Ernst Cassirer would certainly now be recognized as the founder of philosophical structuralism. I say "unfortunate" gratuitously, and without giving Cassirer the chance to reaffirm his preference; but the remark already quoted shows that he was using the term "structuralism" at the end of his life, and under translation its reference to a "general tendency of thought" might almost have been justified by his *Philosophy of Symbolic Forms* alone. That title reflects perhaps too stubborn a fidelity to his Kantian origins; at all events it did not catch the philosophical imagination. The work itself, however, anticipates remarkably most of the insights and concerns of structuralism. The symbolic forms—language, myth, religion, art, and science—represent for Cassirer the different modes in which human thought expresses the world to itself; they are, furthermore, the transcendental conditions of the possibility of this expression: "it is only by their agency that anything real becomes an object for intellectual apprehension, and as such is made visible to us" (1946:8). Each of them, taken alone, seems to require a foundation or a purpose, the search for which has always been eventually frustrated by an encounter with some metaphysically impenetrable limit. What is needed to circumvent this futility, says Cassirer, is a "standpoint situated above all these forms and yet not merely outside them: a standpoint which would make it possible to encompass the whole of them in one view, which would seek to penetrate nothing other than the purely immanent relation of all these forms to one another, and not their relation to any external, 'transcendent' being or principle. Then we could have a systematic philosophy of human culture in which each particular form would take its meaning solely from the *place* in which it stands" (1953:82).

The fundamental insight of this passage is that "meaning" is to be construed as internal to human culture: if one thing men and women do is meaningful it is because of its relation to some other thing they do, not because of its insertion into an absolute or transcendent plan of the world. This realization is not accessible to intuition; it has to be constructed. Intuition will always presume an objective reality or significance in what is delivered to it, but it is just this that philosophical inquiry is unable to justify or render intelligible in its naïve form. "No theory," Cassirer says later, "and particularly no exact one, no mathematical theory of the natural process, is possible unless pure thought detaches itself from the matrix of intuition, unless it progresses to structures which are fundamentally intuitive in nature. And now the last decisive step is taken—now these very structures become the actual vehicles of objective being" (1957:320).

The context of this last passage is, it is true, a discussion of the physical sciences, and the philosophical idealism implicit in it may supply another reason for subsequent neglect of Cassirer's work. But—as I shall argue later—a form of idealism that may be philosophically suspect if applied to the world of nature may be exactly appropiate when applied to the world of society, since although the existence of nature as nature cannot reasonably be supposed to be dependent on minds (the New Physics to the contrary notwithstanding), the existence of society as society can. Cassirer's Kantianism leads him to stress the impossibility of the knowledge even of nature unmodified by the categories of thought, and he points out repeatedly that perception is already structured, but this does not affect the distinction I am drawing here. It does, however, reinforce the view that all knowledge, whether of nature or society, is enclosed with perception in a system that is, as it were (to revert to an earlier metaphor), "freely suspended," and that is by definition incapable to external grounding.

It is this system, and not necessarily the unknowable external world, that exhibits the mathematical structure the mathematicians themselves were discovering. In a remarkable essay written in the late 1930s Cassirer effects the juncture of the two lines of thought, finding in the experimental fact of what he calls "perceptual constancy" (1944:9) under variable conditions an exemplification of the behavior of the mathematical group, which preserves the invariance of a rule under diverse transformations. This view was prefigured by Kant, for whom the concept was "nothing other than the unity of a rule by which a manifold of contents are held together and connected with one another" (Cassirer 1957:287). What group theory provided for the first time was a formal representation of this rule, or rather of the species of rule to which it belongs. "The rule may, in simple and exact terms, be defined as that *group of transformations* with regard to which the variation of the particular image is considered" (Cassirer 1944:22).

The application of this idea to perception lays the basis for a structuralism more radical than the version developed in this book, restricted as that is to the objects of the social sciences.

> Perception, [says Cassirer], is not a process of reflection or reproduction at all. It is a process of objectification, the characteristic nature and tendency of which finds expression in the formation of invariants. . . . The peculiar kind of "identity" that is attributed to apparently altogether heterogeneous figures in virtue of their being

transformable into one another by means of certain operations defining
a group . . . permits us not only to single out elements but also to grasp
"structures" in perception. (1944:19–20, 25)

One of Cassirer's most significant conclusions is that very different concepts
may be generated on the same perceptual base by the application of different
groups of transformations, in other words by the insertion of constants of
perception into different structures. "The perceptual image as well [as the
geometrical one] involves that reference to certain possible groups of transformation. It changes when we refer it to a different group and determine the
'invariants' of perception accordingly" (1944:16; cf. Bourbaki 1966:3). In the
*Symbolic Forms* he had already grasped this point informally with respect to
language: "If the moon in Greek is called the 'measurer' (*měn*), in Latin the
'glittering' (*luna, luc-na*), we have here one and the same sensory intuition
assigned to very different notions of meaning and made determinate by
them" (1955:284–85).

What makes the initial confusion of sensory awareness tractable to
perception is, in other words, the imposition upon it of one or more of a
number of *a priori* structures, now able to be categorized in terms more exact
than Kant had at his disposal. If this account is to be judged correct, certain
assumptions it makes require justification. It assumes, as a minimum requirement of coherent perception, that the structure of the perceived world
and that of the conceiving mind have something in common (the former,
indeed, being in part a product of the latter), and that the intelligibility of the
world can be accounted for in terms of the matching of these structures. (It is
tempting to speculate, if this is so, that it is just the experience of this
matching of subject and world that confers the *sense* of intelligibility.) It
assumes a relatively small number of such structures of intellegibility,
otherwise the original perceptual confusion would just be duplicated on the
conceptual level. And it leads in consequence to the expectation that these
structures will be found to repeat in different contexts, that is, that different
branches of knowledge will show homologies with one another.

The convergence of lines of inquiry that led to the structuralist movement of the 1960s turned precisely on the investigation, under different
stimuli and by different methods, of the structures of a variety of cultural
domains—language, mythology, kinship practices, literature, and so on.
These are domains in which the part played by conceiving minds is on the
whole easier to accept than it is in the domain of perception itself, although
this issue is complicated by the question of how conscious the structuring
activity of the mind may be, a question to which I shall return in connection
with the views of Lévi-Strauss. But the structuralist movement itself appeared on the French intellectual scene as a fashion, as a candidate for public

attention in a tradition of learned exhibitionism that reaches back to the origins of the Paris salon and will no doubt continue indefinitely into the future. It generated enthusiasm and became notorious, and tended in consequence to be dismissed by philosophers—especially outside France— suspicious of ideas whose popular success comes too easily, of cults and name-dropping and verbosity. Ideas, however, are not always to be judged by the company in which they are kept. There was serious content even to the surface manifestation of structuralism in its period of popularity, to an examination of which I now turn.

# 2

# Structuralism in France

## 9. Paris fashions

PRIMITIVE PEOPLE, Claude Lévi-Strauss tells us, have a passion for naming, classifying, and establishing relations among things, without much regard to the accuracy of the classifications or the objective validity of the relations. In this they resemble the French. It is no accident that Paris should be the world capital of fashion, one of the most complex and most arbitrary signiferous systems ever devised by man (and it is no surprise that the structuralist Roland Barthes should have devoted a book, *Système de la mode*, to a solemn analysis of the textual accompaniments of this system). Nowhere is the preoccupation with system—or for that matter with fashion—more evident than in French intellectual life. Since World War II there have been several major fashions in French thought. One was existentialism, which lasted until the early 1950s; another, which took hold in the late 1950s and early 1960s and lasted until May 1968, was structuralism. Yet another, which grew out of the politically shaken ground left behind by the events of that spring, was the New Philosophy, or rather the message of the so-called *nouveaux philosophes*, the New Philosophers, which underwent a metamorphosis into the New Right and evaporated along with the government of Giscard d'Estaing.

The doctrine of the *nouveaux philosophes*, as many people remarked at the time, was neither new nor philosophical, and it was not a competitor for attention in serious intellectual circles. But in the 1970s structuralism yielded also to a rediscovery of semiotics (a regressive shift about which I shall have more to say), to a hermeneutics which had been developing independently in France and in Germany, and to a deconstructionist mode of reading that seemed, in its name and in its practice, to be the very antithesis of structural analysis. At the same time, as remarked earlier, the fact that the only general term available to describe what has happened since structuralism is "poststructuralist" testifies to the importance of structuralism itself. That term still means, for most people, what was going on in the last notable period of coherence in French intellectual life, in the 1960s. It is one of the basic claims of this book that it was let go too soon and for the wrong reasons.

Neither existentialism nor structuralism had the character of a movement in the strict sense of the term, in contrast to such prewar fashions as surrealism and Marxism, with their orthodoxies and exclusions. Marxism was naturally allied with the party; surrealism was identified with André Breton and his followers. In both cases, of course, there extended from the center an intellectual region within which people wished to claim the title "surrealist" or "Marxist," although they might be disowned by the hard-core disciples. The center, for existentialism, was much less well defined; unlike Breton, Sartre never assumed the role of pope. In the case of structuralism there was not really a center at all. The founding father of the movement in France was generally agreed to be Lévi-Strauss, but there were at least four other people who occupied essentially independent leading positions, namely Jacques Lacan, Louis Althusser, Barthes, and Michel Foucault. To make matters worse, structuralist habits and beliefs are quite consistent with those of many other intellectual movements. Such movements may succeed without replacing one another; surrealism and Marxism still survive, however stubbornly or vestigially, and Althusser until his breakdown was a prominent Marxist. Lacan, for his part, was a dedicated and fundamentalist Freudian who was strongly influenced by surrealism. The others had less striking doctrinal commitments, but they came from diverse professional fields—Lévi-Strauss from anthropology, Barthes from belles lettres and literary criticism, Foucault from philosophy. Little wonder that the standards of clarity and distinctness learned from Descartes by every lycée student broke down completely in the face of the structuralist phenomenon. A kind of despair could be detected on the part of French commentators on the intellectual scene; a typical article in the *Quinzaine littéraire* entitled "Où en est le structuralisme?" began: "' . . .In the momentary world of commercialized concepts, eclecticism is the rule.' This statement of Alain Badiou characterizes precisely the intellectual debauch to which the pseudo-school that has been named *structuralism* has given rise." The article made the point that while there was a more or less identifiable set of contemporary activities properly called structuralist, the indiscriminate use of the term had rendered it almost meaningless.

A close examination of what lay behind the fashion, however, would have revealed a common element in structuralist thought fully warranting the view that writers as different as those named above formed a coherent school, not at all deserving of the *Quinzaine*'s epithet "pseudo-," and this chapter will be devoted to an exposition of that common element as it appeared at the time, that is, in the years preceding May 1968. That would have been the moment, if ever, to choose a designation other than "structuralism," since this term, while not actually misleading, did not indicate what was most significant about the movement at that time, nor what bound its members together. The name said something interesting about the origins of the movement in structural anthropology and structural linguistics, but the line of thought that emerged from the confrontation of those disciplines had more to do with linguistic and cultural products (myths, works of literature) and their relation to the problem of human subjectivity than with any concept of structure in the more obvious sense. Clearly there are "structures" in language and in culture, such as Navajo grammar or Tibetan marriage customs, and one might, to consider the anthropological case only, have expected that "structuralism" would have taken as its task the analysis of such objects in terms of the interrelation of their elements, by contrast to the "functionalism" of Malinowski, for example, which conducted its analyses in terms of social and psychological purpose. There is in fact an anthropological structuralism of precisely this sort, associated mainly with the name of Radcliffe-Brown. But the obvious structures, while not unimportant, were not what Lévi-Strauss was chiefly interested in. For him, the really interesting structures were beneath the surface, as it were—though all such spatial metaphors are dangerous—and might have a series of quite different embodiments at the level of apparent structure.

## 10. Mind in its natural state

THE EVENT THAT brought French structuralism most vividly to the attention of the English-speaking world was the publication in 1966 of a translation of Lévi-Strauss's *La pensée sauvage*. Its title in English, *The Savage Mind*, is unfortunate, and in fact manages, with a single literalism, to distort seriously Lévi-Strauss's intention. The book is about systems of thought in so-called primitive societies, and the "savage" mind suggests a contrast with the "civilized" mind to be found in more "advanced" societies. All the terms in quotes, at least to the extent that they suggest a hierarchy of value (as they inevitably do) would be rejected by Lévi-Strauss. The trouble with "savage" in English is that it now has only one level of meaning; while it was once possible to use the term in a more or less descriptive way ("the friendly savages") it has come to mean hopelessly uncivilized or downright ferocious. "*Sauvage*," on the other hand, has the connotations of "wild" in English as it applies to plants and animals that need not be at all ferocious but on the contrary represent a special kind of natural value. "*La pensée sauvage*" is the wild pansy (not the savage pansy!) and an illustration of this flower appeared on the cover of the book; its homonymous form therefore signifies, as Lévi-Strauss himself remarks, "mind in its untamed state," and it refers not just to the mind of savages but to the human mind in general and thus to *our* mind. It was the perceived relevance of his work to contemporary human self-understanding that placed Lévi-Strauss at the center of the intellectual scene.

It is worth noting that the universality that Lévi-Strauss attributes to mind does not involve him in the absurdity, as some have suggested, of maintaining that there is no essential difference between primitive societies and modern ones. The difference, however, he sees as one of social organization and not as involving essentially a disparity of mental powers. In an interview (Charbonnier 1961) he compared the two types of society to two types of machine, clocks and steam engines: primitive societies, like clocks, use a constant input of energy and "have a tendency to maintain themselves indefinitely in their initial state, which explains why they appear to us as societies without history and without progress"; modern societies, on the other hand, like thermodynamic rather than mechanical devices, "operate in virtue of a difference of temperature between their parts . . . (which is realized by different forms of social hierarchy, whether slavery, serfdom or class distinctions); they produce much more work than the others, but consume and progressively destroy their sources of energy." The transition from cold to hot occurs, according to Lévi-Strauss, at the moment of the emergence of writing.

However, culture did not have to wait for writing in order to become articulate. It has by now become a commonplace of linguistics that the oldest languages are not necessarily the simplest: ". . . known languages, ancient or modern, cannot be classed in terms of their level of development. There are neither primitive languages nor highly developed ones, if we take into account only their structural features" (Shapiro 1960:198–99). As far as grammatical structure is concerned this can be seen as a manifestation of a constant mental complexity. Complex lexical structures, however, have often been explained in terms of the practical needs of language users—as reflected in the commonplace that there are seven (or is it seventeen?) Eskimo equivalents of "snow." But Lévi-Strauss amasses a great quantity of evidence to show that the naming of details of variation in the natural environment, among primitive people, goes far beyond any possible considerations of utility and amounts to what he calls a "science of the concrete"—not always accurate by the standards of modern classification (although far more so than early ethnologists were prepared to believe), but having in the primitive intellectual world just the function that science, in its nonutilitarian aspect, has in ours, namely, that of organizing the totality of experience into a coherent whole. Using the resources of this rich descriptive language the primitive mind shows a tendency to build intelligible structures on more abstract levels: magic, which corresponds to science in its practical aspect (and which sometimes works, although that is not of the first importance); myth, which corresponds to literature; totemism, which corresponds to morality in providing rules of conduct of a satisfyingly rigorous nature, offenses against which are suitably dangerous. Modern man thinks of these things as childish curiosities which he has long since outgrown, failing to see that science is his magic, literature and other forms of entertainment his myths, morality his totemism.

Part of what conceals from us our interior link to the primitive is a habit, inculcated by the development of modern science and technology, of looking for the *right* way of building these various structures, on the assumption that the main function of language is to communicate truth and that consistency (except perhaps in art) is a greater virtue than creativity. We have all become engineers with concepts, working from plans and anxious to get the structure right. The primitive however is not an *ingénieur* but a *bricoleur* (a word for which there is no really satisfactory English equivalent, combining as it does the ideas of resourcefulness and ingenuity in practical matters), who puts together his structures from whatever comes in handy, without special concern for the congruity of their elements. *Bricolage* is the kind of thing that is made out of old chair legs and coat hangers, the remnants of former constructions for other purposes; the *bricoleur* is the handyman, the tinkerer, who gets surprisingly practical (and often aesthetic) results from the most unlikely material. One of the fundamental theses of *La Pensée sauvage* is that the structure is all-important, the material largely irrelevant; it is as though the mind had to busy itself about something of sufficient complexity, but cared very little about the nature (or the logical level) of its components. Lévi-Strauss gives many examples of homologous mythical structures—we shall be looking at some of them in chapter 6—in which elements and relations change places from one tribe to another, sometimes arriving at what in Western eyes would be a complete contradiction; the native informer, however, recognizes the same structure beneath the contradiction and cannot understand why an apparent inconsistency matters.

Although the "same" structure can sustain different embodiments, that does not mean that the primitive mind apprehends it as disembodied. This is an elusive but important point. As Jean Pouillon put it in his "Essai de définition" at the beginning of an issue of *Les Temps modernes* devoted to structuralism, "Structuralism is not formalism. On the contrary, it challenges the distinction between form and matter, and no matter is *a priori* inaccessible to it. As Lévi-Strauss writes, 'form defines itself by opposition to a content which is exterior to it; but structure has no content: it is itself the content, apprehended in a logical organization conceived as a property of the real'" (Pouillon 1960:782). The world becomes intelligible as it becomes structured, primarily through the agency of language, secondarily through the agency of magic, totem, and myth. There are many languages and many myths; structuralism finds that they are homologous and capable of being generated out of one another by means of suitable transformations.

## 11. Structural transformations

THE CRUX OF Lévi-Strauss's notion of transformation is that cultural objects are never given singly, but always in groups (like mathematical groups) whose members prove to be transforms of one another; the object of knowledge in the human sciences is therefore not the particular case but the group of transformations to which it belongs. An example from his early work is provided by the acknowledged connection of his book on kinship with Marcel Mauss's *Essay on the Gift*, an account of potlatch practices in the American Northwest. Mauss thought that the exchange of gifts was a way of keeping the social world in motion; what looked like a pointless escalation of extravagance was in fact a highly structured mode of communication between groups that might otherwise have interacted in a far less friendly way. Lévi-Strauss concluded that exogamous marriage was a structural transform of this, produced by substituting women for gifts; the exchange of women kept disparate groups in contact and made them both beholden and accountable to one another. This would sound like functionalism if it were just an explanation of exogamous marriage as a force for social cohesion; the functional aspect is not insignificant, of course, but it turns out that almost anything will do—gifts, women, language, money—as a medium of exchange, so that the account precisely does not explain why it should be gifts in this society, women in that (or why the emphasis should fall on one or the other). Once again, the structure is more important than the elements through which it is realized.

The methodological consequences of this view will be that instead of asking for an interpretation, say, of a myth, right away, one will first ask what other myths exist, of which it might be a transformation, or which might be reached from it by a series of transformations; only when the whole group is established will the question of significance be raised, if it still seems desirable to do this. This last qualification is necessary because it may well be that the whole question of interpretation or significance will look quite different when all the myths belonging to the group are in hand; what seemed arbitrary at first may come to seem natural and necessary when the whole structure is in place. A group, every member of which can be seen only as arbitrary if taken alone, may, if in fact it constitutes a group in the strong sense, have the property that every member is necessary once one is given all the others. In the paradigm case of mythology, no myth in the group can be given privileged or fundamental status; "the world of mythology is round," as Lévi-Strauss puts it (1966a:7)— wherever one starts, one can eventually arrive everywhere, or return to the starting point. So the only strategy for getting under way is to choose a "reference myth" and start the process of transformation from it.

It may be, of course, that all the elements of a group are transformations, not just of one another, but of some other and more basic entity (to express the matter as cautiously as possible) that does not in fact appear in the group. Here the analogy with mathematical group theory has been left behind—the question is as it were an empirical one, if the absence of a conjecturally basic engendering entity can be said to be an empirical matter. This possibility presents itself in several different ways in the literature of structuralism and related movements. The engendering entity may be a schema of which the other entities are said to be realizations; this is roughly the situation in Vladimir Propp's *Morphology of the Folktale*, where from a small number of patterns and their variants it is shown how the whole corpus of legend and fairy tale can be derived. It may be metaphysical, and a number of writers have succumbed to the lure of absolute or absent structures which, if only they could be grasped or would reveal themselves, would provide the meaning that life now so notoriously lacks. It would not be wholly unreasonable to assimilate the standard deep/surface opposition from transformational-generative linguistics (of the vintage of Chomsky's *Current Issues*) to a model of this kind, since the underlying strings are never uttered and may produce by transformation a whole class of terminal strings all of which translate into one another (we might say that the sentences are pronounced but that their meaning never is). The latter case, however, clearly does not *require* a whole group of surface structures, since a semantic interpretation must correspond to each phonetic interpretation, even if the sentence is only uttered once. None of these cases, however, is quite in the spirit of Lévi-Strauss, who in all his analyses insists on staying with the surface structure, as it were. The "science of the concrete," the characteristic form of science for primitive people, is just the mastery of the group of transformations, or enough of it for local purposes, without worrying about some postulated form that would give a theoretical account of them.

There is, it is true, an early text of Lévi-Strauss that might be interpreted as betraying a kind of deep-structural conviction of an almost metaphysical kind. At the closing session of a conference of anthropologists and linguists, at Indiana in 1953, he said ". . . we have not been sufficiently aware of the fact that *both* language and culture are the product of activities that are basically similar. I am now referring to this uninvited guest which has been seated during this Conference beside us, and which is *the human mind*" (1958:81). The remark is ambiguous, but it suggests that the study of different cultural products—that is, directly or indirectly, the products of mind, or minds—might uncover a great transformation group consisting not of languages *or* kinship systems but of both of these *and* of mythology and religion and literature and psychoanalysis and politics and the rest, all of them generated by a structure that could be argued back to and shown to determine the shape of the human world—a global form of Cassirer's project or, in its more schematic way, of Kant's. The ambiguity could be expressed aphoristically by asking whether that world too is round, like the world of myths, or whether it also has a center.

But in either case the center, one way or another, will be human rather than transcendent. Language, myth, and so on represent the way in which human beings have been able to grasp the real, and for humans they constitute the real—they are not structures *of* some ineffable reality which lies behind them and from which they are separable. To say that the world is intelligible means that it presents itself to the mind as a message, to which primitive language and behavior are an appropriate response—but not as a message *from elsewhere*, simply as a message in its own right, as it were. The message, furthermore, is unitary, a fact which we have for the most part forgotten: ". . . we prefer to operate with detached pieces, if not indeed with 'small change,' while the native is a logical hoarder: he is forever tying the threads, unceasingly turning over all the aspects of reality, whether physical, social or mental. We traffic in our ideas; he hoards them up" (Lévi- Strauss 1966:267). And in this way he avoids the fragmentation we frequently lament in our own lives. But it would be a mistake to suppose that he has access to a kind of conceptual stability denied to us, by virtue of some now lost insight into things as they are. He looks for no such insight and therefore does not miss it; it is enough to be engaged in the structuring activity, whatever form it may take, to be relieved of any uneasiness about lack of foundations or of meaning or of the other things for which modern men and women, anguished and alienated as they are, often yearn so eloquently.

## 12. Stability and subjectivity

IF MIND IN its natural state finds this psychic equilibrium so easily, how does it come about that we have such difficulty in adjusting ourselves to the conditions of our existence? We may have moments of equilibrium, significantly enough when we are wholly engaged in some activity (as might by now be expected, it doesn't much matter *what* activity, whether athletic, intellectual, commercial, or artistic), but left to our own devices we tend to be a bewildered and discontented lot. This bewilderment and discontent manifest themselves in all sorts of projects for self-improvement, self-realization, self-discovery, all of which the primitive would find completely mystifying. He is in the fortunate condition of not knowing that he has a self, and therefore of not being worried about it. And the structuralists concluded that he is nearer the truth than we are, that a good deal of our trouble arises out of the invention of the self *as an object of study*, from the belief that "man" has a special kind of being, in short from the emergence of humanism. Structuralism is not a humanism, at least not one of the Western variety, because it refuses to grant humans as such a privileged status in the world. Obviously it cannot deny that human beings constitute a species, that there are individual human beings who observe, think, write, and so on (although it does not encourage them in the narcissistic effort of "finding themselves"). Nor does it deny that there are more or less cohesive social groups with their own histories and cultures. Nothing concrete recognized or valued by the humanist is excluded, only the theoretical basis of humanism.

The point becomes clearer if we consider the status of the *subject*, a topic that in principle tends to be slighted if not rejected outright by structuralism, on the grounds that the structures that emerge in large-scale social and cultural contexts "make themselves" independently of subjects ("myths think themselves through us," says Lévi-Strauss), but which in the passionate discussions of the movement in the 1960s always seemed to surface if not to dominate, and which became a leading preoccupation of some later work, notably that of Foucault. The subject, first of all, is a linguistic category, the "vantage" (to use an expression due to Benveniste) of verbs in the first person. As such it is important if only for purposes of clarity in reference: it avoids confusion between persons. (Strictly speaking the first person refers only to the subject "I"; the other directly personal subject "you" and the indirectly personal and nonpersonal subjects "he" and "it," however, do not lend themselves so readily to overinterpretation. The same is true of their plural forms, but the first person *plural* poses a special problem that will be dealt with later.) The subject is a vantage point in nonlinguistic senses too: *I* look at the world from a particular point of view, *I* act upon it from a particular strategic location.

But—whether under the influence of Greek philosophy, or Christianity, or Renaissance humanism—Western man began to look for a more substantial embodiment of the subject than that provided by his own contingent and transient body as percipient and agent, or by his linguistic habits as a mere point of reference. Just as the assertion that the world is a message now elicits the immediate response "from whom?" so the intelligibility of the world seems to be addressed to something more basic and more permanent than the momentary and evanescent subject of particular utterances or particular actions. If God had to be invented to create and sustain the world, Man had to be invented to perceive and understand it. Men therefore began to ask, "What am I?" in a nonlinguistic sense, much as they also asked, "What is matter?" or "What is gravity?" They began, in other words, the long and frustrating attempt to get the subject out into the world so that it could be examined objectively. But this involves a logical mistake and can easily lead to a psychoanalytic disaster.

## 13. The word of the patient

THE PSYCHOANALYST AMONG the structuralists was Lacan, who devoted a large part of his work to the problem of subjectivity. Lacan's career began at least as early as Lévi-Strauss's, and it is evident from his collected writings, (*Ecrits*, 1966b, and the sequence *Le Séminaire*, 1973–) that he represented a genuinely independent source for structuralism. His reputation in France derived mainly from his seminar at the Ecole Pratique des Hautes Etudes, whose members held him in a regard reminiscent of that in which Wittgenstein was reputedly held by his students in Cambridge and which became a gathering point for the intellectual society of Paris reminiscent of Bergson's lectures at the Collège de France. Lacan in his early career showed no special hurry to get his ideas into general circulation, and there is no systematic development to be traced. Starting always from Freud, he wandered by circuitous paths, and in a highly personal, extremely difficult, and often irritating style, compounded with verbal preciosity, hermetic allusions, and a kind of half-concealed amusement at the whole enterprise, into various problematic corners of contemporary thought. The impressive thing is that (once the barrier of style has been surmounted) he consistently throws light on them from a completely original angle.

Lacan's connection with structuralism shows itself in part in his insistence on the central place of language. "Whether it wishes to regard itself as an agent of cure, of development, or of inquiry," he says, "psychoanalysis has but one medium: the word of the patient. . . . We shall show that there is no word without response, even if it is greeted only with silence, as long as there is a hearer, and that that fact is the clue to its function in analysis" (1966b:247). This shows at once the parallel with Lévi-Strauss, although with a difference of scale: the message is particular rather than universal. The structure of language is, as before, the key to the structure of mind. On the opening page of *Ecrits*, in a short introduction to the collection as a whole, Lacan provides a characteristic example of his own style and a characteristically involuted formulation of a problem:

> "Style is the man himself," we repeat, without seeing in it any malice, nor being troubled by the fact that man is an uncertain reference. . . .

Style is the man, let us adopt the formula, only to extend it: the man to whom one addresses oneself?

This would simply be to satisfy the principle we have put forward: that in language our message comes to us from the Other, and to enunciate it to the limit: in an inverted form. (And let us remember that this principle is applied to its own enunciation . . .).

But if man were reduced to being nothing but the point of return of our discourse, would not the question come back to us what is the point of addressing it to him? (1966b:9).

The stylistic inaccessibility is deliberate—Lacan, like Kierkegaard, seems sometimes to want to make things harder rather than easier. And the question of the subject is difficult; not only our naïve assurance about it, but also our confidence in psychoanalysis itself, or even in a structuralist explanation, may be *deceptively* simple. Lacan wishes to force the reference to self-reference, the idea of language doubling back on itself, examples of the *dédoublement* that haunts structuralist writing (it would not be improper, according to Lévi-Strauss, to think of his own work as "the myth of mythology" [1969:12]). They are important because the subject, for Lacan, turns out to *be* a kind of *dédoublement*, a matching of consciousness with the world, of speaker with hearer, of the signifier with the signified. (These Saussurean terms will be dealt with in more detail later.) Whereas the civilized mind thinks itself capable of taking an objective stance and judging the adequacy of language or symbol (on the side of the signifier) to their meanings (on the side of the signified), the view of mind that emerges from ethnology and psychoanalysis suggests that the two realms are autonomous and that mind precisely *is* this adequacy, so that such objectivity is impossible.

This point is made again and again, in different forms and on different occasions, in the writings of Lacan. The subject is an activity, not a thing; the Cartesian *cogito* comes closer to representing it correctly than any view of the self as substance, but even the *cogito* gives too strong a sense of continuity and permanence, so that it would perhaps be better to say " '*cogito ergo sum' ubi cogito, ibi sum*" (wherever I think "I think therefore I am," there I am). The subject produces itself by reflecting on itself—a crucial stage in ontogenetic development is the "mirror stage," with its associated pathology of the "fragmented body"— but when it is engaged on some other object it has no being apart from the activity of being so engaged. The idea that it had objective being and could be studied scientifically, according to Lacan, was a direct consequence of the success of science in throwing light on the rest of the world, but when Freud looked for the subject in the light of science he found instead the unconscious, the Other.

Freud's own subjectivity, of course, was engaged on this quest, and its discovery by itself would have been, again, a case of impossible self-division. Although Lacan never quite puts it this way one could sum up the conclusion of his argument against the possibility of a science of the subject by saying: *the subject cannot be the object of a science because it is its subject*. When the analyst tries to get at "the subject which he calls, significantly, the patient," what he finds is not the true subject at all, but only something that is called into being by his questioning; "that is to say, the fish is drowned by the operation of fishing." The final image of the subject is the Möbius strip, or as Lacan calls it the "interior eight," which from two surfaces produces one, or from one two, depending on the starting point of the exercise. What Lacan seems to be saying is that the subject cannot give an analytic account of itself, only paradoxes, hints, and images, and this being the case there can be no "science of man." "There is no science of man, because the man of science does not exist, only its subject. It is known that I have always felt a repugnance for the term *sciences humaines*, which seems to me a call to slavery itself" (1966a:6).

## 14. The end of man

ONE OF THE most powerful structuralist blows against traditional humanism was administered by the publication in 1966 of Michel Foucault's *Les Mots et les choses*. Foucault did his best to dissociate himself from structuralism, going so far as to say in the preface to the English translation of that book (entitled *The Order of Things*, perhaps because the title *Words and Things* already belonged to two works, by Ernest Gellner and Roger Brown respectively) that he could not get it into people's "tiny minds" that he had used none of the methods or language of structural analysis—but this was false, except on a construal of "structural analysis" so narrow as to disqualify most of the other structuralists as well. At all events the starting point for the reflections that resulted in *Les Mots et les choses*, says Foucault in the original preface, was a text of Borges, which is worth quoting for itself as well as for the light that it throws on the structuralist enterprise:

> This text cites a "certain Chinese encyclopedia" where it is written that "animals are divided into: a) belonging to the Emperor, b) embalmed, c) tame, d) suckling pigs, e) mermaids, f) fabulous, g) dogs running free, h) included in the present classification, i) which behave like madmen, j) innumerable, k) drawn on camel-skin with a very fine brush, l) et cetera, m) which have just broken their leg, n) which from a distance look like flies."

And Foucault continues: "In our astonishment at this taxonomy what strikes us with sudden force, what, because of its setting, is presented to us as the exotic charm of another system of thought, is the limitation of our own: the stark impossibility of thinking *that*" (1966:7).

Why, Foucault asks, do we find Borges's imaginary Chinese classification so preposterous? Into what intellectual straitjacket has our own history forced us? And he concludes that our resistance to this kind of spontaneous absurdity, our demand for logical coherence even where it is unnecessary, is again a product of the invention of *man* as an embodiment of analytic reason. Until early modern times subjectivity was absorbed in a single discourse, which constituted the world as intelligible and summed up all that could be said about it. The rise of science led to the fragmentation and dissolution of this conceptual and linguistic unity by drawing attention to separable properties of the world—biological, economic, philological—and pursuing them independently. But it then became apparent that in some sense all these inquiries were about the same thing; only instead of recombining into a single activity, they were thought of as pointing to a single entity—Man. Man thus appeared to have achieved his own objectification. The present perplexity of the so-called humanities indicates, however, that that conclusion was premature; the picture of man that they present to us turns out to bear little resemblance to our real contemporaries. Humanism has been a detour from which we may be beginning to return to the main track: Foucault concludes *Les Mots et les choses* with a more or less confident prediction that man will disappear "like a face drawn in sand at the edge of the sea" (1966:398).

This must not be understood as a prophecy of doom. Men and women will still be here, facing the same problems in the same way, with the exception that the particular aberration called *man*, which corresponds to no such actual person, will have been done away with. All attempts to classify and predict *individual* human behavior quickly encounter limits which show them, in all but a few cases (and all these to some extent pathological), to be futile. Rational, humanist aesthetics, for example, yielded when put into practice a wooden imitation of art; art began to revive in this century when the surrealists and others preached liberation from orthodox canons and advocated the free play of the unconscious. Even structuralism, when this is taken as a program for creation rather than understanding, hinders rather than helps the enterprise of art. This was one of the errors, according to Lévi-Strauss, that literary enthusiasts of structuralism fell into: "Because the human sciences have brought formal structures to light behind works of art, there is a rush to fabricate works of art on the basis of formal structures. But it is by no means certain that these conscious and artificially constructed structures, taken as a basis for inspiration, will be of the same order as those that are discovered, after the fact, to have operated in the mind of the creator, most often without his being aware of them" (1971:573). (I note for future reference that this amounts to an admission of the incompleteness of structuralist explanation in the domain of art.) Things are even worse in the social sciences, and the havoc that these are capable of wreaking when the order of explanatory dependence is reversed surrounds us on every side. There is nothing wrong with them, of course, as inquiries into individual or group behavior carried on by somebody for whom that behavior constitutes an object; they become sinister only when people believe uncritically what they are told about themselves and *become what the social scientist says they are.*

Structuralism, in effect, advocates an engagement with the world, an active participation in significant activity, which in structuring the world will bring the subject into equilibrium with it—or rather it does not need to *advocate* any such thing, it asserts that something like it will naturally happen if not inhibited by reflective preoccupations. *What* activity is not a matter of great concern. There is nothing particularly worthy, as the existentialists thought, in political or artistic engagement; any number of other pursuits can embody the structure of mind. Art and politics, nevertheless, as two of the most comprehensive signiferous structures, come in for special attention from structuralism, and above all literature, since it employs directly the very archetype of structure, language itself. But there is more than one kind of structuralist criticism, and the overlap with other techniques is greater here than elsewhere. The great triumph of structural method, which imitated the sciences in producing new knowledge through empirical investigation, remains in fact the work of the Marxist critic Lucien Goldmann on Pascal and Racine, in the course of which he was able to reconstruct some parts of the Jansenist movement which had been forgotten, and furthermore to locate the evidence that they had in fact existed (the relevant works are *Le Dieu caché* and the *Correspondaence de Martin de Barcos, abbé de Saint-Cyran*).

## 15. Critical work

I HAVE NOT included Goldmann in the list of the major structuralists because much of what I have taken to define the movement does not apply to him, and his own method, which he called "genetic structuralism," rested very heavily on the notion of literature as an embodiment (often in spite of the intentions of the writer) of some collective social attitude appropriate to a class or period. Structuralist criticism in the wider sense does not limit itself to collective or social or historical considerations, although it does not ignore them either. The work embodies a structure, or belongs to one; the critic uses it as a point of departure. One of the striking things about this criticism, in fact, is its habit of getting far more out of a work than its author or for that matter its historical period could possibly have put into it. Foucault opens *Les Mots et les choses* with a chapter on "Las Meninas" (The Maids of Honor), a painting of Velasquez from which he extracts by hindsight and free elaboration a whole theory of the "absence of the subject." And Althusser, who has applied structuralist techniques to a "rethinking" of Marx, was said in an essay in *Aletheia* to have developed a complete apparatus "for putting oneself in a condition to read Marx so as to think profitably not only what Marx wrote but also what he thought without writing" (Karsz 1967:233).

This remark was not necessarily meant kindly, but Althusser might well have agreed with it. For him the central concept is that of *ideology*, the structured, unconscious system through which we become aware of and relate to the world. Structuralism itself is an ideology (1971:17), but he uses its methods to show how the Hegelian dialectic transforms into the Marxist one. The ideal (not a word Althusser was in the habit of using—I do so in its nontechnical sense) would be to become "scientific" rather than ideological, as Althusser takes Marx to have done after the *coupure épistémologique* or "epistemological cut" that, he claims, followed *The German Ideology*. His works (*Pour Marx, Lire Le Capital*) present a Marxism Marx himself could not have created, since he did not enjoy the advantages of the intervening hundred years; the article already cited calls them "limiting cases of interpretation."

Such rereading, rethinking, reconstructing are quite in keeping with the principles of structuralist criticism. The clearest statement of these principles is to be found in Roland Barthes's *Critique et vérité*, a response to Raymond Picard's *Nouvelle critique ou nouvelle imposture?* in turn an attack on Barthes's *Sur Racine*. Picard, a typical humanist, had become indignant at the way in which Barthes had, in his view, tampered with literary and historical objectivity, with the "facts" about Racine. Barthes points out that there could be a "science" of literature only if we were content to regard the work simply as a "written object," disregarding its privileged sense in favor of all its possible senses, disregarding its author in favor of its remoter linguistic origins—treating it, in fact, as the ethnologist treats a myth. What criticism does, by contrast, is to produce *one* of the possible senses of the work, to construct alongside, as it were, another work, in the light of which the original becomes intelligible in a new way. "The book is a world," says Barthes. "The critic confronted by the book is subject to the same conditions of utterance as the writer confronted by the world" (1966:69).

The critic cannot do the work of the reader (but rather makes more work for the reader). Readers confront the text, creative or critical—and both are both—at a particular time, in a particular context; it becomes part of their experience, presents itself to them with a certain intelligibility, as a message (from whom?); it engages them in further episodes of the structuring activity that makes them what they are. An old book is not (unless the reader takes pains to make it so) a bit of antiquity, it is a bit of the present; consequently Racine can still be read, and new critical views about Racine, possible only in the light of contemporary events, can find in him without distortion meanings which he and *his* contemporaries could not even have understood. Similarly Althusser is justified in his rethinking of Marx; indeed all works have constantly to be rethought if they are to be more than archaeological curiosities.

## 16. Complexity and humanity

STRUCTURALIST CRITICISM BRINGS us back to Lévi-Strauss. The critic never says all there is to be said about a book; critical reading is always an approximation that we know to be inadequate, even if we do not know what would constitute an adequate reading—even if it makes no sense to imagine such a reading. Similarly language never formulates the world adequately; nor does myth; nor does science, in spite of its (now abandoned) aspiration to completability in principle; nor does history. These structures change in time (they can be considered diachronically as well as synchronically); also, which is not the same thing, they are dynamic, having complex interrelations among themselves. The respect in which I think Lévi-Strauss does not exploit the full resources of his own method in distinguishing between primitive and modern societies has to do with this complexity of interrelation of structures. If mind emerged, as it surely did, under evolutionary pressure which required an order of complexity in behavior greater than that of any other form of life, if when the evolutionary pressure was off it devised language as a means of keeping that complexity in dynamic equilibrium with its world, then it seems to me that the way was opened for a kind of amplification of complexity by shifting language from the side of the object to the side of the subject, where mind (now ramified with language) became capable of handling an even greater objective complexity, and indeed required it in order to maintain equilibrium. We are perhaps today in one of the later stages of such an exponential development.

    If that should be the case we might well cultivate the totalizing quality of the primitive mind, of which Lévi-Strauss speaks at the end of *La Pensée sauvage*. It is there (in the course of a polemic against Sartre) that he refers to "this intransigent refusal on the part of the savage mind to allow anything human (or even living) to remain alien to it." This allusion to one of the oldest mottoes of humanism may seem odd in a discussion of an antihumanist point of view; but I think the truth is that here again Lévi-Strauss does not go far enough. To restrict the sphere of concern to the human, or even to the living, does not do justice to mind as its own history has revealed it. The structuring activity that keeps the subject in balance with the world is and must be all-encompassing. To quote Pouillon once more: "structuralism forbids us to enclose ourselves in any particular reality." The fact that we abandon a restrictive humanism, however, does not mean that we cease to be human. If structuralism had a motto, it might well be: *Homo sum, nihil a me alienum puto.*

The motto that Lévi-Strauss alludes to and that I adapt was no doubt intended by him to reflect creditably on the tenacity of the primitive in the appropriation of his world. Actually it proves to be in the best tradition of *bricolage*—functional, but taken out of its original context. The line occurs in a play of Terence, adapted from Menander, called *Heautontimoroumenos* or *The Self-Tormentor*, and reads: "Homo sum, humani nihil a me alienum puto," ("I am a man, I consider nothing human alien to me".) However, in Terence it is a tribute not at all to the spirit of free inquiry but rather to that of inquisitive meddling. Menedemus, the "self-tormentor" of the title, being interrogated by Chremes about his mode of life, says: "Chremes, are you so much at leisure from your own affairs that you can be concerned about other people's, which are none of your business?" to which Chremes pompously replies, "I am a man . . ." But this background fits the present context admirably: human beings are great self-tormentors, but they are also great meddlers, and in this lies one possibility of escape from torment. I have dealt elsewhere (Caws 1969:1379) with the relation between what psychologists have called "exploratory" behavior and the development of scientific theories, but the point is more general: it is the structuring activity of the mind, its appetite for interrelations among things, that lends intelligibility to whatever systems of the world, or of things in the world, we think of ourselves as inhabiting or having dealings with.

It is important to notice, however, that this need not be construed megalomaniacally. Systems, as I shall have occasion to insist later on, can be local or partial, and our involvement with them temporary or episodic. If Lévi-Strauss, among the French structuralists, is the chief builder of grand systems of significance, whether in the domain of kinship or totemism or mythology, it may be good to be reminded in closing this chapter of the gentler and less pretentious style of Roland Barthes, who after his early attempts at large-scale syntheses in literature (to which I have already referred) and semiology (which, being a more or less direct adaptation of Saussure, will be taken up separately in a later chapter), devoted the last years of his life to the production of a series of masterly texts on limited episodes of meaning and the systems that carry them— not only the passing fashion itself, as in *Système de la mode*, but also the Eiffel Tower, Diderot's *Encyclopédie*, the Italian *castrati* and novels about them, the Marquis de Sade, the exercises of St. Ignatius Loyola, the utopianism of Fourier, Japanese art, reading, love, photography. The text on the Eiffel Tower is a typical case. In it Barthes describes the device used by some writers (Hugo and Michelet, for example) of taking a "bird's-eye view" of Paris, or of France, and remarks that the construction of the Eiffel Tower made such a view for the first time physically realizable by large numbers of people: "Paris and France become under the pen of Hugo and Michelet (and under observation from the Tower) intelligible objects, without however—and this is what is novel— losing anything of their materiality; a new category arises, that of concrete abstraction: such moreover is the sense that can be given today to the word *structure*: a body of intelligent forms" (Barthes 1964:43). Barthes used some-times to speak of "conquest by the intelligible," and his works might be thought of as providing a strategy for that conquest, the task of structuralism itself, claiming once again for intellect a territory that we had all but abandoned to the Absurd. For the Absurd is precisely the *un*intelligible, things and events presented to us in their bewildering or menacing opacity, devoid of meaning.

The contrast between the structuralist view and that of the theoreti-cians of the Absurd who dominated the early postwar period lies in the refusal of the former to accept apparent meaninglessness, its determination to construct its own intelligibility. The question that springs to mind, in reading Camus and other writers in the absurdist tradition, is why anybody should ever have expected meaning to come to us *from the world as a whole*, why anybody should ever have looked for it *in the world as given*. Meaningful-ness in human experience seems to me necessarily episodic—we learn what matters, and what signifies (the two essential components of meaning in the full sense) in local contexts, and the generalization of the concept to global dimensions is both misguided and harmful. Both mattering and signifying are relative to us, not objective properties of anything in the world. (Note however that this does *not* commit us to epistemological relativism.) Structur-alism therefore—except in some aberrant forms—pays no attention to abso-lute or transcendent features of the world, those fatal lures of philosophy in its grandiloquent mode, but concentrates on limited episodes of significance and mattering: works of literature, affective relations between individuals, small-scale examples of social organization, scientific theories themselves, as paradigm cases of human achievement that do not require global principles or transcendent guarantees in order to be lived and appreciated as fully meaningful.

Such at all events is the lesson I take myself to have learned from structuralism in France. This sketch of the movement as it was in what might be called (borrowing from Jamesian scholarship) the "major phase" will be supplemented later by a somewhat more technical account; I have sought to capture here the openness, diversity, and excitement of the period. My conclusion about structuralism and the life of meaning, which will be developed further in Part II, would probably have seemed far too modest to the French structuralists themselves, who indeed have been perceived by their own countrymen as exercising a form of intellectual tyranny (Bouveresse 1984:114–15). But this very likelihood may help to explain why, as a serious entry in the history of philosophy, the major phase came to such a comparatively rapid end.

# 3

# Structuralism in America

## 17. The New World and the Postwar Period

STRUCTURALISM IS IRREVERSIBLY associated with its Parisian flowering and fading, but part of my purpose in this book is to establish some distance between that parochial setting and what I take to be the international (or, as proud terrestrials are tempted to think, the universal) importance of the ideas it embraces. Some of them emerged independently at other times and in other places, so that a standard geography of the subject will refer to Moscow with the Russian Formalists, and to Prague with its linguistic circle, as well as to Paris (cf. Broekman 1974). And there are scattered figures of importance in other places as well, England for example, where Edmund Leach has played with respect to Lévi-Strauss a role reminiscent of the one Ernest Jones played with respect to Freud in an earlier generation. These aspects of the history are familiar enough. What is perhaps less familiar is the way in which thought in America, and especially in the United States, anticipated, prepared, and nurtured the structuralist movement.

I do not mean this treatment to be an exhibition of adopted chauvinism. A bit of everything, of whatever national or international origin, is to be found in America—Russian folklore, German philology, British analytic philosophy. Also there often exist indigenous analogues of such things, sometimes pre-Columbian, sometimes pre-Revolutionary, sometimes merely dating from before the massive invasion of the country by refugees or brain-drained intellectuals. The resulting difficulty, not to say impossibility, of identifying the specifically American component in any complex movement of ideas, presents itself in the case of structuralism no less than in other contexts. "Structuralism in America" means at least four different things. It means the precursors and the independents, like Lewis H. Morgan and Charles Sanders Peirce and the New Critics and the early structural linguists and Zellig Harris and Noam Chomsky—already spanning a century and several ideological rifts; it means the gestation of French structuralism, which took place in New York in the 1940s; it means the scattered enthusiasm of contemporary workers in a variety of disciplines, some of them (but not all) influenced by French thought, who have brought structuralist methods to bear on a constellation of different problems, literary, linguistic, and anthropological; and it means the osmosis of French structuralism into American intellectual life that took place in virtue of visits and exchanges arranged by American academics, some of them more credulous and impressionable than others. Such unity as structuralism in America may be said to have is for the most part borrowed from this last association, since without it the indigenous and imported components would not appear to have the interdisciplinary cross-connections they do in fact appear to have.

The genesis of the postwar emergence of structuralism as an interdisciplinary phenomenon can be traced to New York, where the basic connection between linguistics and anthropology was established in the personal relationship of Roman Jakobson and Claude Lévi-Strauss. Not that these disciplines had previously been unrelated to each other—indeed their interrelations have been intimate from the beginning, language being the characteristic mark of the human, and exotic languages, discovered in other cultures, having stimulated first comparative and then structural linguistics. But without the personal encounter to which I refer there might well have been nothing called "structuralism" outside linguistics proper. In particular Jakobson's earlier association with the Russian formalists and the Prague school, and his long and intimate acquaintance with Troubetzkoy (who, but for illness, might himself have come to the United States as yet another brilliant refugee instead of being badgered to death in Vienna), put at Lévi-Strauss's disposal a powerful linguistic tradition, springing from Saussure, that was already fully "structuralist"; added to his own background in French philosophy and sociology (especially Durkheim and Mauss), and his recent experiences among the Bororo and the Nambikwara in Brazil, this constituted the matrix out of which his thought developed after his return to France at the end of the war. He and Jakobson were, in the latter's words, "one another's mutual students" in linguistics and anthropology (1968:19).

This was structuralism geographically and contingently *in* America, not yet an integral part of its own intellectual life. The extraordinary collection of talent that Nazi oppression and American hospitality had brought to reinforce an already considerable native strength led, however, to the founding of the Linguistic Circle of New York and its journal *Word*, in which Lévi-Strauss published his early article on "Structural Analysis in Linguistics and Anthropology" (Lévi-Strauss 1945) and which became one of the prime sources for structuralist inquiry. Jakobson of course remained in the United States and I shall have occasion to return to his later work. It is worth noting that there was in the United States at the same epoch another group of expatriate scientists, the Gestalt psychologists, whose ideas had a close affinity with structuralism and to whom Lévi-Strauss explicitly admits his debt (Bastide 1962:43). The notion of *Gestalt* in its connection with that of structure was analyzed in a paper read to the Linguistic Circle by Ernst Cassirer (who spent the latter part of his own life in the United States) and published in the second issue of *Word*. Called "Structuralism in Modern Linguistics," it was his last public lecture, and it contained the remark cited in chapter 1 to the effect that structuralism was not an isolated phenomenon but the expression of a general tendency of thought that had become prominent in recent decades. (However Lévi-Strauss by his own account was not present on this occasion and did not discover the parallel between his own work and Cassirer's until much later [Lévi-Strauss, private communication].)

## 18. Morgan and Peirce

THE TENDENCY OF thought to which Cassirer referred went back more than a few decades, although its postwar vogue, as Lévi-Strauss points out in giving credit to Lewis H. Morgan, was a rediscovery rather than a continuous transmission (Bastide 1962:143). Morgan was an American lawyer who studied the Iroquois because he had joined a club whose constitution was supposed to be based on theirs, and who became fascinated with their kinship terminology. Kinship relations, as we have already seen, embody a basic form of social knowledge (indeed later on Durkheim and Mauss in *Primitive Classification* maintained that they were the pattern for all subsequent classificatory schemes, a claim that while ethnographically dubious has not lost its plausibility), and Morgan considered that this knowledge was systematically organized to a high degree. What might be called his characteristically structuralist turn came when he turned his attention from the Iroquois to the Ojibwa; among the latter, he remarks in his treatise *Systems of Consanguinity and Affinity of the Human Family*, "every term of relationship was radically different from the corresponding term in the Iroquois; but the classification of kindred was the same. It was manifest that the two systems were the same in their fundamental characteristics" (Morgan 1871:3). We should now wish to say that the two systems had the same structure.

Morgan himself, later in his book, speaks of the "structure of the system," although he does not define it further. It is to be noticed that kinship relations have this peculiarity, which we shall encounter in other contexts: that the individuals related by them have their place in the system because they are so related, and not for any other reason. Their *being* individuals, in the context of the system, *consists* of their being related, in ways that are now mainly conventional, to other individuals. The case of twins in some primitive societies is instructive: because there are two of them

having the same relations to everyone else in the society, structural individuation no longer works; they cannot be distinguished within the system, and
this anomaly must be dealt with somehow. It is a striking testimony to the
strength of the drive to structural order that, confronted with this problem,
different societies should so frequently have resorted to extreme measures. As
might have been expected from structuralist considerations, *which* extreme
does not matter, as long as the anomalous elements are removed from the
system; so the Bushmen of the Kalahari used to put twins to death, while the
Ashanti regarded them as divine and made a present of them to the king.
However there are other ways of saving the situation, like that of the
Ndembu, who carry out a complex ceremony of differentiation in order to
acknowledge and absorb this natural paradox, which they regard as at once
mysterious and absurd (Turner 1969:84–85).

The origins of kinship relations are no doubt biological, but biological
relations are short-lived and the structure of kinship systems far too variable
to allow even a sociobiological explanation in any detail. Morgan seems to
have anticipated the structuralist insight that such systems come, as it were,
to have lives of their own. He remarks for example on the stability of the
radical form of the family system found in Turanian and Ganowanian (that
is, Asian and pre-Columbian) groups, and adds: "this conclusion is further
strengthened by the extraordinary circumstance that the system, in virtue of
its organic structure, has survived for ages the causes in which it originated,
and is now in every respect an artificial system, because it is contrary to the
nature of descents as they actually exist in the present state of Indian
society" (1871:508). This can legitimately be read as a variant of the doctrine
of the arbitrariness of the sign, especially since Morgan explicitly approached
the problem of kinship by way of its terminology.

The other great nineteenth-century precursor is Charles Sanders Peirce,
who presents, however, a rather more complicated historical problem.
Peirce's brilliant and chaotic writings contain anticipations of almost everything of philosophical importance in the twentieth century, but one of the
domains in which his influence has been most widely acknowledged is that of
semiotics. Semiotics and structuralism, in spite of their very close association, must not be confused with each other: although the principal developments of structuralism took place in the analysis of significant (or, as I prefer
to say, "signiferous") systems, and although the principal recent developments of semiotics have taken place in a structuralist or poststructuralist
context, there is no essential connection between the Saussurean doctrine of
system that led, among his followers, to structuralism, and the other Saussurean doctrine of the sign, whose origins are to be found among the Stoics.
Similarly with Peirce: it is not because of his theory of signs that I count
Peirce among the precursors of structuralism, but (among other things)

because of a quite independent and almost casual remark about the concept of structure itself, which constitutes a startling if obscure adumbration of one of the more difficult structuralist theses.

Peirce's remark occurs in connection with a proposed analysis of the elements of what he calls the "phaneron," a term original with him by which he means "the collective total of all that is in any way or in any sense present to the mind, quite regardless of whether it corresponds to any real thing or not." For this analysis he coins the term "phaneroscopy"; it is in fact an original formulation of what we now call phenomenology, quite unconcerned with the line of development that led through Husserl. He assesses two different strategies: "one is a division according to the form or structure of the elements, the other according to their matter." The second, though, he thing can be said to have structure.

This question is answered by Peirce in terms of the concept of "val-abandons as hopeless: "Fortunately, however, all taxonomists of every department have found classification according to structure to be the most important." This sounds, so far, like Cuvier perhaps, but given the nature of the enterprise the question necessarily arises (in another place, but plausibly juxtaposed by Peirce's editors) of how an indecomposable *element* of some-ence" or "external structure," just in the sense in which the latter term was used in chapter 1. His idea is that the structure of the elements of a system may be regarded as a function of the relations that interconnect them, rather than as an independent property of each element separately (1931:141ff). In other words the phaneron is, to revert to Saussurean language, a system of differences; the structuralist question is not addressed to the structure of the element in a conventional sense, but to the structure or structures of which its constitutive relations form a potential part. At the same time Peirce does not suppose that the relations displayed in the phaneron are surds; on the contrary, he seems in other passages to share (though in a stronger, more Kantian form) the structuralist conviction that their intelligibility is to be explained by a second-order relation of matching between them and us: "there is an energizing reasonableness that shapes phenomena in some sense, and . . . this same working reasonableness has molded the reason of man into something like its own image" (1958:291); "man's mind must have been attuned to the truth of things in order to discover what he has discovered" (1958:372).

## 19. Structural linguistics

MORGAN'S NOTION OF the systematic interrelations of systems of kinship, and Peirce's notion of structure as something things belong to rather than something they have, are easily recognizable as early variants of structuralist doctrine, but neither of them bore the label "structuralist." In linguistics, on the other hand, there did grow up in America a school bearing this label, but its doctrines were almost the opposite of those now called structuralist. This fact has led to great confusion and accounts among other things for the anomalous position occupied by Chomsky with regard to the structuralist movement. For whereas structuralism in linguistics, from the French point of view, means the investigation of structures common to many if not all languages, it meant from the American point of view in the early twentieth century the investigation of structures specific to particular languages. In part this was only a terminological difference, arising from an ambiguity in the term "structure" itself. In the *Handbook of American Indian Languages* the structure of a language means less its syntactic structure than the structure of its lexical forms (and in fact at about the same epoch this was the way in which it was understood by Saussure, who never used the term in a "structuralist" sense). But in the Introduction to that work Franz Boas clearly recognizes the universality of grammatical structure, although not by that name: ". . . the occurrence of the most fundamental grammatical concepts in all languages must be considered a proof of the unity of funda-mental psychological processes" (Boas 1911:71). The reason why in the end linguistic differences rather than linguistic similarities came to be stressed by American linguists was in part the evident diversity of rapidly vanishing linguistic and cultural material that had, as it were, to be salvaged, and in part no doubt a sense that linguistic differences were clues to far-reaching conceptual ones, a sense that found later expression in the Sapir-Whorf hypothesis.

The dominant trend in American linguistics between the wars was behaviorist as well as "structuralist" in this narrow sense. Its aim was to articulate descriptive and noninterpretative data about particular languages as complex forms of human behavior; with a kind of puritanical single-mindedness (also found as we shall see among the New Critics) it sought to rid itself of all historical, and for the time being at least of all comparative, prejudices: "Features which we think ought to be universal may be absent from the very next language which becomes accessible. . . . When we have adequate data about many languages, we shall have to return to the problem of general grammar and to explain these similarities and divergences, but this study, when it comes, will not be speculative but inductive" (Bloomfield 1933:19). This positivist suspicion of speculation no doubt had a dampening effect in linguistics as in other domains. But after the Second World War two developments took place that tended to open the discipline toward new possibilities. One has already been alluded to in the discussion of the Linguistic Circle of New York, but it may be worth adding here that this involved one of the first explicit presentations of the work of Saussure in English, in an article published in *Word* (Wells 1947). The other was the independent development, by Zellig Harris, of yet another form of structuralism, based on the notion of "distributional structure" (Harris 1954). Harris's concern was not so much comparative as mathematical; he sought a way of expressing in formal terms the data obtained from descriptive studies. This led to the working out of an abstract mathematical system whose structures (hereditary processes, redundancies, transformations, and so on) are characteristic of natural languages and presumably determined by the "semantic burden that [they] alone can carry" (1968:207). It led also to discussions of the "reality" of linguistic structure and the existence of a "parallel 'meaning structure'" (1954:29, 31).

In the light of these antecedents it is hardly surprising that when Harris's student Noam Chomsky embarked on the independent line of linguistic inquiry for which he became famous he should, while not avoiding the term "structure" altogether, have resisted classification as a structuralist. For Chomsky the more important grammatical notion is that of the *rule*; a grammar is a "system of rules" (1964:8), and while these rules "express structural relations among the sentences of the corpus" (1957:49), a more significant fact about them is that there are many structural relations that they do not express. The purely structural information to be derived from the study of languages is not very interesting (1968:65), but what is remarkable is the fact that grammatical rules actually in use seem to generate a highly restricted class of structures, "that there are innumerable 'imaginable' languages that violate these restrictions and that are, therefore, not possible human languages in a psychologically important sense" (1967:8).

In other words the structural features of language need for linguistically significant or interesting purposes to be supplemented by other considerations. Here again, however, the issue is partly terminological. It has often been pointed out that the term "structure" can without much effort be shown to apply to everything whatever, and the interest of structuralism has always in fact been in a restricted class of structures, namely, just those that reveal themselves in cultural products, including language. If we accept the definition of structure as a set of systematic relations, then we can contrast an inclusive sense that covers all kinds of possible relations (which yields mathematics) or all kinds of actual relations (which yields science) with an exclusive sense that covers a few kinds of actual relations, selected by cultural practice; these tend to show up as systematic *constraints*, and they are the ones in which structuralism is interested.

Everything hinges on the choice of system. The universe, as physicists point out, is in one sense a total system having a structure; since everything in it appears to be composed of similar basic elements and to occupy (or constitute) a connected space-time framework, everything in it is related to everything else. Precisely for this reason, physical structures as such are of no interest to structuralism. In fact no system that would have been as it is independently of the human mind calls for structuralist investigation, with one exception. The exception is the human mind itself, a natural product (hence not dependent on itself but on prior determinations) whose structure can however not be examined directly but can only be inferred from the structures of its products.

In this light Chomsky's position appears much closer to that of structuralism. Although his chief interest, on the academic side at any rate, remains language, he has taken an explicitly mentalistic view of its underlying mechanisms and associated himself with a philosophical tradition that saw in mind and in reason an autonomous province of being. This does not commit him or the structuralists to philosophical idealism, in whatever form (although as I shall argue in Part 2 there is a domain in which such a commitment makes sense), but it does mean a rejection of doctrinaire positivism or reductionism and an insistence on taking human phenomena as capable of explication in their own terms, not merely as recalcitrant deviations from biological or chemical norms.

Whether or not it will ever be possible to establish the continuity, which practically everyone admits in principle, from the inorganic through the organic to the mental—a task undertaken, for example, with mixed success, by the American philosopher Suzanne Langer (1967, 1972, 1982)—it is the task of structuralism to inquire into the coherence of the latter domain. As Kenneth Pike puts it, ". . . man has certain structural traits which are more pervasive than has previously been suspected, and which therefore tell us something important about man himself. . . . The struggle to understand is the struggle to sense structure and its criteria" (1967:641, 663). The work from which these citations are taken, *Language in Relation to a Unified Theory of the Structure of Human Behavior,* is a monumental attempt to unite linguistics with the other behavioral sciences, and it deserves mention in a chapter on structuralism in the United States not only because of its structuralist orientation but because of the light it casts, incidentally and perhaps unintentionally, on some paradigmatic banalities of life in the United States—evangelical church services, college football matches, family breakfasts. In an extremely slow and detailed argument Pike introduces the notions of the "etic" and the "emic"—borrowed from the standard meanings of "phonetic" and "phonemic" (see chapter 5)—to embody the contrast between physical description and structural analysis, between external appearance and internal significance. The technical terminology he develops on this basis seems unnecessarily heavy, but the intention behind it can only be applauded: "to build a conceptual framework which will provide a bridge over which, on the one hand, the linguist can travel in order to understand more easily certain problems of the anthropologist or sociologist and, on the other hand, over which the anthropologist may pass in order to understand some of the problems of the linguist" (1967:641).

## 20. Structural anthropology

ANTHROPOLOGY AND LINGUISTICS have always been closely associated, and in the United States they have in some ways followed parallel paths, owing partly to the fact that the same stock of indigenous cultures provided an obvious empirical resource for both, even though a good proportion of the attention of American anthropologists was directed elsewhere (one thinks, for example, of Ruth Benedict and Margaret Mead). The interest of anthropology for structuralism, however, lies more in anthropological theory than in the details of field studies, important as the latter are if the theory is not to be hopelessly abstract. In this connection it is worth remembering that one of the early stimuli of Levi-Strauss's anthropological career, some years before his New York period, was a textbook by an American anthropologist (Lowie 1920). But the discipline was not recognizably structuralist in those days, indeed Kroeber somewhere remarks that the interest in structure is just a passing fad. Some of those who conducted field studies on American Indian populations, however, did begin to see beyond the accumulation of data to underlying structural patterns.

A good example is Gladys Reichard, whose long and penetrating inquiry into Navaho culture involved the analysis of thirty-five hundred genealogies. In all this evidence, said Reichard, she never came across a relationship that was doubtful as seen from ego's point of view—a powerful testimony to what now appears as a human appetite for structure: "The members of the family themselves will always know—at least they will have settled upon —their own clan membership and all that goes with it. There is then no large category into which persons of doubtful connections are thrown for to them connections never *are* doubtful" (1969:15). And elsewhere she speaks of the "religious system which has for years enabled the Navaho to retain their identity in a rapidly changing world," of an "interlocking system of associations" (1950:xxi–ii). It is just this preoccupation with the stability of human structures and their synchronic complexity that marks later structuralist thought.

Reichard's thirty-five hundred genealogies recall (or, in the order of this exposition, anticipate) other examples of the range and intensity of the empirical base required by serious structuralist studies—the hundred distinct languages that Troubetzkoy felt he needed before venturing on any phonological generalizations (see chapter 5), the 813 myths assembled by Levi-Strauss in his *Mythologiques* (see chapter 6). A further case is provided by a work that began a new variant of structuralism in American anthropology, in which Murdock analyzed data from 85 societies documented by the Yale Cross-Cultural Survey (a late realization of a project of Spencer's to accumulate sociological data from all societies in summary form) and another 165 described in a more fragmentary way in the literature (Murdock 1949). The special interest of Murdock's work lies in the fact that, like Morgan, he approaches the anthropological question of social structure through the linguistic medium of kinship terminology. The anthropologist depends for the most part on spoken information, but what the informant says may or may not reflect accurately the reality of social relations; in a society in which any kind of historical development takes place there is likely to be a lag between the social structure, which is partly determined by external (for example, economic) factors, and the structure of the kinship terminology that to some degree reflects and adapts to it. Both are synchronic but they do not exactly match. The problem of this relationship between semantic structure and social structure, but more particularly the intrinsic interest of the semantic structure, became prominent in theoretical anthropology in the United States under the names of "componential analysis" or "formal semantics."

A general account of this is given by Harold Scheffler (Ehrmann 1966:69ff.), and an apology and defense by Floyd Lounsbury (Goodenough 1964:351ff.), where he says: "It is the parsimony of formal accounts—the fact that they do not tell one more than the barest necessary minimum—that is precisely the characteristic that can give them their value in terms of cross-cultural generality; and it is the habit of overexplanation, so common in attempts at functional description, that robs the latter of their generality." But the formal account he goes on to give of the Crow and Omaha kinship terminologies is a perfect case of what in a Lévi-Straussian context would be called structural analysis: the Crow and Omaha systems are transformations of each other with a change of sign, everything on the father's sister's side in the Crow terminology showing up on the mother's brother's side in the Omaha terminology, and vice versa. Scheffler and Lounsbury also collaborated on a much more detailed treatment of a specific case (Scheffler and Lounsbury 1971).

In this part of the literature and in the present context it is worth calling attention to a couple of articles that draw their data from the nonindigenous population of the United States—Ward Goodenough's "Yankee Kinship Terminology" (Hammel; 1965:259ff.) and Schneider's "American Kin Categories" (Pouillon and Maranda 1970:377ff.), the latter stressing a distinction (reminiscent of Kant) between the "order of nature" and the "order of law" as embracing two different kinds of relation which nevertheless are complementary to each other: while in structuralist studies the relevant relations are primarily those in the order of law, these are generated and sustained in non-trivial ways by relations in the order of nature. But of course American scholars continue to work on non-American cultures, and a similar point is made by Clifford Geertz in his study of the Balinese: ". . . certain sorts of pattern and certain sorts of relationships among patterns recur from society to society, for the simple reason that the orientational requirements they serve are generically human. The problems, being existential, are universal; their solutions, being human, are diverse" (Geertz 1966:5).

The uses such scholars make of structuralist insights (under whatever name) are as might be expected tempered by their refusal to buy any given doctrinaire pattern. Geertz, in the study just cited, warns against overdoing the search for structural interconnections: "Systems need not be exhaustively interconnected to be systems. They may be densely interconnected or poorly, but which they are—how tightly integrated they are—is an empirical matter. . . . And as there are some rather compelling theoretical reasons for believing that a system which is both complex, as any culture is, and fully joined cannot function, the problem of cultural analysis is as much a matter of determining independencies as interconnections, gulfs as well as bridges" (Geertz 1966:66). And Victor Turner warns, in his analysis of the Ndembu ritual called *Isoma*, whose function is to counteract barrenness in women, against the tendency to suppose that structuralist accounts are the only ones that matter: "The symbols and their relations as found in *Isoma* are not only a set of cognitive classifications for ordering the Ndembu universe. They are also, and perhaps as importantly, a set of evocative devices for rousing, channeling, and domesticating powerful emotions, such as hate, fear, affection, and grief. They are also informed with purposiveness and have a 'conative' aspect. In brief, the whole person, not just the Ndembu 'mind,' is existentially involved in the life or death issues with which *Isoma* is concerned" (Turner 1969:42).

## 21. Structure and violence

TURNER'S BOOK (WHICH contains also his account of the twin-differentiation ritual referred to earlier) is called *The Ritual Process: Structure and Anti-Structure*, and its subtitle reflects the ambiguous or at any rate reserved attitude to structuralism common to many social scientists in the United States. Its preoccupations lead by a kind of thematic parallel to structuralism in literature and to the central work of a French writer who has been for many years a member of the American academy, and who was instrumental in bringing some of the main figures of Parisian structuralism to the United States in the late 1960s—René Girard and his study of the relation between violence and the concept of the sacred. Girard's thesis, to translate it somewhat freely, is that structural order not only serves to dominate the world in a conceptual sense but also neutralizes or channels more violent aspects of human character, which break out precisely at those points where structural differentiation fails. Brothers are in almost the same situation as twins, and the theme of the "warring brothers" is a fundamental one in sacred and classical literature; the sacred has its origin, in fact, in real episodes of violence whose recurrence has to be ritually guarded against.

If structure is a system of constraints we must look for the *origin* of the constraints elsewhere than in the structure; but this need not deprive the structure of its explanatory power, because it explains synchronic features rather than origins (and explains them, to be sure, in terms of one another). The trouble as Girard sees it is that in stressing the positive or systematic side of the matter the fundamental importance of the constraint may be lost sight of. In connection with kinship, for example, he criticizes Lévi-Strauss's explanation of the incest prohibition as a positive means of ensuring the social exchange represented by the family: ". . . we must think of the family as a function of the prohibition and not of the prohibition as a function of the family. If there is an essential structuralism, it is there. . . ." (Girard 1972:330). All symbolically significant customs and beliefs go back to an originating violence, and this is precisely why they are important and need to be maintained against the dissolution of structure that is characteristic of our age, because without structural constraint the violence will inevitably break out afresh—as indeed it continually shows signs of doing.

Girard's work is not primarily one of literary theory, but it takes literary texts, particularly those of Greek tragedy, as its prime sources. Such texts, of whatever genre, in whatever language, and from whatever period, can be expected to show structural patterns because they are quintessentially cultural products, doubly structured, once by language itself and again by the extralinguistic preoccupations of the writer, narrative or didactic or whatever. Characteristically, however, it is only when freed of such extraneous considerations that the structural features of literature appear, and in this the emergence of literary structuralism in America follows the pattern already seen in linguistics and anthropology. As long as the prime function of language was taken to be communication, or the prime function of social activity the stability of the group, structure tended to be hidden; these things had to be bracketed—not abandoned—while structuralism developed.

## 22. Criticism, new and even newer

AN INDEPENDENT MOVEMENT in the United States between the wars, which came to be known as the New Criticism, deserves credit for having helped to free the literary text from a great deal of historical, biographical, and sentimental baggage, thus beginning to illuminate its structure, although still in a functional-aesthetic context. Kenneth Burke stresses the autonomy of criticism: "The critic may quite legitimately confine himself within any rules of discussion he prefers. He may, if he prefers, treat the poem structurally as though it had not been written by a private individual at all, but had been made merely by the tossing of an alphabet into the air" (Burke 1967:73). But he goes on to develop his own technique of structural analysis, based on the two relations of equality and "calling forth" as holding between elements of the work judged on purely internal grounds, and claims for it "that the mode of analysis I would advocate will give you ample insight into the purely structural features of a work, but that the kind of observations you will make about structure will deal with the *fundamentals* of structure, and will deal with them *in relation to one another*, as against the infinite number of possible disrelated objective notions that can be made" (Burke 1967:74).

We find here the characteristically self-referential modality of structuralism but not yet an extension to the domain of literature as a whole that would be analogous to Troubetzkoy's 100 languages or Murdock's 250 societies. René Wellek and Austin Warren come closer to a synchronic structuralist position when they distinguish "between a view of literature as a simultaneous order and a view of literature which sees it primarily as a series of works arranged in a chronological order," but they too deal mainly with the individual work, as "a whole system of signs, or structure of signs, serving a specific aesthetic purpose" (Wellek and Warren 1949:30, 141). Clearly the intention of structuralist criticism must be, among other things, to throw light on particular works, but as we have seen not all that refers to structure is structuralist, and for a critical text simply to point out with respect to a work that it has a structure, or even to show what that structure is, does not by itself justify the designation. As a rough rule, and following the insight of Peirce discussed earlier, we may say that a structuralist analysis of a given entity always involves as an essential component the location of the entity in question *within* a structure, that is, the specifications of its relations to other entities with which it is systematically connected; it need not (although of course it often will) involve a consideration of the *structure of the entity* at all, as long as the relations that constitute the *structure of the system to which it belongs* are made clear.

There is a sense, of course, in which literary texts belong to the system of language as well as to the system of literature as such. It is therefore possible to carry out a structuralist analysis of a work as a linguistic object, by showing how it, or some aspect of it, is located with respect to other linguistic forms or usages. A classic analysis of this kind is that of a sonnet of Baudelaire ("*Les Chats*"), carried out by Jakobson and Lévi-Strauss (1962), a collaboration whose American origins have already been established. In the "*note liminaire*" to this article Lévi-Strauss claims that an individual literary work may contain within itself the "system of variants (always indispensable to structural analysis)" that I have referred to, because each work is vertically layered, consisting of the intersection, as it were, of phonological, phonetic, syntactic, prosodic, and semantic structures superimposed on one another. But it remains a disputed question whether this kind of exercise is of specifically literary value. Structuralist criticism in the United States at any rate has since tended to treat works in context and has not limited itself to, or indeed greatly interested itself in, technical linguistics narrowly defined. But as Wellek and Warren already realized the line between literary criticism and theory, linguistic or literary, is sometimes a fine one, and the treatment of a particular work is often incidental to the demonstration of a broader thesis. A certain blurring of boundaries is inevitable in view of the diverse currents that have influenced all workers in the field. We have already seen this phenomenon in Girard, and it also occurs—although space will not allow its illustration—in Samuel Levin's Chomskyan analysis of poetic language (1962), in Paul de Man's study of psychological blindness, in Jacques Ehrmann's assimilation of "literature" to other textual products of contemporary culture, and so on. One of the few American critics to have resisted this diversification is Michael Riffaterre, whose structural stylistics take in a wide range of works but rarely venture outside an essentially closed literary domain (1971).

All the recent writers to whom I have referred have been influenced by structuralism, some in more polemical contexts than others, but in spite of their habitual use of (some of) its concepts and methods, none of them would claim to belong to a structuralist movement. As I said at the beginning of this chapter, it was the reflection of the movement in France that lent coherence to the diverse lines of thought I have been describing—to which might be added elements from scattered fields outside the anthropological-linguistic-literary orbit, such as George Kubler's treatment of art as a "system of formal relations" to be studied historically not through an analysis of styles but as embodied in "a linked succession of prime works with replications" (Kubler 1962:vii, 130), or Gunther Stent's reinterpretation of musical style in structural terms (Stent 1969:100–03). That coherence was borrowed, however, does not mean that it was not genuine. Academic literary structuralism achieved almost canonical status in the mid-1970s in what might be called its international form in a deservedly well-received work by an American critic,

Jonathan Culler's *Structuralist Poetics* (1975); since that time it has been a standard part of the landscape.

It has been my aim in this chapter to show that structuralist ideas emerge independently under certain conditions, which have obtained in the United States in the last hundred or so years and which it may now be possible to specify in the light of the foregoing account: an openness to ethnographic and linguistic diversity coupled with a resolve to look for human constants that underlie it; freedom from doctrinaire commitments—to positivism, to traditional criticism, indeed to any canonical view, historical, metaphysical, or ideological; and a disposition to take seriously the results of other and perhaps apparently unrelated inquiries as possibly relevant, if only contextually, to one's own concerns.

Structuralism goes beyond comparative studies, although it is clear that comparative studies are propaedeutic to it. It was no doubt in part Lévi-Strauss's openness to primitive culture that prepared him for his structuralist discoveries; conversely, I have no doubt that self-satisfaction within a single culture (and especially within a single language) makes structuralist insights well-nigh inacessible, and I suspect that this may have something to do with the unevenness of their reception, particularly in the United States (and particularly among philosophers). I shall however resist the temptation to digress into reception theory in order to shift attention from the social and historical context of structuralism that has occupied the last two chapters, back to the movement in its disciplinary embodiment, first of all in the founding discipline of linguistics.

In the more technical chapters that follow some of the material treated in the last two will be covered again, more extensively and in more detail. Such repetition and redundancy is also a structural feature of human discourse. The relations that constitute the structures of intelligibility in particular cases (as distinguished from the logical and grammatical relations that underlie them) are not laid down once and for all in the mind, as they might be in a computer, but establish themselves by repeated perusal on different occasions and in different orders and embodiments. This means that they are hardly ever, except in the simplest cases, straightforward transcriptions of particular linguistic formulations. The implications of this observation will however be saved for Part II.

# Part IB

## Language and the Human Sciences

# 4

# The Linguistic Base I: The *Cours de linguistique générale*

## 23. The natural history of language

THE BASIC IDEA that underlay the emergence of the structuralist movement is expressed in a principle of linguistics that seems first to have been formulated explicitly by Ferdinand de Saussure, namely the principle that *language is purely relational*. Two insights quickly followed the apprehension of this idea: first, that in this respect language is only one among the structures of human intelligibility, of which however it serves as the obvious paradigm because of its dominance; and second, that as such a structure of intelligibility it is a product and a reflection of the structure of the human mind itself.

It was by no means obvious to early students of the subject that language was in fact a human product. Words, to be sure, are uttered by individuals, but individuals do not invent them, nor can they use them as they please. The origin of language is therefore puzzling: on the one hand, as Lévi-Strauss puts it (Charbonnier 1961:160), "language has not always existed, but on the other hand it is incomprehensible that it should have come into being, because it is not enough, for it to come into being, that somebody should invent discourse, it is necessary in addition that the person opposite should understand what is being said to him,"—that is that he should have *prior* knowledge of the language in which the discourse is couched. Language has not always existed, yet at every moment of its existence it must already have existed.

But in this it hardly seems to differ from the rest of the world; the immediately plausible though unreflective hypothesis is that of deliberate creation. Thus Plato, in the *Cratylus*, envisages a lawgiver, a demiurge of the Word, whose business it once was to create words appropriate to their significations, just as other things in the world were created to serve adequately their own proper functions. With the passage of time etymological

59

changes have obscured this appropriateness, which can now only be conjectured or reconstructed. How seriously Plato intended the doctrine of the *Cratylus* to be taken is a matter of argument: the main conclusion of the dialogue seems to be that names have become contradictory and that the investigation of things is a surer way to knowledge than speculation about language. "Nobody knows," as Holger Pedersen insists, "whether Plato was in jest or earnest when he put a series of astonishing etymologies in the mouth of Socrates. If it was Plato's intention to make fun, he was sadly misunderstood, for his etymologies found acceptance, and he himself was regarded in ancient times as the founder of etymology" (1962:4). But at all events the idea that words *have* a meaning, that they *already* have it when they are encountered for the first time, is clearly for Plato a perfectly plausible one.

"Words are proximally present-at-hand; that is to say, we come across them just as we come across Things" (Heidegger 1962:201); they were therefore generally regarded until the eighteenth century as belonging to Nature, "a fourth natural kingdom," as Saussure puts it (1959:4). And the natural history of language, as of the other kingdoms, consisted for a long time of the collection of exotic specimens. Not that studies within more familiar languages had been lacking; there was a grammatical tradition that went back to classical times, and philological speculation abounded. The Stoics, for example, already had a sophisticated theory of meaning that permitted a form of the distinction between sense and reference (Mates 1961:19), and Priscianus formulated in the sixth century an early version of the principles that the order of language reflects the order of the world, and that if law is anywhere, it must be everywhere (Porset 1970:242). Maupertuis, in imagining what it would be like to be transplanted among a distant people and try to communicate with them, adopted a position that has the flavor of Quine's radical intranslatability blended with the Sapir-Whorf hypothesis: "the diversity of their Philosophy," he wrote, "would come from the accustomed language of each nation" (Porset 1970:49)

The search for the exotic, helped along by British imperial ambitions, resulted in the discovery of Sanskrit in the early nineteenth century. This had the force in linguistics that the discovery of fossils had at about the same time in geology. The comparison, for example, of the verb "to be" in Sanskrit:

*asmi, asi, asti, smas, stha, santi,*

with the same verb in Latin:

*sum, es, est, sumus, estis, sunt,*

obviously suggested, by exhibiting the comparative anatomy of the two languages, an evolutionary hypothesis. (It might, of course, as in the case of Morgan, have simply suggested a structural one—note that evolutionary transformations are always structural, but not vice versa, since in the case of evolution we need also an order of priority in time and some plausible mechanism of causal production.) The study of language therefore shifted from the grammatical and philological to the comparative and historical, all the time however taking the *concept* of language for granted.

Comparisons tended to be between elements of languages, and grammar to deal with one form at a time, not the language as a whole. It was Wilhelm von Humboldt who, in his work on the Kawi language of Java, proposed the idea that each language had an "inner form" that made it a unity expressing the *Geist* of the people who spoke it. For von Humboldt this inner form was specific to each language. But languages collectively exhaust the possibilities of human conception and expression. We may move from one to another but never escape from language altogether: man "spins language out of himself, spins himself into it, and thus draws around the people to whom it belongs a circle from which it is possible to step out only in so far as one steps into the circle of another language" (1836:LXXIV). And in moving from one language to another, while we encounter a new world outlook, we also find again features of our own, in other words of the common intellectual endowment of the race: "All speech, beginning from the simplest, is a conjunction of individual felt experience with the general nature of mankind" (1836: LXX).

Here too we find an anticipation of the intranslatability thesis, which arises out of the fact that for von Humboldt words do not refer directly to objects but to the ideas we have of them, or as Cassirer puts it to "the soul's image of the object. In this sense, the words of different languages can never be synonyms" (1953:285). And Chomsky seems to see in von Humboldt also an adumbration of the view that the reality of language is distributive as well as being an aggregate. Language as a concrete object is simply the totality of human acts of speech, but "the form of language is that constant unvarying factor that underlies and gives life and significance to each particular new linguistic act. It is by having developed an internal representation of this form that each individual is capable of understanding the language and using it in a way that is intelligible to his fellow-speakers" (Chomsky 1964:17).

The central problem here is that of the ontological status of the "inner form." Idealism provided a comfortable home for entities like this, but there seems to be no good reason to postulate an objective domain for them distinct from the familiar domains of ordinary physical objects and our personal thoughts, though philosophers from Plato to Popper have succumbed to the temptation to do this. I do not raise here the question of the relation between physical things and our thoughts, but it seems hard to deny the existence of either, and the (occasional) coherence of the latter leads naturally to the hypothesis that there is some system (in the sense defined above) that sustains them. This system we commonly call "mind"; I take it to be the individual mind, not mind in any other sense. Unless some being is postulated whose mind it is (God, for example), there are no grounds for assuming that there is such a thing as mind in general.

Nor are there any grounds for assuming that particular minds are necessarily alike. (The concept of mind is one concept among others that individual minds, in their various ways, entertain.) In the case of language the situation is parallel, and indeed very closely related. There are no grounds for postulating the "inner form" as objective. When Chomsky speaks of an "internal representation of this form" it sounds as if there were an external object whose representation had to be internalized, and von Humboldt does seem to have meant this. (It is tempting to reinterpret his "inner" as referring to individuals, but he would probably have rejected that; inner/outer has for him something of the force of the more recent opposition deep/surface, meaning that the inner form does not show itself directly but is as it were hidden within each utterance, making it an expression of the *Geist* in question.) Only when we realize that the form of language *consists entirely of internal representations* does the mystery of its origin begin to dissipate, and to transform itself into a question about the acquisition of inner structures by individual speakers. The difficulty that now presents itself is that of reconciling the particularity of the internal representation (which there seems no reason not to call a mental structure) with the undeniable fact that language is a collective phenomenon, found only in more or less stable and continuous social groups (and constituting one of the structures characteristic of such groups). This requires, in Lévi-Strauss's phrase, "an inventory of the internal determinants" of language as such, rather than a historical or comparative or metaphysical examination of it. And this was what Saussure attempted to provide.

## 24. Language as system

"IF I HAD not been poor," says Socrates to Hermogenes in the *Cratylus*, "I might have heard the fifty-drachma course of the great Prodicus, which is a complete education in grammar and language—these are his own words— and then I should have been at once able to answer your question about the correctness of names. But indeed, I have heard only the single-drachma course, and therefore I do not know the truth about such matters." It is a historical curiosity that the chief source of the structuralist movement should be a modern analogue of the fifty-drachma course of Prodicus, the course in general linguistics given by Saussure in Geneva between 1906 and 1911. Saussure's claims about his course were certainly more modest than those of Prodicus, in fact his modesty was such that except for a few technical points he published none of the theoretical material in it during his lifetime, and his editors suspected that he himself would not have authorized their publication of it. The *Cours de linguistique générale* was put together posthumously from the notes of Saussure's students Bally, Sechehaye, and Reidlinger, and in spite of the inaccuracy of their memories and the prejudices of their editing—which have been brought to light by the critical works of Godel (1957) and Engler (Saussure 1967/8) among others—it established itself rapidly, on the Continent at least, as the chief classic in its field, a position it still occupies in spite of an enormous amount of work, some of it modifying basic propositions of the *Cours*, that has been done by European linguists since.

Saussure has been called, by George Mounin, the "structuralist without knowing it" (1968), and while it is not true, as Benveniste claimed (1966:92) that the word "structure" does not occur in the *Cours*, it is used there only to describe the orthographical structure of words and not the significative structure of language. Structure is associated with the idea of construction, to which Saussure objects because of its implied suggestion that the linguistic relations into which words enter are put together item by item, whereas in fact they come into being all at once (*"il s'agit pour la langue d'une construction subite,"* 1968:405). At the same time he insists that language constitutes a *system*, and one in which "everything hangs together" (*tout se tient*); no bit of linguistic evidence can be ignored or brushed aside, the challenge to the linguist is precisely to understand the nature of the system and *how* it hangs together. The notion of language as systematic can hardly have been novel; Saussure's contribution was to take it seriously and raise the question of the locus and material of the system as well as of its rules of operation and development. It must be emphasized though that "everthing's hanging together" in language can only have had for Saussure the status of a conjecture, however firmly he may have held it. But then science progresses through firmly held conjectures that are vindicated in the event.

Given that language has been an object of interest at least since the time of Plato, and no doubt long before, how did it come about that the full realization of its systematic character was delayed until the twentieth century? The fact is not so surprising when we remember that even the physical world was not generally regarded as a system until well into the Renaissance, and that the character of language as the system in terms of which knowledge of everything else has to be expressed conceals its own workings from those who use it. Our acquaintance with the world shows us that some things are intelligibly connected and others, apparently, not; it took centuries of research to show, for example, that the different forms of energy (light, heat, mechanical and electrical energy) belong to the same system, and the systematic character of the physical world, while virtually unchallenged, still has the status of a conjecture.

What does it mean, in fact, to say that language is a system (or has a structure)? That its elements are essentially interconnected; but the crucial question is *how* this connection operates, assuming, that is, that the elements themselves have been correctly identified, which assumes in turn an understanding of what language concretely is. As we have seen, the dominant linguistic theory in the nineteenth century was an evolutionary one. Saussure was not opposed to evolutionary theories—they belong to the *diachronic* structure of language, the study of which is both necessary and interesting— but what concerned him more was its *synchronic* structure, that is, language not in relation to its ancestral forms but considered in its own right as a contemporary entity, as it were arrested at a given moment in time and laid out for systematic study. The possibility of such a theoretical detachment of the synchronic follows from Saussure's view that linguistics is a double science, both static and evolutionary, a conviction that in 1894 he had already "nourished for many years" (Godel 1957:33).

It has been said of Saussure that he was after all a historical linguist, but that unlike other historical linguists he asked himself what it was that he was studying (de Mauro 1968:22). In so doing he exemplified the structuralist conviction that there is not much point in offering historical explanations until the nature of the object whose history is to be studied has been understood, since at best they displace the problem to an earlier time. Saussure assumed that there was such a thing as language, that is, that there did exist an object for linguistic study, historical or otherwise, and he was concerned to discover its "intrinsic reality," to constitute linguistics "as a science, formal, rigorous, systematic" (Benveniste 1962:5). For this assumption he was taken severely to task by C. K. Ogden and I. A. Richards, who in *The Meaning of Meaning* devote a number of somewhat uncharitable pages to his work.

> How great is the tyranny of language over those who propose to inquire into its workings [they write] is well shown in the speculations of the late F. de Saussure. . . . This author begins by inquiring, "What is the object at once integral and concrete of linguistic?" He does not ask whether it has one, but obeys blindly the primitive impulse to infer from a word some object for which it stands, and sets out determined to find it. . . . De Saussure does not pause at this point to ask himself what he is looking for, or whether there is any reason why there should be such a thing. He proceeds instead in a fashion familiar in the beginnings of all sciences, and concocts a suitable object—"la langue," the language, as opposed to speech. (1949:4)

The fact that Saussurean linguistics was ignored for so long by English-speaking philosophers may indeed be partly due to the failure of Ogden and Richards to understand what Saussure was doing. They accuse him of simple-mindedness—as if he thought language a simple object—but give no evidence of having mastered the technical discipline out of which his conjectures about the reality of language sprang. But their book was extremely influential.

Saussure's initial conclusion, following von Humboldt, was that language exists uniquely in the sum total of acts of speech; these constitute the given reality confronted by the linguist and provide his empirical base. This view helped to correct the "isolation of speech from the speaking individual" which is said by Mathesius to have been one of the chief failings of nineteenth century linguistics (Vachek 1964:26), but it also demanded a new type of linguistic explanation: whereas comparative or historical studies had made it possible to refer an element of the language to a corresponding element in another language, or in the same language at an earlier epoch, the new static linguistics allowed reference only to other elements of the same language at the same epoch.

Not only does Saussure stress the synchronic aspects of the system of language over the diachronic ones, he also stresses its internal over its external aspects. The image of the game of chess illustrates both distinctions. Chess is a game in which history is irrelevant; given the configuration of pieces on the board at a given point in the game, the sequence of moves by which it happens to have been arrived at is, strictly speaking, a matter of indifference to the players, whose task is to confront the configuration as it presents itself at that time, that is sychronically. (The history may be instructive to one of the players as evidence of the other's style or habits of mind, as leading up to a familiar endgame and so on, but these are second-order considerations; the state of the game, regarded objectively, as, for example, in a chess puzzle published in a newspaper, is not in any way dependent on them.) By contrast, as Pouillon points out, in a game such as bridge the history is of the essence—the prospects of a given hand at a given point can be assessed only in the light of the history of the game in progress—the bidding, the earlier tricks, and so on; bridge, unlike chess or language, forms an essentially diachronic system (Lévi-Strauss 1961:119).

> Language [writes Saussure] is a system that has its own arrangement. Comparison with chess will bring out the point. In chess, what is external can be separated relatively easily from what is internal. The fact that the game passed from Persia to Europe is external: against that, everything having to do with its system and rules is internal. If I use ivory chessmen instead of wooden ones, the change has no effect on the system; but if I decrease or increase the number of chessmen,

this change has a profound effect on the "grammar" of the game. One must always distinguish between what is internal and what is external. In each instance one can determine the nature of the phenomenon by applying this rule: everything that changes the system in any way is internal. (1959:22)

Historical and comparative linguistics take the "system" as it is and deal primarily with its external features; the internal features constitute what came to be called the "structure" of the language, or in Saussure's terminology its "arrangement."

In spite of his insistence on speech as the primary mode of being in language, Saussure admits that it may be necessary, in the study of languages that are remote in time or space, to consider written texts; but for him these are clearly inferior sources of data, to be resorted to only when the linguist is unable to make direct observations of speech. This is in contrast to the view, dominant among earlier linguists and still frequently encountered, that written language is in some way the more real or more official form. One manifestation of this view is concern for accuracy in spelling, even in orthographically deviant languages like English; nothing, from the point of view of Saussurean linguistics, could be more absurd, since the particular code in terms of which spoken utterances are converted into written ones can come into play only after the language has been established. Of course in literate societies there will be feedback from the written to the spoken, but such influences are not privileged—they simply constitute one more external factor among the many that are always at work, which collectively account for the diachronic changes in the language. Still it is easy to understand how, in a culture saturated by the written word and paying exaggerated respect to books and writers, this mistake in ontological priorities should have been made. "The literary language," says Saussure, "adds to the undeserved importance of writing. It has its dictionaries and its grammars; in school, children are taught from and by means of books; language is apparently governed by a code: the code itself consists of a written set of strict rules of usage, orthography; and that is why writing acquires primary importance. The result is that people forget that they learned to speak before they learned to write, and the natural sequence is reversed" (1959:25).

## 25. *Langue* and *parole*

LANGUAGE, THEN, IS wholly embodied in the aggregate of acts of speech. But our idea of what it is is not exhausted by this fact. For these acts would not be acts of speech if there were not a norm according to which each manifests itself, and this too is language. The distinction between language and speech is crucial but these terms express it clumsily in English. Every act of speech is individual and is executed by some person. To designate this executive side of language Saussure chose the French word *parole*. For the general phenomenon of language, undifferentiated as to form or function, he used the term *langage*, while the synchronic system of norms whose internal structure and workings he was concerned to study he called *langue*. These lexical distinctions do not have exact parallels in English and it is simpler to leave the terms in French. *Langue* (literally "tongue") and *parole* (literally "spoken word," or "discourse" understood as an activity rather than an object) then become complementary aspects of *langage*. *Langue* for Saussure belongs to the collectivity of the speakers of a language, *parole* to the individual; *parole* gives *langue* its concrete embodiment, *langue* gives *parole* its significance (thus exemplifying the structuralist thesis that elements derive their significance from the relations into which they enter, not the other way around). If it were not for *langue*, *parole* would be a series of meaningless noises; if it were not for *parole*, *langue* would be a series of mute abstractions. The accompanying diagram (figure 4.1) was given to his students by Saussure himself (Godel 1957:153), and the scheme beneath it (figure 4.2) represents a reconstruction of the relationship between the two terms by Godel (1957:250).

Godel's schema shows that the distinction between these two complementary aspects of language is not clear cut. As might be expected, while *langue* carries the burden of (synchronic) system, *parole* carries the burden of (diachronic) history, since it is through modifications in spoken language from one individual to another over intervals of time that linguistic evolution occurs. But Saussure insists that language "always implies both an established system and an evolution; at every moment it is an existing institution and a product of the past. To distinguish between the system and its history, between what it is and what it was, seems very simple at first glance; actually the two things are so closely related that we can scarcely keep them apart" (1959:8). The practical difficulty of disentangling system and history does not, of course, destroy the validity of the distinction between them for analytic purposes. And in fact Saussure's chief importance as the founder of structuralism may prove to lie in his insistence on binary oppositions of this sort. In a notebook he wrote: "Language is reducible to five or six DUALITIES or pairs of things" (1967:27); these were signifier/signified, individual/mass, *langue/parole*, synchrony/diachrony, comparison/exchange. In spite of subsequent criticism they still stand up as remarkably good first approximations to the truth about language and as invaluable methodological devices for an understanding of its structure. The general point is worth making here that almost all distinctions can be challenged in borderline cases without in the least impairing their usefulness for cases that are not

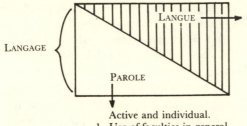

LANGAGE

LANGUE

Passive and residing in the collectivity. Social code organizing language and forming the tool necessary for exercising the faculty of language.

PAROLE

Active and individual.
1. Use of faculties in general (phonation, etc.)
2. Individual use of the code of language according to individual thought

*Figure 4.1*

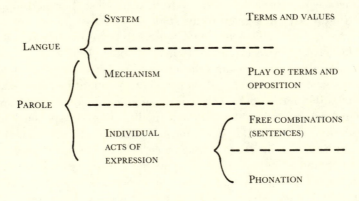

LANGUE
  SYSTEM                TERMS AND VALUES

  MECHANISM            PLAY OF TERMS AND OPPOSITION

PAROLE

  INDIVIDUAL ACTS OF EXPRESSION
                       FREE COMBINATIONS (SENTENCES)

                       PHONATION

*Figure 4.2*

borderline. (It would be silly to criticize the distinctions between plants and animals or men and women on the grounds that there exist zoophytes and hermaphrodites.)

The duality of *langue* and *parole* might be called *orthogonal*, in contrast to other dualities that might be called *parallel* (cf. Caws 1974d). This distinction is intuitively clear—in that its metaphorical base is obvious: two lines that cross at right angles as contrasted with two parallel lines—even if difficult to render technically precise, and it is helpful because the two types are often confused, and this hinders the understanding of how language works. The terms of an orthogonal duality belong to different dimensions, as it were, the terms of a parallel duality to the same dimension. Temporal/spatial, diachronic/synchronic, perhaps individual/collective are orthogonal dualities; speech/writing, English/French, sound/sense are parallel ones. Reference and other semantic relations, as well as paradigmatic substitution, are orthogonal to the signifying chain, while syntactic determinations as well as plain syntagmatic linking are parallel to it.

The affinity between the examples in the orthogonal case is instructive. Time and space are represented in the geometry of four dimensions as having a relationship analogous to the relationship between the various dimensions of space itself. It is characteristic of that relationship that a line segment in one dimension intersects a plane in the other two at a point, and it is legitimate to represent the intersection of a linear time segment with the three-dimensional spread of space as having pointlike properties: it will be a moment at a place, or a place at a moment, occupying a specific instant of time at a specific location in space. Now this is the characteristic situation of the human subject, the user of language, through whom indeed the whole language enters into the world. As the subject speaks, choosing words, using them to refer, and so on, he or she is located at a point on an individual spoken chain, the unfolding of *parole* in the temporal dimension. At the same time the speaker confronts other speakers, interlocutors, who at each point bring the norms of *langue* to bear on what is said, in understanding or judgment; in this way the plane of *langue* is metaphorically intersected by the orthogonal line of *parole*.

In the parallel case it is to be noted that the dimension in which the parallel runs is not specified. On the one hand the interlocutors follow what is said through time, so that speaking/hearing is a parallel duality in the temporal or diachronic dimension. On the other hand the hearer's system of *langue*, which enables what is said to be understood, may be considered at any moment to double (approximately) the speaker's system which enables it to be uttered: the duality of the two embodiments of *langue* is a parallel one in a momentary or synchronic dimension, metaphorically spatial rather than temporal. Sometimes the same parallel duality holds in different dimensions: if a running translation into French is provided for a speech given in English, English/French is a parallel duality along the diachronic axis, whereas the two languages as alternative forms of *langue*, each covering without remainder the whole extent of linguistic space, show the same duality in the synchronic plane. Similarly with sound and sense: we can think of the sense of an utterance as doubling its sound while the utterance proceeds, but also of the whole system of sound as doubling the whole system of sense. In general we might say that the paradigm of orthogonal duality is given by the *opposition* between history and structure, while the paradigm of parallel duality is rather a *matching* of structure with structure.

The notions of duality and of matching are central to Saussure's understanding of the linguistic sign, the element of the system of *langue*. Earlier theories of the sign had treated it as a unit, carrying significance because of its external relations to other entities. Depending on the nature of these relations, the study of signs assumed different forms: relations between signs in the spoken or written chain were codified in syntax; relations of signs to the objects they signified (their sense and reference) were the subject matter of semantics; pragmatics, finally, dealt with the relations of signs to their users and other features of the environment. The understanding of the "sign situation" owed a great deal to Peirce, who used the notions of *object* and *interpretant* in relation to the sign as respectively *that which* the sign signified and *the one to whom* it signified what it did, or more exactly the reaction it invoked, the idea it determined in the hearer's or reader's mind (Peirce VIII:232). This account, while accurate as far as it goes, does not reflect the details of Peirce's view, which calls for two objects and three interpretants; for him, in fact, the triad is only the starting point of a complex inquiry into the nature of signs, which demands the consideration of "$3^{10}$, or 59049, difficult questions." It has been suggested (Wells 1954:116) that the interpretant as idea rather than person gives the sign relation four terms rather than three, since we require to know when the idea is invoked in the person. But it is the three-term relation, often represented by the familiar triangular diagram of figure 4.3, that has become a standard feature of theories of meaning in the English-speaking world at least. It is to be found prominently, for example, in Ogden and Richards (1949:11).

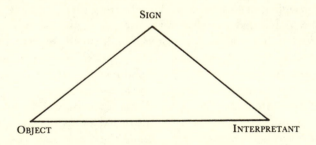

Sign

Object          Interpretant

*Figure 4.3*

## 26. The doctrine of the sign

SAUSSURE'S DOCTRINE OF the sign takes a quite different point of departure. For him the sign is not a unit but a complex entity, having two elements both of which are necessary to its constitution as a sign and neither of which in the

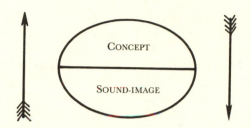

*Figure 4.4*

*Figure 4.5*

first instance can exist without the other. These elements Saussure called *signifiant* (literally "signifying," usually in its substantive form rendered "signifier") and *signifié* ("signified"). He compared them to the two sides of a sheet of paper, which face in different directions but are nevertheless inseparable. It is tempting at first to think of the signifier as a word, inscribed or uttered, and of the signified as a thing. But a word by itself is not, for Saussure, a sign at all. "The linguistic sign unites, not a thing and a name, but a concept and a sound image. . . . The linguistic sign is then a two-sided psychological entity that can be represented by the drawing [see figure 4.4]. . . . I call the combination of a concept and sound-image a *sign*, but in current usage the term generally designates only a sound image, a word, for example (*arbor*, etc.). One tends to forget that *arbor* is called a sign only because it carries the concept 'tree' [see figure 4.5], with the result that the idea of the sensory part implies the idea of the whole" (1953:66–67).

The expression "sound-image" in the original French is "image acoustique," the sound as *heard*; Saussure explicitly rejects the expression "image vocale," the sound as *spoken*, probably because speech requires a physical action. Language is thus placed squarely in the psychological domain, and this seems reasonable when one reflects that books without readers, for example (in Peirce's language signs without interpretants) revert to the merely physical and cannot be said to have anything linguistic about them except potentially, for future readers. Later structuralists have not always been careful to follow Saussure on this point, sometimes talking as if words were signifiers and objects signified directly by them, thus missing an essential feature of the relation between signifier and signified, namely, that it is effected by speakers and does not inhere in the terms related—or, in other words, that once again the determinateness of the relation is prior to that of the things.

What can be said of this relation? Saussure's doctrine of the sign has two cardinal principles, the first of which is that the association between the signifier and the signified is *arbitrary*. This does not mean, obviously, that we can choose any sound image we like and associate it with any concept we like—the sign once established "always eludes the individual or social will" (1959:17)—but only that there is no internal or necessary connection between the two elements of the sign. This lack of necessary connection also means the lack of any ground of dispute about the appropriateness of a signifier to its signified, and this according to Saussure "is really what protects language from any attempt to modify it" (1959:73); there can be no rational preference for one signifier as against another.

One might, of course, by etymological study, arrive at theories about the expressive or onomatopoeic origins of given signifiers, as in Plato's *Cratylus*, but this would be of purely historical and not of the slightest systematic interest. What makes the sign signify is not now and could not even in its origins have been any positive property of the signifier, its spontaneity or its similarity to some natural sound or (in Peirce's terminology again) its indexical or iconic value. These things have to be supplemented by an orthogonal and intentional relation between signifier and signified, animated by a speaker (although Saussure would not have put the matter in just these terms), and once this is present, they are unnecessary. The crucial consideration for Saussure is negative, and consists in the capacity of the user of the sign *to distinguish the sound image in question from other sound images*.

Language is a *system of perceived differences*—a double system, as we shall see. The fundamental differences obtain not just between the complex sound images that function as signifiers, but between elementary sound images called by Saussure "syllables" or "phonemes." The chief characteristic of the phoneme is simply that it is different from all the other phonemes—what it is in itself is a matter of comparative indifference. Saussure suggests, in fact, that it would be quite reasonable for a linguistic analysis to designate the phonic elements of a language simply by numbers (Godel 1957:27). The phonemes actually available to us are limited by the physiology of the human organs of speech and include the spoken sounds with which we happen to be familiar, but different organs might have produced different sounds, and from the point of view of linguistic principle this would not matter. Similarly our organs of perception and of thought segment the world of appearance in more or less arbitrary ways—arbitrary in that different organs of perception or of thought might have segmented it differently. What is striking about language (and this is one of the fundamental insights of structuralism) is that the arbitrary association of two contingent systems of *difference* is capable of producing a system of *significance*.

The positive character of the sign, produced from the arbitrary association of signifier and signified, Saussure called its "value." The following passage from the *Cours* makes clear how positive value arises out of negative differences:

> . . . in language there are only differences. Even more important: a difference generally implies positive terms between which the difference is set up; but in language there are only differences *without positive terms*. Whether we take the signified or the signifier, language has neither ideas nor sounds that existed before the linguistic system, but only conceptual and phonic differences that have issued from the system. The idea or phonic substance that a sign contains is of less importance than the other signs that surround it. But the statement that everything in language is negative is true only if the signified and the signifier are considered separately; when we consider the sign in its totality, we have something that is positive in its own class. A linguistic system is a series of differences of sound combined with a series of differences of ideas; but the pairing of a certain number of acoustical signs with as many cuts made from the mass of thought engenders a system of values; and this system serves as the effective link between the phonic and psychological elements within each sign. Although both the signified and the signifier are purely differential and negative when considered separately, their combination is a positive fact; it is even the sole type of fact that language has, for maintaining the parallelism between the two classes of differences is the distinctive function of the linguistic institution. (1959:120)

In other words the orthogonal duality of the signifier/signified relation in the case of individual signs is what lends stability to the parallel duality of the conceptual and phonic system. I call the former duality orthogonal because what fixes a signifier (or the signified) in its place in the system is on the one hand a set of relations of difference in the plane of its own system, as it were,

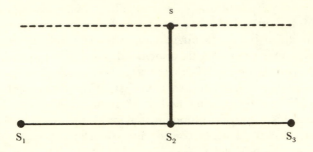

*Figure 4.6*

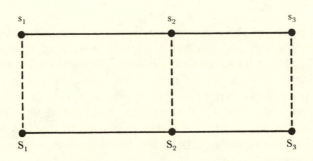

*Figure 4.7*

on the other a relation of arbitrary association in another dimension. If we adopt the convention of using an uppercase *S* for the signifier and a lowercase *s* for the signified we might represent the orthogonal relation as in figure 4.6 and the parallel one as in figure 4.7. The diagrams suggest, in the interchange of solid and broken lines, an ambiguity in the signifier-signified relation that has plagued Saussurean linguistics and other disciplines influenced by it.

    This ambiguity has been stressed by Lacan, who represents the relation as *S/s*, "the signifier over the signified, 'over' corresponding to the line separating the two levels," thus inverting Saussure's own schema in figure 4.4. This is the formula, says Lacan, "by which, in spite of the differences among schools, the beginning of modern linguistics can be recognized" (Ehrmann 1966:115–16). The question is, is the bar a link or a separation between *S* and *s*? The doctrine of the sign suggests the former, but the notion of the *para-allelos*, the "other alongside," stresses the incommensurability, perhaps the mutual inaccessibility, of the two domains, which have no essential connection but only an arbitrary and artificially forced association. The answer is clearly "both," although its understanding requires the theory of intentional apposition to be developed in Part II. In the *Cours* Saussure is at pains to insist on the inseparability of the two sides of the sign, once their arbitrary association has been established, and this might be seen as a version of the principle of the "stacked deck."

There is a further difficulty with the notion of the signifier which surfaces in the second of the principles that constitute the doctrine of the sign, namely, the *linearity of the signifier*. There is nothing particularly "linear" about a given sound-image as a pole of the signifier-signified relation; but the sign does not signify until it is used, and its use in speech involves the deployment of signs in a linear order. Once drawn attention to this is obvious enough: language, whether spoken or written, unfolds in time as a chain of utterances or inscriptions, and it is the one-dimensional character of this chain that permits the sequences and substitutions on which the open-ended variety of a discourse formed from the recursive use of a limited number of phonemes depends. But Saussure is unable to distinguish clearly between the (relatively long) syntagmatic chains characteristic of discourse, which belong to *parole*, and the (relatively short) chains that constitute words or other standard and repeatable expressions, which belong to *langue*.

Even within an element of *langue*, however, he wishes to insist on linearity if more than one phoneme is involved. Later authors, as we shall see, suggest that a single element of the signifying chain may consist of the simultaneous deployment of several significant components or "distinctive features," but Saussure seems to anticipate this criticism when he says, "sometimes the linear nature of the signifier is not obvious. When I accent a syllable, for instance, it seems that I am concentrating more than one significant element on the same point. But this is an illusion; the syllable and its accent constitute only one phonational act. There is no duality within the act but only different oppositions to what precedes and what follows" (1959:70).

The linearity of the signifier makes a later and probably independent appearance in the work of Suzanne Langer, who contrasts the "discursive form" of language with the "presentational form" of visual art and of thought in its conceptual rather than its linguistic mode. Her notion of "form" is borrowed from Cassirer. This contrast poses a problem to the Saussurean doctrine of the sign. For Saussure insisted on the generality of this doctrine: "if we are to discover the true nature of language we must learn what it has in common with all other semiological systems" (1959:17). Now Langer draws special attention to music, which alone among the nonverbal arts has discursive or syntagmatic form. Music is a paradigm case of non-linguistic significance, but it is difficult to apply to it the Saussurean analysis of the sign, since the signified of a musical expression does not obviously exist at all. In this case it might seem that Peirce's theory of the sign is more promising, since it can fall back on the series of interpretants even if no object can be found. I shall have occasion to come back later to the notion of a chain of signifiers, without signifieds, as a characteristic form of literacy as well as of musical art, but it may be worth dwelling for a moment on the absence of the interpretant in Saussure's system.

## 27. Interpretation and linguistic value

THE FACT IS that the role of the interpretant in Saussurean linguistics is played by the *linguistic community*. "The signifier, though to all appearances freely chosen with respect to the idea that it represents, is fixed, not free, with respect to the linguistic community that uses it. The masses have no voice in the matter, and the signifier chosen by language could be replaced by no other. This fact, which seems to embody a contradiction, might be called colloquially 'the stacked deck.' We say to language: 'Choose!' but we add, 'It must be this sign and no other'" (Saussure 1959:71). In the standard account of Peirce and others the sign $x$ means the object $y$ for the interpretant $z$; Saussure explains, in effect, that it can do this only because the corresponding signifier $x$ is a member of a class $\{x\}$ of signifiers, while the corresponding signifier $y$ is a member of a class $\{y\}$ of signifieds, and because $x$ can be distinguished from the other members of the class $\{x\}$ and $y$ can similarly be distinguished from the other members of the class $\{y\}$. $x$ is the signifier for $y$ because of a conventional association between them that is accepted by a class $\{z\}$ which constitutes a linguistic community, but no individual $z$ or subclass of $z$'s who protest that $x$ doesn't signify $y$ to *them* can prevent its doing so in Saussure's sense. The relation of significance arises out of the matching of the $x$'s and $y$'s—out of the *structure* of this matching, given that $\{x\}$ and $\{y\}$ both embody systems of differences and that these systems are apprehended as such by members of $\{z\}$. One might speak similarly of a musical community, an interpretive community, and so on as a generalization of the interpretant in other cases of significance. And in fact many ontological problems, not only of meaning but of other linguistic functions, not only of language but of other intellectual domains, can be seen to be resolved when this strategy is adopted.

The value of the sign is what gives it its place in the system. This place is specified in a double sense; for the sake of a certain symmetry that does not, I think, distort the situation, we may say that the (parallel) relation of *difference* detaches the sign from other signs, while the (orthogonal) relation of *reference* attaches it to its object. "Even outside language," says Saussure, "all values are apparently governed by the same paradoxical principle. They are always composed:

> (1) of a *dissimilar* thing that can be *exchanged* for the thing of which the value is to be determined; and
> (2) of *similar* things that can be *compared* with the thing of which the value is to be determined." (1959:115)

After applying this to the case of money he goes on to say that "a word can be exchanged for something dissimilar, an idea; besides, it can be compared with something of the same nature, another word. Its value is therefore not fixed as long as one simply states that it can be 'exchanged' for a given concept, i.e. that it has this or that signification: one must also compare it with similar values, with other words that stand in opposition to it" (1959:115).

It is important to be clear about the difference between the status of a word as a term of a static linguistic system (its value) and its status as an element of a syntagmatic chain. It is of course the former that makes the latter possible—when we speak we choose words with appropriate values. But in the spoken (or written) chain the parallel (or linear) syntagmatic relations are doubled by at least two sets of orthogonal ones, respectively *paradigmatic* and *associative*. Of these Saussure explicitly deals only with the associative. Words that stand in a paradigmatic relationship to a given word are those that could be substituted for it in the syntagmatic chain without destroying the intelligibility of the utterance, that is, that could fill the same slot. The paradigmatic substitution classes for most words in most settings are nearly equivalent to syntactic categories under the most liberal interpretation of intelligibility (that is why they are called paradigmatic), and supplementary limitations that may be imposed on these classes will correspond to different standards or conceptions of intelligibility. Thus in the sentence

Mary wore a brown coat

the adjective "brown" could be replaced by any adjective whatever without violating the canons of grammar:

Mary wore a gray coat<br>
a therapeutic coat<br>
a grammatical coat<br>
a Triassic coat<br>
a speechless coat, etc.

although some of these strain intelligibility, at least for purposes of ordinary discourse. It may be worth remarking, however, that it is a good deal harder to write grammatical nonsense, in the strict sense, than it has sometimes been thought to be. From the sentence

Socrates drinks hemlock

we might form, by free paradigmatic substitution,

Quadruplicity drinks procrastination

which was thought by Bertrand Russell to be a good case of meaninglessness, and yet it is not hard to see in it a kind of sense (See Caws 1965:188).

What gives, metaphorically speaking, depth and color to language and makes it possible to find a sort of intelligibility even in paradigmatically strained sentences is the class of associative relations that each word carries with it. "A particular word is like a constellation," says Saussure; "it is the point of convergence of an indefinite number of coordinated terms" (1959:126). The forms of coordination also are diverse: Saussure gives four different associative series for the term *"enseignement"* (see figure 4.8), but many others are clearly possible. The location of a word in a language, whether *langue* or *parole*, is in short a matter of the simultaneous holding of some among a great variety of possible relations with other words and with things, not all of which were envisaged by Saussure, but which can be developed on the basis of his minimal theory of the sign. It is this complexity, conjoined with the complexity of actual linguistic communities, that renders hopeless a priori any attempt to establish a general theory of meaning or reference for expressions not reduced to that minimal level.

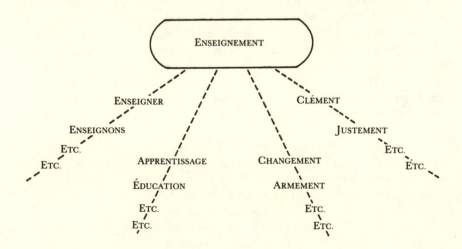

*Figure 4.8*

Another crucial concept that Saussure did use is that of *opposition*. His frequent invocation of dualities has already been alluded to; opposition is a strongly dichotomous duality, the setting of one thing over against another rather than merely distinguishing them as they remain juxtaposed. This alternative, however, is a matter of emphasis for Saussure, and the terms of a linguistic opposition need not be irrevocably fixed—they may be single elements, or more complex expressions. "There is no radical difference, in linguistics, between the phenomena and the units of which they are composed: everything is a relation, and between complex terms; all the phenomena are relations between relations. Or again: everything is just difference utilized as opposition, and the opposition confers value" (Godel 1957:71).

The conferring of value in this way (that is, by difference rather than by reference) is, again, arbitrary; nothing prescribes the use of a particular difference as an opposition. But this arbitrariness is not that of the sign. The latter is absolute at first, before the signifier becomes attached to the signified; then, once the linguistic community has accepted this attachment, it vanishes altogether. The only constraint on the choice (to speak loosely) of a signifier for a particular signified is that it should differ from the signifier of other signifieds, and even this is not absolutely necessary, as is shown by cases of homophony. Here difference is merely difference. The structure of the language takes shape only when relationships between signifiers are established; the whole complex is arbitrary in the original sense, in that another complex might have done as well (and does so, in any other natural language), but within it the relations are positive and functional. So the aim of the linguist is the "reduction, throughout the system of language, of absolute arbitrariness to relative arbitrariness, which constitutes the 'system.' If it were possible for a language to consist uniquely of the naming of objects, the different terms of this language would have no relations whatever among them, they would remain as separate from one another as the objects themselves" (Godel 1957:53).

Two things need to be stressed: first that, in spite of the contingent link between them provided by the concept of difference, the doctrine of system and the doctrine of the sign are essentially independent, and second that the doctrine of system remained, for Saussure, conjectural and programmatic to the end. With respect to the first of these points, it is easy to see that even if the relation between signifier and signified were natural or necessary rather than arbitrary, the character of language as a system of differences would be unchanged, and that on the other hand even if language did not hang together systematically the sign would still be arbitrary and linear. Some Oriental languages, indeed, seem quite to lack the systematic syntax with which we are familiar, and to rely instead on syntagmatic juxtaposition;

whatever relation between terms may be needed is produced ad hoc by the spoken sequence, so that grammar comes as it were to belong to *parole* rather than to *langue*. "This instrument of word order," remarks Cassirer, "which the Chinese language has developed to the highest consistency and sharpness, might indeed, from a purely logical point of view, be regarded as the only truly adequate means of expressing grammatical relations. For it would seem possible to designate them more clearly and specifically *as* relations pure and simple, possessing no perceptual base of their own, through the pure *relation* of words expressed in their order, than by special words and affixes" (1953:305). One might speculate that this property of Oriental languages springs from the fact that as written they represent a development of the conceptual rather than the acoustic side of the sign, but there seems to be little evidence that grammatical structure is determined by the form of writing—although there may be a relationship in the other direction, in that an ideographic form might be adequate to a grammar operating with many detached roots but inadequate to a grammar operating with a few inflected ones. However this may be, the existence of languages with virtually no surface grammar poses afresh the question of just what the systematicity of language consists in. And to this question Saussure had no really satisfactory answer.

## 28. A Saussurean aberration: the anagrams

IT IS KNOWN, however, from Saussure's notebooks, that he did have a passionate interest in what he conceived of as an underlying set of rules governing some examples of one particular manifestation of language, namely Latin verse, an interest that infected his perception of other literary works as well and eventually seems to have driven him to a kind of madness. What the relationship of this work was to his theoretical linguistics it is hard to conjecture. The question of particular uses of language, what people do or make with it in the pursuit of particular ends, is quite distinct from the question of the articulation of language that enables them to do anything at all with it. Saussure himself perceived that the communication of anything by language needed to be marked extralinguistically before it could be recognized as such; in an untitled school notebook he says: "Language is created only with a view to discourse, but what is it that distinguishes discourse from language, or what, at a given moment, allows us to say that language *comes into action as discourse*? . . . . The sequence of words, however rich it may be in terms of the ideas it evokes, will never indicate to a human individual that another individual, in pronouncing them, might wish to signify something to him" (Starobinski 1971:14).

Conceivably, however, the required indication might be carried by the sequence of words but on another linguistic level, as though discourse could bear within itself a kind of concealed certificate of authenticity. This would be particularly desirable in the case of written communication, since, in speaking, the necessary authentication is normally provided by context—the obvious fact that someone is speaking *to* someone else, the accompanying attitudes and gestures and so on. Saussure devoted quantities of time and scholarship to an attempt to discover, in the verses of certain Latin writers, anagrammatic evidences of authorship or address. Among other devices Saussure suspected and tried to demonstrate the existence of "hypograms" or theme words separated into elements scattered through one or more lines of the text "hypographically" or "paragrammatically" (Starobinski 1971:31). Thus from the lines

    6. Meque suis fassa est artibus esse parem
    7. Marmoreo tumulo Medices Laurentius hic me
    8. Condidit; anti humili pulvere tectus eram

he recovers "PICTOR," from *p*arem, med*ic*es Lauren*ti*us h*ic*, *t*umulo, Mar*mor*eo, and also "MEDICES" itself, which, "named in line 7, is hypographed 6–7–8": *M*eque, es*t* ar*ti*bus (where *t-ti* is taken for a weakened form of *d-di*), *M*e*q*ue *s*uis, *es*t, *esse*; also *M*armoreo *t*umulo, Lauren*ti*us, h*ic* me; and finally *m*e, con*didi*t, humi*li*, *c*ondidit, an*te*, pulver*e*, tec*t*us (Mounin 1968:164). This is a typical case, overdetermined with respect to the number of elements and quasi-linear. "We know what his hopes were," writes Starobinski, "to recover a traditional rule of poetic composition. . . . It seems to have the rigor of a law that would impose itself on the poet *in spite of himself*. But in addition Saussure wishes to retrace the *conscious* path which, starting from a word or a small group of words, leads, through a 'phonic paraphrase,' to the elaboration of the poem" (1967:1906). This search became obsessive and in the end frightening. Once he had started to look for hypograms he found them everywhere, often in the wrong places; having determined, for example, that the name of Fra Lippo Lippi's mistress was to be found in the epigram

    Artifices potui digitis animari colore,

he produced "LEONORA": co*lore*, co*lore*, a*n*imari co*lore*, a*n*ima*r*i co*lore*, *a*nima*ri*; unfortunately it was the wrong name, since the mistress in question was called Lucrezia (Lotringer 1973:8).

Here Saussure has strayed far from the doctrine of the *Cours*, but no change in that doctrine is called for—language still adheres to the world through the association of sounds and concepts, even though on the side that faces away from the world, as it were, it has an eccentric life of its own. Its structure is multiple, its ramifications virtually unlimited; with a little imagination almost anything can be found there. This is a principle to be borne in mind when we come to attempts to specify "correct" readings of literary texts. Saussure was perhaps too rigid a philologist to acknowledge or welcome it, and subsequent structuralists also have been slow to reach the conclusion that follows from this principle of multiplicity taken in a completely general sense, namely, that there is an unlimited number of potentially intelligible relationships among things in the world, and hence of coherent structures, so that on the one hand no paradigm of coherence can constrain novelty, and on the other no empirical inquiry is immune from it.

# 5

# The Linguistic Base II: After Saussure

## 29. The structure of the system

WHAT STRUCTURALISM LEARNS from Saussure is that on the one hand significance is produced by the pairing of elements from previously available systems of differences, and that on the other the systems of significance thus generated (which I shall call in Part II "signiferous" systems, because significance is to be found in their manifestations as gold is to be found in auriferous deposits, and at the same time they can be used to carry it from emitter to receiver as Christopher carried the infant Christ from bank to bank of the river) are both ramified and self-contained, that in them everything hangs together (*"tout se tient"*). The reason Saussure remained at the level of system and did not move on to that of structure is that he never arrived at any specification of *how* it was that the systematic whole "hung together." As Jakobson remarks, all questions in the *Cours* "that no longer concern the word, but extend to the organization of the sentence, seem perplexing" (1972:43).

Words are only the elements of the system of language, they do not carry in themselves the relationships that constitute its structure. And they are of course not its only elements, in fact for the most part they are not *elements* at all but complexes of elements. The elements of a spoken language, phenomenologically speaking, are sounds, but sounds as heard are not the same as sounds functioning in language. The fact that regional accents do not normally impede understanding shows that the same significant sound can be perceived under a wide range of heard sounds. In fact it may take a certain effort to hear the *sounds* at all, since what we normally hear when somebody speaks are already whole words.

This distinction is embodied in the division of labor, in the study of spoken language, between phonetics on the one hand and phonology on the other. Phonetics attempts to codify all the sounds the human organs of speech are capable of producing, and to characterize them in standard terms. Phonology studies the structure of the system of sounds that makes speech intelligible even under phonetic variation. Saussure himself seems to have thought that phonology in this sense was impossible (Ducrot and Todorov 1972:220). In the *Cours*, as we have seen, the element of sound is the phoneme; how a particular phoneme happens to be pronounced in a particular linguistic community at a particular time, and how this pronunciation changes, are answerable questions, belonging to phonetics, but the relations among phonemes as the units of differentiable sound are purely negative. To make the phonemes themselves into a system, independently of their value-conferring relations, as signifiers, to *specific* signifieds, would be the first step toward an analytic structuralism of language, but Saussure did not take it.

The study of the structure of such a system might be called "phonemics," although it happens to have been generally called "phonology." The opposition phonetic/phonemic is nevertheless worth dwelling on for a moment, because it exemplifies in the case of language a duality of approach that can be observed in other domains as well. A phonetic study, as the term is now understood, might be made from a completely external viewpoint of a language the linguist did not understand at all, since from the point of view of phonetics sounds are what they are independently of their functioning in meaningful discourse. A phonemic study, on the other hand, would require an internal viewpoint, so that the significant differences among sounds could be distinguished from the irrelevant ones; sounds may be phonetically different but phonemically identical (for example, the two pronunciations of "ei-" in "either"), and this cannot be accounted for without knowledge of the language.

The generalization of this distinction by Kenneth Pike into an opposition between "etic" and "emic" has already been alluded to (See chapter 3): "The etic viewpoint studies behavior as from outside of a particular system, and as an essential initial approach to an alien system. The emic viewpoint results from studying behavior as from inside the system" (1967:37). The etic, he goes to say, represents the creation of an analytic scheme, the emic the discovery of a structural scheme; or alternatively, the etic represents physical description, the emic structural analysis.

Structuralism is, obviously enough, mainly concerned with the emic. But the emic always has an etic correlate; even though, as Pike points out, there can be etic identities with emic difference and vice versa (1967:43–44), still there is an asymmetry between the cases, due to the fact that it is possible for an event to be emically null, as it were (and as indeed most events are), whereas no event can be etically null. The problem is to know what etic features are emically significant. And this was the task that was first accomplished for linguistics (although he could not, and perhaps would not have wished to, characterize it in this way) by Prince Nicholas Troubetzkoy.

Troubetzkoy was a precocious linguist who was already as a schoolboy conducting researches into the variety of languages available in Russia. In his autobiographical notes he writes casually: "I discovered a series of surprising resemblances in the vocabulary of kamtchadale and of tchouktche-koriak on the one hand, and of samoyed on the other. Unfortunately I had to interrupt this work in order to take the *baccalauréat . . .*" (1967:xvi). His learning was immense. Writing to Jakobson in the early stages of his systematic investigation of the phonology of the natural languages he says: "I set out clearly all the vocalic systems I knew by heart (34 in all) and tried to compare them to one another . . . the results are extremely interesting. All the systems reduce to a small number of types and can always be represented by symmetrical schemas" (1967:xxvi). For the purposes of the eventual work he found his own thirty-four languages too small a sample, and supplemented them with data from informants to bring the number up to a hundred.

The results of Troubetzkoy's researches were published in his *Grundzüge der Phonologie* (1939) as part of the work of the Prague Linguistic Circle to which he belonged in the latter part of his life. The distinction between phonetics and phonology had been laid down in an earlier article, where he had written: "for the phonologist sound is only the *phonetic realization of the phoneme*, a material symbol of the phoneme. . . . Roughly speaking, phonetics inquires about *what one actually pronounces* in speaking a language, and phonology *what one imagines one is pronouncing*" (1933:232). Phonology, therefore, has the internal character of the emic. It is evident that the phonetician can, and indeed must, be an atomist, since phonetic elements are what they are at each occurrence independently of their neighboring elements, whereas atomism is not a possibility for the phonologist because the elements are relational and differential, in other words structural—they cannot even be recognized in the absence of someone's "having imagined that he was pronouncing something," and hence having meant to say something.

The Prague school was consciously structuralist, and represents the meeting point of Moscow (the Russian formalists) and Geneva. The general theory of language from which Troubetzkoy takes his departure is therefore essentially Saussurean, although with some philosophical generalizations added. "*Langue* has no other *raison d'être* than to render possible the act of *parole*," he says; "it does not exist except in so far as concrete acts of *parole* refer themselves to it, that is to say only to the extent that it realizes itself in concrete acts of *parole*" (1967:1). But later he goes on to say: "Since human language always presupposes at once a speaking subject, a listener (or more than one) and a state of affairs that the conversation is about, it follows that every spoken episode has three aspects: it is at the same time a *presentation* (or an *expression*) of the speaking subject with a view to its characterization, an *appeal* to the listener (or listeners) with a view to producing a certain impression, and a *representation* of the state of affairs, the object of the conversation" (1967:16).

This more sophisticated version of the tripartite theory of the sign is not however the main contribution of the *Grundzüge*, which lies rather in the understanding that Troubetzkoy exhibits of the fine structure, as it were, of spoken language. He takes over the Saussurean concept of difference but links it firmly to the notion of opposition. Saussure's intuition of the dual or oppositional structure of language did not succeed in conquering the multiplicity of differences among phonemes, because phonemes can differ from one another in different ways and because one phoneme may differ from several others in the same way. What is required is an analytic scheme that would reduce all these differences to pairwise choices. "Difference utilized as opposition" is not good enough—the binary character of the relationship should be necessary rather than accidental if it is to be the foundation of a rigorous system.

## 30. Oppositions

NOW THE CONCEPT of opposition has roots as ancient as those of two-valued logic, and its looser rhetorical use goes back even further, being found in Anaximander and Heraclitus. For the Aristotelians (with their "square of oppositions") it is a formal principle; for St. Augustine it is a moral and aesthetic one:

> For God would never have created any, I do not say angel, but even man, whose future wickedness He foreknew, unless He had equally known to what uses in behalf of the good He could turn him, thus embellishing the course of the ages, as it were an exquisite poem set off with antitheses. For what are called antitheses are among the most elegant of the ornaments of speech. They might be called in Latin "oppositions". . . . As, then, these oppositions of contraries lend beauty to the language, so the beauty of the course of this world is achieved by the opposition of contraries, arranged, as it were, by an eloquence not of words, but of things. (1950:361)

Not only the beauty but the very existence of the moral order is due to the resolution of an opposition, between the good and bad angels, and this ontological force of the concept (which will be seen to recur in more recent contexts) is reminiscent of Anaximander's cosmogony as reported by Simplicius: "He did not ascribe the origin of things to any alteration in matter, but said that the oppositions in the substratum, which was a boundless body, were separated out" (Burnet 1957:53).

Opposition is, in fact, the most fundamental component of structure. In Troubetzkoy it acquires technical status. A term of an opposition is for him what Aristotle called "an opposite which does not survive" ($190^a$ 27), and, like Aristotle, he requires a substratum for it. "An opposition presupposes not only characteristics which distinguish its terms from one another, but also characteristics which are common to the two terms. These characteristics may be called the 'basis of comparison.' Two things which have no basis of comparison, that is, no characteristic in common (for example, an inkpot and free will), do not form an opposition" (1967:33). Here of course we are operating with a restricted concept for linguistic purposes, and not everything that might be said about the general concept (for example by Ogden in his book on the subject) will be applicable. Ogden holds, among other things, that "where there is no neutral point between the two extremes of a series there is no opposition, only heterogeneity. Difference, however great, does not create opposition" (1967:37), but this clearly would not work in the case, let us say, of voiced/unvoiced. On the other hand he is correct in saying that it is not the *degree* of difference that constitutes opposition, since this may be minimal: "opposition is not to be defined as the maximum degree of difference, but as a very special kind of repetition, namely of two similar things that are mutually destructive in virtue of their very similarity" (1967:41). The similarity of the terms lies in their suitability as components of the syntagma—either will do, but never both.

Troubetzkoy makes the concept of opposition prior to that of difference; "two things," he says, "can be differentiated from one another only to the extent that they are opposed one to the other, that is to say to the extent to which there exists between them a relation of opposition" (1967:33). One might say that differences are built up from oppositions: no opposition at all, and we have identity; add one opposition to another, and the degree of difference gradually increases. But this is no more than to say that a sufficiently detailed specification will enable a complete description to be expressed in a series of yes/no choices, something that with the development of the computer has become more obvious than it was at the time of the *Grundzüge*.

We need, then, a taxonomy of oppositions, and this Troubetzkoy sets out to provide. *Bilateral* oppositions are those in which the basis of comparison is exhausted by the two terms in question (as in male/female, which in principle covers the whole class of human beings or other sexually reproducing species), whereas *multilateral* oppositions have bases of comparison shared among more than two terms (as in human/canine, which is only one among a whole set of possible oppositions between mammalian species). In *proportional* oppositions the relation between the terms is the same as the relation between the terms of some other opposition (as in high/low, which may refer to altitudes, sounds, social position, and so on), while in *isolated* oppositions the relation is unique to the terms in question (as in husband/wife, which specifies uniquely the relation of marriage). Troubetzkoy's examples, unlike the illustrative oppositions I am inventing here, are of course all drawn from the phonology of natural languages, and he offers a statistical generalization in that domain as to the frequency of these various types: multilateral proportional oppositions are the most frequent, followed by bilateral proportional and finally, as a rare exception, by bilateral isolated.

Oppositions may further be *privative*, if one term is "marked" as having a certain character and the other can be anything at all as long as it does *not* have that character (as in friend/stranger), *graduated*, if both have the same characteristic but in different degrees (as in friend/acquaintance), or *equipollent*, if each has its own marked character and they are, as it were, of equal logical strength (as in friend/enemy). And they may be *constant* if operative under all circumstances, or *neutralizable* if operative in "positions of relevance" but inoperative in "positions of neutralization" (as for example the king in chess is always white or black but is checked or unchecked only during a game). This taxonomy is perfectly general and is intended in its application to phonology to cover all cases from all languages, though not all types of opposition are utilized in all languages.

Jakobson, in his notes to the *Grundzüge*, attaches the greatest importance to privative oppositions. He speaks of Troubetzkoy's "fundamental discovery" that "one of the two terms of a binary opposition 'is conceived as lacking the mark in question," (Troubetzkoy 1967:xxvii). Marking in this way permits differentiation even when only one side of the opposition is specified. Simple negation is of course a case in point: every name or class attribution yields a closed marked class (say, $p$) and an open unmarked one (not-$p$); other obvious cases outside logic or linguistics are here/elsewhere, same/different, self/other. (The use of privative oppositions rather than equipollent ones may in itself have semantic or even ideological force: consider for example the significance of the shift in American usage from the privative opposition white/colored in speaking of racial types to the equipollent opposition white/black. In general privative oppositions are powerful reinforcers of social structure, and examples could easily be multiplied: Roman/barbarian, Jew/Gentile, Christian/heathen, and so on.)

To return to linguistics: the upshot of Troubetzkoy's work is that we now have a structure for the phonological system, because the possible relations between its elements have in principle been exhaustively specified. But the oppositional structure of phonology is only the beginning. What was true of Saussure's linguistics remains true of Troubetzkoy's, namely, that so far language remains static, or, as we might say, dispositional: ready for use, but not in use. The repertoire of oppositions is something like a dictionary; the relations it specifies among the elements do not hold in an active sense until they come into play in an actual episode of language use, but when that happens all sorts of other relations also emerge.

## 31. Double articulation

THE PHONOLOGICAL STRUCTURE of language, then, cannot by itself account for its function as a carrier of significance. We have already seen that this involves a doubling of the acoustical by the conceptual side of the sign, or better, a doubling of the system of acoustical or phonological differences by a system of conceptual differences (whose structure is as yet unspecified). But we have also seen that this doubling is not by any means a one-to-one matching. Most sounds that function as signifiers are complex; also a relatively simple signifier may correspond to a concept whose analysis is far from simple. There is however yet another kind of parallel duality, internal to the linear signifier, which is implicit in what has already been said but has been elevated to the status of a principle—the principle of "double articulation"—by Martinet. In language both as spoken and as written it is possible to partition the syntagma in two distinct ways: into a sequence composed of a small number of elements frequently repeated (the phonemes or alphabetic characters), or into a sequence composed of a large variety of elements less frequently repeated (words or other meaningful expressions or "monemes"). The latter segmentation is more natural to ordinary speakers and is called by Martinet the "first articulation"; its essential characteristic is that its elements are independently significant, while those of the "second articulation" are merely differential.

It is this duality that explains the versatility and endless resourcefulness of language. It is a familiar truth of elementary mathematics that the number of different ways in which a set of elements can be arranged rises very rapidly as the size of the set increases: two elements permit of only 2 arrangements, but three permit of 6, four of 24, five of 120, six of 720, and so on. The general expression, for $n$ elements, is $n!$, which is given by

$$n.(n-1).(n-2). \ldots 3.2.1.$$

The number of possibilities is greatly increased if the $n$ elements themselves are selected from a still larger group, and if repetitions are permitted. Now the elements of the first articulation are formed by grouping elements of the second articulation, a few syllables or characters at a time; for example, the words on this page are all formed from the twenty-six characters of the Roman alphabet taken in groups having an average of about eight elements.

Assuming no restriction on the initial letter, but assuming that thereafter only about five of the available letters will, on the average, be possible next letters in sequences that would be possible English words, there are still more than two million eight-letter combinations available, not to mention combinations of more or fewer letters.

The gives some idea of the combinatorial power of the alphabet we actually use.

> With a few dozen units of the second articulation [says Mounin], several thousand units of the first articulation. The learning and the production of millions of messages is achieved in the most economical fashion possible. It is double articulation which explains the property of language that has been the most mysterious for all who have tried, up to now, to distinguish it from other means of communication, especially from those found among the animals: its inexhaustible richness in relation to the poverty of all other systems. (1970:74)

Double articulation is in fact a special—perhaps the paradigm—case of what Herbert Simon has called a "hierarchical system," in which stable complexes of elements at one level become elements of stable higher-order complexes at the next higher level. Systems with this sort of structure occur in many domains, not only linguistic in the strict sense but textual, social, economic, and so on, as well as having obvious physical embodiments in, for example, the articulation of atoms into molecules, molecules into drytalline or cellular structures, and so on.

Ontogenetically speaking the second articulation comes first. Children make sounds before they speak words, in fact it is well established that they usually make all possible sounds, and not only those characteristic of the language spoken by the members of the culture into which they have been born. They have at their disposal, therefore, all the elements of a system of spoken language; they do not have a language, since that requires relations between certain elements (and not others)—in other words the specific structure of the language in question. It is sometimes alleged that the emergence of speech from what Jakobson has called the "babbling stage" is simply a matter of selection, among the available sounds, of those heard by the child in its spoken environment. This is certainly a more accurate view than the one it supersedes (namely, that children acquire sounds by imitation), but Jakobson has shown that the sequence is more complicated than that. He remarks, following Grégoire, that "the child at the height of his babbling period 'is capable of producing all conceivable sounds,'" but continues:

As all observers acknowledge with great surprise, a child then loses nearly all of his ability to produce sounds in passing over from the pre-language stage to the first acquisition of words, i.e. to the first genuine stage of language. It is easy to understand that those articulations which are lacking in the language of the child's environment easily disappear from his inventory. But it is striking that, in addition, many other sounds which are common both to the child's babbling and to the adult language of his environment are in the same way disposed of, in spite of this environmental model that he depends on. Indeed, the child is generally successful in recovering these sounds only after long effort, sometimes only after several years. (1968a:21-22)

The explanation of this phenomenon, as we might now expect, lies in the imposition of a structure on the linguistic elements. As Jakobson puts it:

Alongside the purposeless egocentric soliloquy of the child . . . there arises and grows by degrees in children a desire for communication. . . . To the desire to communicate is added the ability to communicate something. The dummy dialogue becomes a true dialogue, and as soon as sound utterances "are employed for the purpose of designation" the actual stage of language formation is launched, as Wundt correctly realized.

It is precisely these arbitrary sound distinctions aimed at meaning which require simple, clear and stable phonological oppositions, and they must be capable of becoming impressed on the memory, and of being recognized and reproduced at will. The original self-sufficiency of the many disunited, individual perceptions is replaced by a conceptual distribution of articulated sounds, parallel to that of colors. In place of the phonetic abundance of babbling, the phonemic poverty of the first linguistic stage appears, a kind of deflation which transforms the so-called "wild sounds" of the babbling period into entities of linguistic value. (1968:24)

Sounds become significant only in context, and until they become significant they do not count as language. Context-free features of language properly so called can be arrived at, therefore, only through context-dependent ones, since otherwise we could not know whether or not they were features of *language*. This suggests a general caution for etic analyses. Not that it is impossible to describe the sound structure of some episode of speech in an unknown language, but even if we could be sure it was speech (as opposed to ritual chanting, for example) the exercise would soon lose its point in the absence of some emic insight. Also etic perceptions are never pure, colored to some extent as they inevitably are by our own conditioning to a particular language, or to particular structures of other kinds. Jakobson, again with his collaborators Fant and Halle, offers striking testimony to this fact:

> . . . interference by the language pattern affects even our responses to non-speech sounds. Knocks produced at even intervals, with every third louder, are perceived as groups of three separated by a pause. The pause is usually claimed by a Czech to fall before the louder knock, by a Frenchman to fall after the louder; while a Pole hears the pause one knock after the louder. The different perceptions correspond exactly to the position of the word stress in the languages involved: in Czech the stress is on the initial syllable, in French on the final and in Polish, on the penult. When the knocks are produced with equal loudness but with a longer interval after every third, the Czech attributes greater loudness to the first knock, the Pole, to the second, and the Frenchman, to the third. (1952:10)

We all come to consciousness of the phenomenon of language from within a language acquired from a social group, and this emic commitment makes etic objectivity all the harder.

## 32. From distinctive features to free discourse

ONTOGENETIC CONSIDERATIONS APART, the code of a given language is made up from elements selected from among the vocally possible phonemes. But the Saussurean phoneme does not survive as the unit of linguistic opposition, a more basic unit being the "distinctive feature" introduced by Jakobson. The set of pairs of such features (grave/acute, compact/diffuse, and so on) exhausts the vocal resources of language, and every phonologically distinct sound can be analyzed into a set of features containing only one element from each pair. However this shift is not seen by Jakobson as contradicting Saussure's views, "because, here as often elsewhere, the editors of the *Cours* have deviated from his authentic teaching. In the original record of Saussure's lectures, we find that it is not the phonemes but their ELEMENTS that take 'une valeur purement oppositive, relative, négative'" (1962:442). Nor does this further analysis of the phoneme involve the abandonment of the Saussurean doctrine of the linearity of the signifier, since although the distinctive features are simultaneous rather than sequential only their combination can function as an element of the signifier.

A full treatment of the notion of distinctive feature is to be found in the work of Jakobson, Fant, and Halle already cited. They list twelve pairs, or binary oppositions, that underlie "the entire lexical and morphological stock" of the languages of the world (1952:40). Assuming that either of each pair could occur in a given phoneme, this would yield $2^{12}$ or 4096 different phonemes. But of course they cluster: "No language contains all of these features. Their joint occurrence or incompatibility both within the same language and within the same phoneme is to a considerable extent determined by laws of implication which are universally valid or at least have a high statistical probability: X implies the presence of Y and/or the absence of Z" (1952:40).

For Jakobson, then, the idea of duality or binary opposition remains primary. Not only speech, but thought itself is built up by a series of "dichotomous scissions"; this pattern indeed is the dominant feature of structural development. The following passages from Henri Wallon's *Les Origines de la pensée chez l'enfant*, quoted *seriatim* by Jakobson, give some idea of the importance that is to be attached to it:

> Thought exists only through the structures that it introduces into things. . . . it is possible to observe from the beginning the existence of coupled elements. The element of thought is this binary structure, not the elements that constitute it. . . . The couple, or the pair, are anterior to the isolated element. . . . Without this initial relationship of the couple the whole eventual edifice of relationships would be impossible. . . . There is no punctiform thought. . . . The simplest distinction, the most striking, is opposition. It is by its contrary that an idea defines itself at first and most easily. The connection between yes-no, black-white, father-mother, becomes automatic, as it were, to such an extent that they seem sometimes to come to the lips at the same time, so that it is necessary to make a kind of choice and repress from the pair the term that is not appropriate. . . . The couple is at once identification and differentiation. (Jakobson 1962:451)

Martinet's duality shows up in Jakobson on two distinct levels: on the semantic level there is the duality of morpheme and utterance, while on the feature level there is the duality of feature and phoneme. One might speak, in fact, of an ascending hierarchy of levels with which is associated an ascending scale of linguistic freedom.

> In the combination of distinctive features into phonemes, the freedom of the individual speaker is zero; the code has already established all the possibilities which may be utilized in the given language. Freedom to combine phonemes into words is circumscribed, it is limited to the marginal situation of word-coinage. In the forming of sentences out of

words the speaker is less constrained. And finally, in the combination of sentences into utterances [or, we might add, texts], the action of compulsory syntactical rules ceases and the freedom of any individual speaker to create novel contexts increases substantially, although again the numerous stereotypical utterances are not to be overlooked. (Jakobson and Halle 1956:60)

This continuity appears (and has been said) to involve the demise of the opposition between *langue* and *parole*, but again the force of the distinction is not lost simply because intermediate cases present themselves. "What F. de Saussure describes as 'parole,'" says Trnka, "is regarded by the Prague linguists as utterances (or parts of utterances) in which a code of inherent structural rules is to be detected" (in Vachek 1964:76)—but of course for Saussure *langue* precisely was the set of rules (the "norm") that manifested itself in *parole*. *Langue* can in fact be regarded as itself having a hierarchical structure whose rules become more permissive at higher levels.

That there should be more freedom at these higher levels clearly depends on there being less at the lower ones. As we move down the scale we encounter a transition from linguistic to physiological constraints: it is our possession of a larynx, and of a tongue and buccal cavity whose configuration can be modified at will, that makes speech possible and sets its boundary conditions. The basis of linguistic duality at this level is the doubling of possible configurations of the vocal mechanism (and hence of possible sounds) by neural structures, as yet incompletely specified, that correlate these configurations with the heard sounds they produce and link them with the network of memories and concepts. Culture realizes only some of the possibilities represented by this complex of natural endowments. One might say that it is natural to be able to have a language, cultural actually to have one. "Language straddles the divide between nature and culture," says Jakobson, and hence "linguistics has become a connecting link between the natural sciences and the sciences of man" (1968b:18). Language belongs to nature not only because it is biologically possible but also because it is a universal form of behavior among the members of the human species, and it belongs to culture because any developed form of it requires social interaction and is accompanied by the development of other kinds of collective organization, no longer universal but mediated by the universality of language. It is the most advanced biological phenomenon (on a scale prejudiced, to be sure, by the human viewpoint from which it is regarded) and the most basic cultural one. If language *in its free and creative use by human individuals* manifests a coherent structure, then it will not be unreasonable to look for such a structure in any product of culture.

## 33. Distributive and mathematical structure

ALTHOUGH JAKOBSON WORKED for many years in the United States, his origins as a linguist were obviously European. Linguistics in America has had its own independent history (not all of which has been obviously "structuralist" but nearly all of which has had implications for structuralism) whose variety is partly due to the extraordinary empirical resources represented by the various American Indian languages. The investigation of these languages, which had been begun in an informal way, as we have seen, by Morgan and others, was undertaken systematically by the Smithsonian Institution at the turn of the century and resulted in the publication of the monumental *Handbook of American Indian Languages*, under the editorship of Franz Boas.

Boas took a Humboldtian view of the association of language with culture and rejected speculation about the determination of language by external conditions such as climate. It had been suggested, for example, that the guttural languages found among the Indians of the northern Pacific coast could be explained by the fact that the moist climate induced catarrh, while the drier conditions in California explained the euphonious languages of the Indians living there. "I do not believe," says Boas, "that detailed investigations in any part of the world would sustain this theory" (1911:53). But on the other hand, as was briefly mentioned in Chapter 3, he did conclude that some linguistic unity must underlie cultural differences. "In all languages certain classifications of concepts occur. . . . The behavior of primitive man makes it perfectly clear that all these concepts, although they are in constant use, have never risen into consciousness, and that consequently their origin must be sought, not in rational, but in entirely unconscious, we may perhaps say instinctive, processes of the mind" (1911:67). From one point of view, therefore, he regards linguistic structure as culturally bound, from another point of view he regards it as universal. But, like Saussure, he does not use the term "structure" except to refer to the way parts of words (prefixes, suffixes, and so on) are put together, and of course this differs from language to language.

Two other figures in the independent development of American linguistics (before it turned toward positivism and behaviorism) were Edward Sapir and Benjamin Lee Whorf. Sapir has a concept of linguistic structure, but it is a classificatory concept, and in the end has more to do with style than with grammar. "It must be obvious to anyone who has thought about the question at all or who has felt something of the spirit of a foreign language that there is such a thing as a basic plan, a certain cut, to each language. This type or plan or structural 'genius' of the language is something much more fundamental, much more pervasive, than any single feature that we can mention, nor can we gain an adequate idea of its nature by a mere recital of the sundry facts that make up the grammar of the language" (1949:120). He rejects any intimate association of language with culture, but does suppose that language has a determining epistemological force; it is, in his words, "a particular *how* of thought" (1949:218). This view was shared by Benjamin Lee Whorf and has become known as the "Whorf hypothesis" or the "Sapir-Whorf hypothesis," according to which the segmentation of the conceptual and even of the perceptual world differs among speakers of different languages. Whorf provides striking examples of this, especially from the Hopi (cf. e.g. 1956:112ff.).

But behavioristic and positivistic tendencies dominated American linguistic theory between the wars. The Chicago school, associated with the name of Leonard Bloomfield, attempted to represent language in terms of stimulus and response; Bloomfield's classic account, involving Jack, Jill, and the apple, suggests that the "speechless reaction"

$$S \to R,$$

where the stimulus S is Jill's seeing the apple and the response R her reaching for it, may be replaced under suitable circumstances by a "reaction mediated by speech,"

$$S \to r. \ldots . s \to R,$$

where the same stimulus S leads to the "linguistic substitute response" r (Jill's asking Jack to get the apple), which in turn produces the "linguistic substitute stimulus" s (Jack's hearing the request) the outcome R being effectively the same as before (Jill's getting the apple) (1933:22ff.). But Bloomfield's views on the status of language as an object for linguistics are to some extent independent of this doctrinaire behaviorism:

> . . . all historical study of language is based upon the comparison of two or more sets of descriptive data. It can only be as accurate and only as complete as these data permit it to be. In order to describe a language one needs no historical knowledge whatever; in fact, the observer who allows such knowledge to affect his description, is bound to distort his data. Our descriptions must be unprejudiced, if they are to give a sound basis for comparative work. The only useful generalizations about language are inductive generalizations. (1933:19)

While (as we saw in Chapter 3) these views reflect the positivist prejudice against hypotheses and tend therefore to paralyze fruitful conjecture, they do endorse the synchronic study of language, independently of its history.

An important departure in descriptive linguistics came with the invocation of statistical and other mathematical techniques. The spoken or written syntagma can be regarded as a complex object and examined in abstraction from its function as a carrier of significance. Here the etic/emic distinction becomes blurred. The descriptive linguist knows perfectly well that the syntagma has an emic function, indeed it is selected for study just because of this. Every syntagma drawn from the corpus of a language in use will be fulfilling some such function—that is what makes it language. But the way in which significance *fits over* the syntagma is problematic, and the fact that there may not be a one-to-one matching of emic and etic elements makes the separate consideration of the latter not only plausible but necessary.

This failure of fit has sometimes been taken as an essential characteristic of language, for example by Louis Hjelmslev, who writes: "in order for a structure to be recognized as a language, the reciprocal relation of presupposition between the content and the expression must not be accompanied by another identical relation between each element on one level and an element of the other level" (1966:138). Not just a duality of structure, but a duality of structures that differ in some significant respect from one another—this may plausibly be taken as a necessary condition for the functioning of any sign system. Hjelmslev's glossematics has been identified as the third independent stream of structuralist linguistics, the other two being Prague functionalism (with which it shares its Saussurean antecedents) and Bloomfieldian descriptive linguistics; its specific difference is its disinterest in phonetics and its insistence on the variety of diverse elements on the level of expression, such as word order, intonation, etc., collectively called "glossemes."

Glossematics tends toward abstract formalism and has been taken to task for this (Vachek 1964:469). It is rather the empirical investigation of the formal properties of texts that has led to the development of mathematical linguistics. Texts are available as data and constitute a domain of objects whose properties are rarely found in nature. But it is important to notice that the mathematical properties of the relations exhibited in texts are not, in so far as they are mathematical, especially "linguistic" or "cultural." Perfectly general mathematical results may be stimulated by the study of artifacts: for example, the study of probabilistic sequences that led the Russian mathematician Markov to the concept of the "Markov chain" involved an analysis of the first twenty thousand words of Pushkin's *Eugene Onegin* (Herdan 1960:141ff.).

The syntagma, in other words, is an object in the world, susceptible of objective investigation. Composed as it is of elements drawn from finite sets (the relatively restricted sets of distinctive features, phonemes, morphemes, and so on, or the relatively open set of words), it is, unless the sequence of these elements is random—which in the nature of the case is implausible, randomness being the complete absence of internal constraint, that is, of structure—obliged to exhibit patterns of the repetition and distribution of these elements. It will of course be possible to connect these patterns back to the significance they bear, but for purposes of analysis any text in the language will do to begin with. After each morpheme in a spoken chain comes another morpheme; after each letter in a written text comes another letter, or a space, or a diacritical mark; every word has a definite length, and with every text therefore is associated a definite mean word length; every element that occurs more than once will occur at points in the syntagma bearing definite relations to one another, and a given text will be character-ized by a number representing the average number of other elements falling between two occurrences of it.

All this suggests a concept of structure quite different from the binary or oppositional or dual structures so far discussed. "Distributional structure" is characteristic not of language in general or of the grammatical or phono-logical aspects of particular languages, but of particular texts or utterances, or bodies of text or utterance, regarded as empirically given objects. The structural features discovered in these objects may be accounted for by reference to properties of language in general or of particular languages, but they may require other explanations as well, or instead. A striking example is provided by statistical research into the distribution of initial letters of words in English texts. It appears that each speaker of English has a specific pattern of frequency in the use of words with various initial letters, and this is explained by the fact that the vocabularies of English speakers are made up, *grosso modo*, of words from two different stocks, Teutonic and Romance, but that each speaker acquires a slightly different mix (Herdan 1960:158ff.).

A major contribution to work on distributional structure has been that of Zellig Harris. His analyses have been based on a corpus of standard utterances, represented as sequences of elements subject to internal con-straints. Each element enters into two kinds of relation, one (in my terminol-ogy) parallel and one orthogonal, called by Harris relations of "serial dependence" and of "parallel substitutivity." This conflict of terminologies is only apparent—my use of "parallel" exploits the fact that a line may be said to be parallel with itself and is primarily directional, Harris's exploits the fact that an alternative utterance, with different substitutions, may be thought of as parallel with the first. But this means that one would have as it were to reach over to the second parallel for an element to be substituted in the first, a move that would be orthogonal to the serial line of the syntagma. This is an example of the risks of dependence on spatial metaphors. The distinction that Harris is making is clearly similar to Jakobson and Halle's between "combination" and "selection," or to the familiar distinction between the "syntagmatic" and "paradigmatic" axes (the basis in Jakobson's work for the contrast between metonymy and metaphor).

What the structure of an utterance or corpus is found to be depends, for

Harris, on the features that inquiry chooses to stress, so that his informal definition of structure is given contextually as follows: "A set of phonemes or a set of data is structured with respect to some feature, to the extent that we can form in terms of that feature some recognized system of statements which describes the members of the set and their interrelations (at least up to some limit of complexity)" (1954:26). The object of study is the "structure of relative occurrence (i.e. of distribution)" of elements in a language (1954:28). It is useful to be reminded that structure is always to be relativized in this way, on pain of involving everything in the universe.

But selecting the features is not always so easy, and here again the dialectical relation between etic and emic becomes apparent (dialectical because it is at once an opposition and an interdependence, which changes with time). We have already seen that the question which phonemes (or oppositions constitutive of them) are operative in a given language cannot be answered on etic grounds, and Harris points out that on the morphemic level analysis resorts to meanings and other internal evidence. As an example he offers the morphemic analysis of "persist" and "person," according to which "persist" is assigned two morphemes because of the existence of a set of related terms ("consist," "pertain" and the like) in which these elements are recognizably distributed, whereas "person" is assigned only one because no such set of true associations can be found (1954:32). There are of course plenty of words incorporating "per-" or "-son," but we know from etymological evidence that they are unrelated to "person"; this knowledge however comes from global considerations about the language that far transcend anything that could be read from the data at the level where the analysis is being conducted.

The structure of language, however, cannot be identified with the structure of meaning, even though at the level of discourse there is a striking correlation between the two (the correlation is less marked at the morphological level and negligible at the phonological level). One might wish, Harris suggests, "to speak of language as existing in some sense on two planes—of form and of meaning" (1954:32); the fact that these evolve independently in individuals and are sometimes unconnected ("the way a person's store of meanings grows and changes through the years while his language remains fairly constant, or the way a person can have an idea or a feeling which he cannot readily express in the language available to him," (1954:31) implies a limitation on what can legitimately be inferred about the one from a study of the other. At the same time it confirms the basic truth about signiferous structures that has been exhibited in different contexts throughout this discussion of language, namely, that significance arises from the matching of two structures independently generated. In this respect Saussure's original insight seems still to hold good.

## 34. Diachrony and the acquisition of language

THE SYNTAGMA, IT must be remembered, is produced by human individuals; it has the character it has because of this fact. One might program a device to produce something like it, varying the distributional parameters, and so forth, but this product could not be recognized or function as a human language unless it reflected more or less accurately the main features of actual speech or writing. On the other hand the human individuals who produce the syntagma do not do so spontaneously but only after having learned how it is done. It used to be thought that language was natural to human beings and that there was *a* language (whether or not one among those actually spoken) they would naturally speak if history and convention did not intervene. Thus it was supposed, for example, that a child to whom nobody spoke might grow up speaking Hebrew, and experiments were proposed (I do not know whether any of them were carried out) to test this hypothesis. It is now clear, however, that language is almost entirely a social phenomenon—not that individuals, once they have it, may not make private use of it or introduce private variations into it, in the limit perhaps attaining something like a "private language," but that if it were not for their insertion into a social context they would never by themselves acquire a language at all, or even the idea of a language.

The languages we actually use are the products of an extremely long and extraordinarily diverse and multiple diachronic development, full of false starts and dead ends, and their apparent stability is due to the very great disproportionality between the time scale of language use and that of linguistic evolution, the former being of the order of minutes and the latter of the order of generations, or (once the language is codified in writing and embodied in literature) of the order of centuries. Any actual episode of language use is limited by the attention span of the user, and this is rarely such as to take in more than a few sentences together; the gist of an argument can be followed for much longer periods, but (except in the case of people with abnormal memories) the details of the syntagma are fleeting. On the other hand the establishment of a genuinely new linguistic form (not counting the relatively rapid changes in vocabulary or style that may be the result of fashion or technological innovation), its adoption and acceptance across a whole population, may not be finally achieved for very many years, even if it is encouraged by official pronouncements or legislation. Most of the changes in form that have taken place in the last few centuries have been simplifications, the suppression of former distinctions, such as the gradual disappearance of the subjunctive in English. It is worth noting that, for any individual who is conscious of the structure of language and attaches normative value to it, these changes can be only in the direction of error, which accounts for the perpetual sense of linguistic degeneration experienced by purists.

The problem that poses itself in the light of all this is *how* the individual comes to have a language. And this introduces a form of linguistic change, if I may so put it, whose timescale is intermediate between those of the two processes I have been discussing. I mean of course the acquisition of language, or language learning. This is generally supposed to take place in the first five or six years of life, although as Carol Chomsky has shown (1969) there continues to be a refinement of detail until about the age of ten. As far as that goes one can reasonably maintain that, when account is taken of the range of vocabulary and the characteristics of style, the process never stops. However the point is that *a* complete language is learned by a relatively early age. Saussure maintained that *langue* resided in the collectivity, but I would add that it can do so only distributively; each English speaker has acquired a system of *langue* approximating that of each other English speaker. Just how does this get internalized in members of the collectivity, so that episodes of *parole*, of speaking and hearing, can be mutually intelligible?

The answer essentially given by Noam Chomsky is that to a much greater degree than is usually thought it does not have to be internalized, because it is innate. Before taking up Chomsky's views, however, a further word must be said, to supplement the earlier remarks made in chapter 3, about the appropriateness of including him in this book at all. Chomsky does not consider himself a structuralist. He is a grammarian, and the line of inquiry that his grammatical researches have followed leads him to a model of language as a mental process, with a dynamic and creative character which is at apparent variance with that of the abstract synchronic structures insisted upon by some of the disciples of Saussure. I say "apparent variance" because I think there is some mutual misunderstanding between the positions, or perhaps more accurately some unilateral misunderstanding by the post-Saussureans of their own position which has forced Chomsky to maintain a public distance from it.

For Chomsky the linguistic evidence is to be found in what people actually say, their *performance*, and in this he does not differ from Saussure and his followers. But the task of linguistic theory, as he sees it, is not so much to analyze the performance as to account for the *competence* that underlies it. "The central fact to which any significant linguistic theory must address itself is this; a mature speaker can produce a new sentence of his language on the appropriate occasion, and other speakers can understand it immediately, though it is equally new to them" (1964:7). Further, the mature speaker acquired this ability not through learning explicit rules for the production of sentences, but simply through immersion in the linguistic environment; out of the data provided by the miscellaneous utterances of others he has himself been able to invent the rules, not to be sure as conscious prescriptions but as patterns of behavior unerringly followed.

Three sequences of events, then, need to be accounted for: (1) the sequence from "primary linguistic data" to a generative grammar, mediated by a learning device, (2) the sequence from a specific utterance to the understanding of it (equivalent in formal terms to providing a structural description of it), mediated by perceptual and information-processing devices, and (3) the sequence from having something to say to saying it, mediated by a productive or creative device. (The latter turns out to be the grammar.) The character of the learning device can be inferred from the restrictions it appears to impose on its output. "Each natural language," says Chomsky— conjecturally but with conviction—"is a specific realization of a highly restrictive schema that permits grammatical processes and structures of a very limited variety. . . . there are innumerable 'imaginable' languages that violate these restrictions and that are, therefore, not possible human languages in a psychologically important sense, even though they are quite able, in principle, to express the entire content of any possible human language" (1967:8).

Where do these restrictions come from? The obvious answer—and one that Chomsky fully accepts—is that they come from the structure of mind. This structure remains "mentalistic" and abstract; the theory of linguistic competence "can at the present stage of knowledge draw no evidence from and make no direct contribution toward the study of the mechanisms that may realize the mental structures" (1966:91). The theory does not rule out an eventual materialism at the ontological level but it is not compatible with a *reductive* materialism. The basic structures, whatever the form of their concrete realization, generate in a recursive fashion whole families of possible linguistic structures, some of which are realized as grammars and in detail as particular utterances. But these "basic structures" are not the "deep structures" of language, which are contrasted with its "surface structures." Deep structure belongs to utterances, not to the underlying mental apparatus (although the use of a term like "underlying" may contribute to misunderstanding, suggesting as it does a contrast between surface and depth, and it is indeed this contrast that is exploited in the usual metaphorical use of "deep structure").

The deep structure of a sentence is provided for it by the syntax of the language (by the "syntactic component" of the grammar). Its function is to be *semantically interpretable*, or in other words to make the sentence meaningful. The surface structure is also provided by the syntax, but its function is to be *phonetically interpretable*. One might say, as a first approximation, that the surface structure is the structure of what we hear, the deep structure the

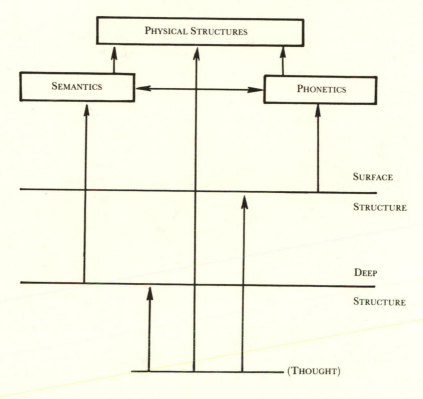

*Figure 5.1*

structure of what we understand by what we hear. The divergences of deep structure that may underlie identical or closely similar surface structures have been dramatized by familiar examples: "Flying planes can be dangerous," or "John is easy to please"/"John is eager to please." Both the deep and surface structures are abstract (or mental) correlates of more evident structures, referential or acoustic, studied in their own right by other disciplines—the natural sciences, phonology, and so forth. The relations between these various structures are set out in figure 5.1.

Chomsky's distance from structuralism is marked by a methodological disagreement with other American linguists of the structural school and a strategic disagreement with the European structuralists. The methodological point turns on the inductive and behaviorist tendencies of earlier American linguistics, according to which a roughly Lockean mind acquired "habits and know-how" from experience. Chomsky rejects this view and aligns himself explicitly with Descartes, implicitly with Kant, although he is on firmer ground than either because he has at his disposal technical resources unknown to them. Language cannot be learned inductively from scratch. The mechanism of generation that governs the production of new sentences appears to be recursive, that is, to proceed by the successive application of transformation rules to some initial formula. In order to get an end product adequate to the facts of creative language use, on the basis of the available rules, one is forced to assign characteristics to the initial formula that cannot be derived inductively from any finite set of antecedently available sentences. "If one follows behaviorism to its logical conclusion, which has never really been done, one arrives at a system of models that governs behavior and one knows in principle how to represent these models by means of mathematics. Now it can be demonstrated that language has formal properties which cannot be expressed by means of these models . . . " (1969:18)

This situation resembles a familiar one in the philosophy of science, where a rather confused debate about induction has been going on for centuries. New events are always happening; no set of principles derived inductively from what has already happened can be counted on to anticipate them. But hypotheses, together with principles learned inductively, may lead to the specification of whole sets of possible events, among which the novel ones may actually be found. Where do the hypotheses come from? Their generation, I have suggested elsewhere (Caws 1967, 1986), is a perfectly natural function of the mind, which might in the light of Chomsky's work be said to be among other things a creative use of language. The grammar of any possible science will be one among a restricted set of logical structures characteristic of mind; this is a Kantian point, or, if we assume a homology of some sort among these structures and the world, a Peircean one.

Chomsky's linguistics is Cartesian in that it invokes a mental component independent of individual experience. But its mentalism grows not out of an a priori conviction of dualism, but out of an a posteriori necessity for an abstract and non-behavioral level of linguistic activity. It is hard to see what is objectionable in this. The quarrel here however is not between a structural and a nonstructural linguistics but between those who think that the structure is constructed through experience and those who think that some of it at least is biologically given. I shall return in Part II to the whole question of "instruction," that is, the question of how mental structures are internalized, remarking here only that it now seems quite inconceivable that anyone should ever have believed that the internal complexity of the organism had nothing to do with its ability to learn, and that once this connection is conceded the opposition between innate and learned structure ceases to be one of principle.

## 35. Formalism and complexity

"AS TO CONTINENTAL structuralism," Chomsky once said in an interview (and it seems worth quoting him at length),

> I have learned much from it, but I reproach it for remaining superficial in its recognition of structures. The goal of structuralism is to extract from performance a certain number of elements linked among themselves by a set of relations in formal models. Such a disposition of elements in formal models constitutes the structure of language. An example has been Jakobson's theory of phonology, studies in which he has extracted distinctive features whose structure he has investigated. But in going further with the investigation of language one discovers that underlying the system of characteristics and properties disposed in a certain way, there are much more abstract principles and rules which link the systems with the formal structures studied by structuralists. These therefore appear as epiphenomena resulting from much more profound operations. And even if it is true that the study of epiphenomena is interesting, it seems that it ought to be the deep principles which one would explore and expound. They have a recursive character, that is to say they characterize and engender in their turn an infinite ensemble of possible structures. This property has not been perceived even by the most advanced research under the rubric of structuralism. It seems to me that the generativity of language is not a marginal property. For this reason I am in agreement with structuralism, but I think that one can build on its results and carry researches on language much further. (1969:18)

This is good advice but it is not easy to follow. It is safe to say, I think, that any structuralist, given in connection with some set of mutually transforming structures the choice between a paradigmatic structure and some transformation rules on the one hand, and a device for generating all the structures of the set on the other, would unhesitatingly choose the device; the trouble is that outside linguistics structuralism is still at the stage of identifying and establishing the sets, while inside it Chomsky's version of the device is not universally accepted.

In fact the stress on "formal models" in this statement of Chomsky's points up a general problem for structuralism. It is perfectly true that outside some domains of linguistics very little progress has been made in developing interesting or fruitful formalisms; as we shall see in the next chapter, Lévi-Strauss's attempts, which count among the most ambitious, seem often at once simplistic and contrived. But even within linguistics the results have not been much happier, and my own view is that the whole attempt to conduct the structuralist enterprise in terms of rigorous mathematical models is a case of what I call "spurious formalism." A nonspurious formalism has to meet two conditions: what it deals with must be *precisely* specifiable in formal language (in the ideal case, moreover one frequently encountered in the physical sciences, it will be quantifiable), and this specification must make possible formulations and operations *that would not be possible in ordinary language.* This last condition is hardly ever met in structuralist studies; the main points can nearly always be conveyed discursively, and the introduction of formulas and technical expressions is often merely ornamental and plays no real role in the argument.

The point of structuralism, after all, is to show that the entities in play are relational rather than substantial, and to show which relations are involved, how they are generated, and how the structures they compose transform into one another; it is not to claim that those relations are so complex that they require mathematical expression. On reflection it appears that the need for such complexity is unlikely, since the relations in question constitute the relatively familiar structures of human and social institutions, while most interesting nonspurious formalisms (apart from those of pure mathematics itself, which exists just in order to explore possible complexities) have been called for and developed to deal with the constitution of relatively unfamiliar features of the physical world. That some of them have become familiar through our exposure to the natural sciences does not affect this observation. To put the point in another way: we do not, as individuals, have to sustain the complexity of nature, which can therefore be as complex as it likes (thus making us possible). But we do have to sustain the complexity of the social world, and that world cannot therefore be more complex than the mental operations by means of which we do sustain it—or if it should become more complex it will at the same time risk instability, since individuals may fail to do what is required of them if it is to be sustained.

I do not mean here to suggest that we always have to be consciously aware of the complexity of everything we do. In particular our use of language requires no doubt unconscious complexities as great as, if not greater than, those of any other neurophysiological activity. So really necessary and nonspurious formalisms are likely to develop in psycholinguistics. One of the routes of access to this material lies through cognitive science and studies on artificial intelligence, and the obstacles in the way of a formal representation of something as basic as pattern recognition show how formidable the task is. However I take this work to lie outside the purview of structuralism, just as particle physics does. The structures dealt with in structuralism are those of which we can become reflectively aware, from grammatical usage to the appropriate treatment of kinfolk to the recognition of literary allusions to the conflicts and transformations of economic and political institutions, and here I believe my conclusions about complexity—which will return in Part 2 as the "optimum complexity principle"—can be shown to hold.

It is important to see that it is *as individuals* that we sustain the social world. Each of us has a *whole* language, each of us internalizes *all* the relations that determine our membership and comportment in groups and other social institutions. There is nowhere for these relations to subsist except as embodied, distributively, in us. And that brings up another general difficulty. Mentalists like Descartes and Chomsky seem to find the assumption of mind, with its abstract and formalizable structure, unproblematic. It is no doubt a useful hypothesis. But all we actually have at our disposal are individual minds, embodied in speakers and listeners, readers and writers, parents and children, masters and slaves, buyers and sellers; and the assumption that from an observation of the speech and behavior of these individuals "profound operations" and "deep principles" can easily be inferred seems optimistic if not Utopian.

In addition to his doubts about the level at which structuralist activity in European linguistics has been carried on, Chomsky also has serious reservations as to the legitimacy of any extrapolation from linguistics to other branches of inquiry. He commends Lévi-Strauss for his study of the categories of primitive mentality (in *La Pensée sauvage*) but criticizes the use of structural linguistics as a model: "the structure of a phonological system is of very little interest as a formal object; there is nothing of significance to be said, from a formal point of view, about a set of forty-odd elements cross-classified in terms of eight or ten features. . . . the real richness of phonological systems lies not in the structural patterns of phonemes but rather in the intricate systems of rules by which these patterns are formed, modified, and elaborated" (1969:18). Once again it is a question of actually identifying the patterns before presuming to ask for the rules, and from the far side of the boundary that marks linguistics off from the other *sciences humaines* it seems ungenerous of the linguist to criticize the ambition of his more backward colleagues to be like him. There is at all events no doubt that it was the apparent success of linguistics in extracting structural patterns and rules that encouraged Lévi-Strauss and others to make the same attempt in anthropology and the rest of the social sciences.

# 6

# The Social Superstructure

## 36. Semiotics, linguistics, structuralism

JOSEPH STALIN, IN his essay *On Marxism in Linguistics* (a work which earned him Kolakowski's ironic praise as The Greatest Linguist in the World) felt called upon to correct Academician Marr's overzealous doctrines by the following exemplary bit of pedagogy:

> Question. Is it true that language is a
> superstructure resting on a base?
> Answer. No, it is false. (1951:12)

The philosophical view that Marr had sought to strengthen by his theory of language as a class phenomenon, namely Marxism, has a strong affinity with structuralism, not only conceptually but also historically. Lévi-Strauss acknowledges his debt to Marx; what is perhaps less well known is that Marx acknowledges *his* debt to Lewis H. Morgan, the American forerunner of structuralism whose doctrines were touched upon in chapter 3 (Hobsbawm, in Marx 1964:24–25). What must have pleased Marx in the work of Morgan was precisely the latter's insistence on the fundamental status of human relations, including the property relation. For Marx such relations were the reality underlying the appearance of commodities and capital; the economic relations between human beings, between members of an exploiting class and potential members of an oppressed one (already really oppressed, potentially members of a class), formed the *Struktur* on which the *Ueberbau* of bourgeois culture was erected. The translation of these terms as "base" and "superstructure" has served to obscure Marx's connection with the foundations of structuralism.

This connection becomes clearer when we recall that the reinterpretation of familiar and apparently substantial entities in terms of unfamiliar but, once grasped, perspicuous relations was one of Marx's characteristic strategies. The case of money is illustrative: it appears as a commodity but is in fact the formal embodiment of a value relation based on human labor. Again, money is what it is only because of the relations into which it enters; in itself it is nothing, or rather it does not matter what it is, provided it satisfies certain purely practical requirements (durability, distinctiveness, and so on). The same can be said, *mutatis mutandis*, of that other great medium of human exchange, language. The economy of language is not limited to its own circulation, but it enables other commodities to enter the circuit of intelligibility.

Language, in other words, is the chief currency available to us for the structuring of the world, for making it communicable. Marr's mistake was to put it in the superstructure; even in Marxist terms, it now appears more like part of the base. Indeed the parallel between language and money has become more and more obvious (see Shell 1985), to the point where it is worth remembering one immensely significant difference between them, a difference that in a more generalized form is the great stumbling block to all Marxist theories of culture, namely, that although there *can* be a form of economic oppression even in the linguistic and epistemological domains, *in principle* language and the knowledge it conveys can, unlike money or other material commodities, be shared without being divided. As a base, then, linguistics seems more promising and more humane than economics.

As we have seen, Barthes thought language more fundamental than significance itself; in his *Eléments de sémiologie* he made a deliberate effort to derive from the linguistics of Saussure a theory of the sign adequate to the proliferation of cultural objects with which structuralism might wish to deal. The work was indeed derivative, from other linguists such as Hjelmslev as well as from Saussure, but it provoked thought about the parallels between language and other domains of significance. In the linguistic case each act of *parole* has actually to be performed somewhere, at some time, by some individual; but each has also to be judged by the canons of *langue*—to be a more or less correct realization of some grammatical possibility, to conform more or less closely to some accepted rule of linguistic usage—if it is to be intelligible as an utterance of the language. Applied to other signiferous systems, this opposition between case and rule, between code and message, suggests that for any set of customs, practices, works of art or literature, and so forth, that may constitute a coherent domain of culture (kinship, table manners, technology, fashion, and so on) it makes sense to look for the structuring principles that account for all the members of the set, each of which is an object, event, or episode produced or played out by individual agents, as realizations of the same pattern or archetype or prototype or paradigm case, or show them to be transformations of one another.

The new science of semiology, whose place among the other sciences Saussure "staked out in advance" (1959:16), was intended by him to be more general than linguistics. "If we are to discover the true nature of language we must learn what it has in common with other semiological systems. . . . By studying rites, customs, etc. as signs, I believe that we shall throw new light on the facts and point up the need for including them in a science of semiology and explaining them by its laws" (1959:17). What these things have in common is presumably what I have called signiferous structure; their laws will be the laws of this structure. It follows that, while we may look for structure where we find significance, we will not explain the structure in terms of the significance but the significance in terms of the structure.

This point is relevant to what has happened since structuralism, especially in France, which I take to have been a regressive move toward semiotics (as semiology has generally come to be known) as part of the amorphous manifestation of "poststructuralism." The trouble with semiology was that its very name suggested some independent recognition of what counted as significant, that is, functioned as a sign; Saussure (and Peirce independently at about the same time under the name "semiotic") derived the name from the Greek *semeion*, a mark, device, flag, seal, omen from heaven, all particular objects or events recognized as already invested with significance. But it seems clear that a sense of the significance of some activity may and often does precede the identification of the specific carriers of this significance. The whole system appears as fraught with significance, as having a signiferous structure, and investigation will show which structural relations are chosen for embodiment in acts or utterances. This will require something like the *langue/parole* distinction (so that we can be sure that this episode—a marriage, a ceremonial recitation of a myth, a sacrifice or whatever, really does count as a case of the kind of thing the system sanctions and determines, otherwise it will fail to be significant and we will just be going through the motions) but it does not require, on the contrary it is required by, an understanding of how the particular signs function as such.

What structuralism offers, in other words, is a way of encircling and zeroing in on the sign, as it were, without prejudice as to its constitutive nature. It is therefore more fundamental, in the order of explanation, than semiotics. What happened in France was once again, I suspect, a function of fashion and of professional style: the work that needed to be done to show how it comes to be the case that anything at all is significant proved less attractive than the discursive elaboration of cases that already obviously involved significance. (It would be an oversimplification, but an instructive one perhaps, to see in this development a contrast between philosophical doggedness and literary excitability.) At all events it is I think a mistake to equate structuralism and semiology, as Jonathan Culler for example does (1975:6), and misleading to conclude that structuralism "realized that it had become . . . a branch of that semiology which Saussure had envisaged," even though this conclusion may have been reached about their own disciplines by some people who came to be known as structuralists (Lévi-Strauss, for example, as Culler correctly indicates). (For structuralism to be said to have realized anything is an example of the "fallacy of misplaced agency" to which so many structuralists so willingly succumbed.)

The relations between structuralism, linguistics, and semiotics are thus worth careful restatement. Barthes cites Saussure's conviction that linguistics will prove to be a special case of semiology and suggests that it puts the disciplines in the wrong order. "It seems increasingly difficult," he says, "to conceive of a system of images or objects whose *signifieds* could exist outside language: to perceive that a substance signifies is, fatally, to have recourse to the divisions effected by language: there is no sense unless it is named, and the world of signifieds is none other than that of language"; and he goes on a little later to conclude, "From now on the probability must, in short, be admitted that Saussure's proposition may one day be reversed: linguistics is not a part, even a privileged one, of the general science of signs, it is semiology which is part of linguistics"(1965:80–81).

This seems to me quite perverse, but is in line with a general tendency to assimilate all forms of intelligibility to language, with which I shall deal at greater length in Part II. To some extent the question is terminological. By stipulating, for example, that thought itself is necessarily conducted in a kind of language, as Fodor does in *The Language of Thought* (1975), the issue is resolved without contest—but at the same time what I take to be a valuable distinction between language and a more fundamental structuring activity of the mind is lost. To put the difficulty in another way: if language is not only the paradigm but the very foundation of intelligibility, what accounts for the intelligibility of language?

If language is, as I believe, only a special case—the most obvious and the most developed—of the use of signs, its intelligibility has to be accounted for in nonlinguistic terms. However I wish to go still further, and say that the intelligibility of signs has to be accounted for in nonsemiotic terms. The structuralist explanation of intelligibility rests for me on the conviction that *the matching of structured systems is experienced by us as primordially meaningful,* and that this experience can be broken down for analytic purposes into two components, one of affective involvement and the other of formal understanding, or respectively *mattering* and *signifying.* In practice the two components are virtually inseparable; the affective involvement after all need not be melodramatic, and may be no more than a sense of satisfaction or adequacy that brings closure to an otherwise unresolved situation. The absence of resolution need not have previously been felt as a lack, since we may be quite unaware of it until the matching draws our attention to it retrospectively.

Consider the following minimal case: among a random collection of irregular shapes are two that are congruent; nobody notices this until one day someone idly brings them into coincidence and suddenly recognizes that one fits exactly over the other. The fact of this recognition, and the "shock"

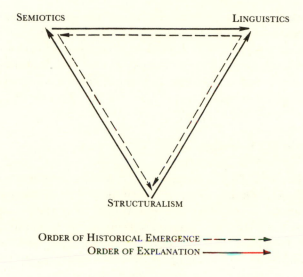

*Figure 6.1*

of it (an exaggerated way of speaking for such a modest example, but indicative nevertheless of the kind of experience such matching engenders), constitute in my view the phenomenological basis of meaning. Getting shapes into congruence—solving jigsaw puzzles, for example—is a satisfaction in itself, and it is our appetite for this sort of thing, conjoined with our ability to do it in many modes and contexts, that accounts for the development of signiferous structures. In particular the arbitrariness of the elements to be matched (the irregular shapes in the example just given) may not be a consequence of random causes but part of a productive function exercised intentionally by us, as in the case of the arbitrary association of a concept and a sound in the Saussurean sign; it is on the *repetition* of the same sound with the same conceptual association that the matching and the recognition take place, that the sign as it were acquires significance.

The triad structuralism-semiotics-linguistics might be represented as symmetrical (see figure 6.1). In the historical order of their emergence linguistics came first and in a sense gave rise to or provoked the other two, although the claim, made for example by Fredric Jameson in *The Prison-House of Language* (1972), that structuralism is merely the projection of a linguistic model of cultural products, replacing an earlier organic model, seriously oversimplifies the case. But in the order of explanation structuralism is the more fundamental and accounts for the other two, one of them (linguistics) in its turn a special case of the other. If this were not so there would be little point in working on structuralism at all—the concept of structure would be one useful tool among others for the analysis of cultural artifacts, but it would have no special explanatory force. A lot of what has been called structuralist analysis is in fact only "structural" in this weaker sense, and this accounts for its lack of interest to philosophers. The claim made here is that structure is fundamental to intelligibility, not merely one aspect of it.

## 37. Signs without language

IN CONTRADICTING WHAT I take to have been Saussure's deeper insight into the relation between linguistics and semiotics Barthes introduces some confusion into the structuralist debate. But just before the passages cited on p. 112 he makes a related and in my view far more telling point, which, while it still claims too much (note the "never" in the citation to follow), indicates something of major importance for the understanding of contemporary culture. Remarking that pure semiological analysis has been restricted to banalities like traffic signals, he alleges that all interesting sign systems are *accompanied* by language:

> Certainly, objects, images, behaviors can signify, and they do so abundantly, but never autonomously; every semiological system has language mixed into it. Visual material, for example, confirms its significations by duplicating itself with a linguistic message (as is the case for the cinema, for advertising, for comics, for press photography, etc.), in such a way that at least a part of the iconic message is structurally related to the system of language as redundant with respect to it, or as serving to draw attention to it; as to aggregates of objects (clothing, food), they do not attain the status of systems except in passing through the stage of language.(1965:80)

What this reasonably suggests is that the linguistic accompaniments of other cultural forms, the captions and manifestos and commentaries and critiques, offer material to structuralist analysis along with their referents. But Barthes himself, in *Systéme de la mode*, found that it was impossible to talk about fashion directly, so that he had to concentrate instead on what was said about it in women's magazines, or as he puts it "not really on clothes nor on language, but as it were on the 'translation' of one into the other" (1967:8). And in his review of Jean-Louis Schefer's *Scénographie d'un tableau* he makes a similar point about art: "The painting . . . exists only in the account I give of it; or again: in the sum total and the organization of the readings that can be made of it: a painting is never anything but its own plural description"

(1969:16). In Schefer's own words, "the image has no *a priori* structure, it has textual structures . . . of which it is the system" (1969:162).

Once again these are wild overstatements. But they draw attention to an important truth, namely, that we do all indulge in ceaseless linguistic commentary on the significant events of our lives, that these become to some degree structured in the telling, and that in many cases—perhaps most, in a developed and self-consciously verbal culture—the recounting of crucial episodes may come, in time, to supplant in the order of significance the episodes themselves. The keeping of diaries, the desire to record or to tell all about what happened, are witnesses on the level of the commonplace to this powerful tendency, which has found expression historically in literature itself. Literature began as a recounting of what was supposed actually to have transpired in the lives of gods or heroes: that supposed real lives can become fictional paves the way for fictions without a corresponding supposition of real lives. In the case of literary culture the recent proliferation of criticism represents a supplanting of one *linguistic* form by another.

This drive to verbalization is no doubt due to the fact that for a long time language, spoken or written, has been, if not the only, at all events the most effective way of communicating and perpetuating the impact and significance of meaningful events. At the same time it must be remembered that written language was preceded in the evolution of culture by cave paintings, pictographs, and the like, and there seems no reason to doubt that the visual, even while it was spawning, on the part of learned commentators, the language of iconography and art criticism, continued to be directly significant, *without* any verbal supplement, to generations of men and women, many of them illiterate, who had access to the religious and secular art of Italy or Flanders or the other centers of European painting, not to mention their analogues at other times and in other civilizations. The comic strip and the cinema, among other contemporary forms, attest to the continuity of this tradition, even though neither is a pure case of it.

But we need not be so tentative about it—there are plenty of pure cases of the signiferous without language: not only painting without art history and movies without sound or titles, but mime, for example—and above all, music. Music, in fact, is the absolute stumbling block for any theory that maintains the primacy of language in the matter of significance. Barthes seems to have had little concern for music; apart from two short essays in *Mythologies* on popular songs and the music hall, and his treatments of the castrati in *S/Z* (all, it is to be noted, cases in which music is systematically associated with language), he hardly mentions it at all. Lévi-Strauss, on the other hand, makes an elaborate metaphorical use of it in the construction of the first volume of his four-volume magnum opus, *Mythologiques*. *The Raw and the Cooked* opens with an "overture" and continues the musical theme with characteristic preciosity throughout the book ("Fugue of the Five Senses," "The Oppossum's Cantata," "Rustic Symphony in Three Movements," and so on).

Although he is not entirely lucid on the point—he calls music a language, and contrasts it with language, in the same paragraph (1969:27) —Lévi-Strauss's choice of music as a paradigm of structure confirms his own view that significance is carried by objects and practices as well as by language.

> The aim of this book [he says] is to show how empirical categories— such as the categories of the raw and the cooked, the fresh and the decayed, the moistened and the burned, etc., which can only be accurately defined by ethnographic observation and, in each instance, by adopting the standpoint of a particular culture—can nonetheless be used as conceptual tools with which to elaborate abstract ideas and combine them in the form of propositions. (1969:1)

The whole series, it is true, is about mythology—a linguistic form—but it precisely demonstrates how the significance that the myths embody comes not from the language in which they are couched but from the non- or prelinguistic relations and oppositions that constitute the structure of the world and of society for those who recount and listen to them. They are directly meaningful—in themselves, as music is, but also in their embodiment of features of the natural order: animals, weather, landscape, the directionality of space (upstream, downstream, and so on), earth, sky, gender, birth, death.

## 38. The mythical structure of the world

MYTHS USE THE vehicle of language, but the structure they lend to the world does not derive from this fact; language serves to embody a structure that is first encountered in prelinguistic form. Because of the generality of its grammatical (and even more fundamentally its logical) structure, language can embody discursively any empirical structure whatever, just as mathematics can do this formally. Of course, the languages we actually speak, like the mathematics we actually work out, and even the logic we are capable of formalizing (on this point see Caws 1975), reflect in their way the pregiven structure of the world, although it is difficult from this late linguistic vantage point to say just where the line is to be drawn between what is given before language gets to it and what owes its structuring to something linguistic, however primitive. What does seem incontrovertible is that the present evolutionary stage of language use must have been preceded by a stage in which language was not yet used, and further that even when language had appeared it could not by itself determine what was to be said in it.

I have suggested that meaning has two components, one affective and the other, in effect, formal. In trying to account for the mythical structuring of the primitive world it is easy to forget the affective component—indeed one of the weaknesses of structuralism, as we have already observed and will have occasion to observe again before the end of this book, is its lack of a subjective and intentional standpoint. In *Mythologiques* Lévi-Strauss deals almost exclusively with the formal oppositions that are in play in the names and places, the categories and sequences of the mythological corpus. What he does not manage to convey is the intensity and excitement that are actually invested in the recounting of the myths. In the case of some northern Brazilian tribes at least this has been recorded on film. The narrator wears a sort of minimal loincloth and sits on his haunches in a clearing, his arms free; he tells the story with the sort of animation that says to the listener, you must hear this, this is tremendously important; he gestures wildly, imitating the movements and sounds of the animals and birds whose exploits are re-counted. Toucans fly down from the mountains with great swoops, they transfix enemies with their beaks.

If the myth were to be translated into the idiom of the comic strip there would be huge exclamation points everywhere and balloons saying ZIZZ! and SPLAT! and KABOOM! It seems to me worth stressing this, before giving a further account of Lévi-Strauss's mythological analysis, as a remin-der that structuralism is about *human* relations, not just relations among humans (as in his earlier studies of kinship) but the relations that humans experience as meaningful in the double sense of intelligibility and affect. It is on the affective side that the primitive proto-logic that preceded the articula-tion of language is to be looked for, and since the primary affective relations are those of kinship it is not surprising that some social scientists (for example Durkheim and Mauss in *Primitive Classification*) find in gender, parentage, and so on the earliest models of any sort of categorial arrange-ment of things in the world. Such relations build up into structures that in spite of their greater complexity are still available for animation by the involvement of subjects. But beyond the simple cases of affect it is not easy to say a priori which imaginable structures will prove to be psychologically possible (to borrow Chomsky's terminology from p. 102), as myths or eventually as literature, which explains why structuralist studies have to be empirical.

Lévi-Strauss's *Mythologiques* is a great empirical compilation and struc-tural reorganization of (mainly North and South American) mythology. Each volume starts from a reference myth arbitrarily (but not entirely arbitrarily!) selected from a corpus gathered in the field; the analysis pro-ceeds by setting out the code proper to a group of myths to which the reference myth belongs, and showing how within this code other myths can be generated from the reference myth by a series of transformations, and how myths in other groups can be shown to be homologous with other myths in the first group. The code in *The Raw and the Cooked* is culinary. In *From Honey to Ashes* the same code is extended, honey and tobacco being opposite ends of the spectrum of cuisine—the first linking it to nature (since honey is prepared, but not by human beings) and the second being purely cultural (since tobacco has no nutritional value but is as it were completely cooked). In *The Origin of Table Manners* the code incorporates ritual customs of diet and hygiene, extending to good manners in general and to the upbringing of children, especially girls, who, as periodic beings, must respect the ordering of nature for fear that their own equilibrium might be disturbed. The notion of natural and human periodicity occurs also in *From Honey to Ashes* in the analysis of "limping dances," which, according to Lévi-Strauss, introduce an asymmetry into behavior in order to correct (and at the same time pay tribute to) the asymmetries in the length of day and night produced by the seasons, which without this recognition might get out of hand.

---

| $M_{23}$–$M_{24}$ | $M_{26}$ |
|---|---|
| A husband (affinal relationship) | A mother (blood relationship) |
| has a wife jaguar | has a son snake |
| destructive through the mouth | protective through the vagina |
| of a husband who has climbed a tree | of a son who has climbed a tree |
| looking for animals (birds) | looking for vegetable food (fruit) |
| that the wife ought not to eat (but does); | that the mother ought to eat (but does not); |
| disjunction through the agency of the husband | disjunction through the agency of the mother |
| mother killed by affines (=children, in the the case of patri- lineal descent) | son killed by relatives (=maternal uncles, in the case of matri- lineal descent) |

burning of the victim,
origin of tobacco

It may be worth giving here an example of the kind of transformation schema that Lévi-Strauss concocts (I choose the term deliberately in view of its context) to show the interrelatedness of his myths. I take it from *The Raw and the Cooked* (1969:99–104). Three myths about the origin of tobacco have been recounted, $M_{23}$ and $M_{24}$ from the Toba and Tereno respectively and $M_{26}$ from the Bororo. They are full of details that distinguish them quite starkly from one another: the first begins with a woman and her husband going to catch parakeets, the second with a sorceress who defiles plants with menstrual blood and feeds them to her husband, the third with men returning from the hunt who whistle to their wives to come and help them carry game. Lévi-Strauss stirs these ethnographic ingredients and comes up with the "strictly symmetrical" rendering on p. 118. In this highly selective process most of the content of the myths is suppressed; as one small example among many others, the "son snake" of $M_{26}$ is conceived miraculously (his mother picks up a piece of boa her husband has killed and its blood penetrates and fertilizes her) before Lévi-Strauss's plot summary even begins. The symmetry is thus purchased at what some critics reasonably feel is a rather high price.

In the last volume of the series, *The Naked Man*, Lévi-Strauss sums up his whole enterprise as the description and closure of "a vast system, whose invariant elements can always be represented under the form of a combat between earth and heaven for the conquest of fire" (1971:535). Heaven and earth, after male and female, represent perhaps the most obvious and fundamental opposition of all, the first to have imposed itself on the primitive mind as it sought to orient itself in the natural environment. If heaven is the opposite of earth, the opposite of fire is water; supplement these oppositions with that of excess to defect, of the alimentary (which goes into the mouth) to the linguistic (which comes out of it), of the conjugal to the nonconjugal, and so on, and there is at hand the material for the whole world of myth. It is by manipulating this material, says Lévi-Strauss, that thought itself develops.

> The problem of the genesis of myth is therefore identical to that of thought itself, whose constituting experience is not of an opposition between the self and the other but of the other apprehended as opposition. Failing this intrinsic property—the only one, in truth, that is *absolutely* given—no constitutive grasping of the consciousness of self would be possible. The conditions of the appearance of myth are therefore the same as those of every thought, because thought can only be the thought of an object, and because an object is not such, however simply and barely one conceives of it, except in virtue of the fact that it constitutes the subject as subject, and consciousness itself as consciousness of a relation. (1971:539)

Not only does this make the essence of myth prelinguistic, but it seems to be a restatement of Sartre's doctrine of the prereflective *cogito* in a phylogenetic rather than an ontogenetic context. And indeed Lévi-Strauss's thought, as it approaches its term, becomes progressively more fundamental and more general.

Such philosophical reflections, tagged on at the end of an ethnological work, require supplementary argument if they are to stand. Applying his scheme of oppositions to structuralism itself near the end of the book, Lévi-Strauss makes one grand metastructural generalization that is worth noting: he sets down "as a working hypothesis, that the field of structural studies includes four major families of occupants which are mathematical entities, natural languages, musical works, and myths" (1971:578). These families are generated by taking positive and negative values along two axes, those of sound and sense: mathematics has neither sound nor sense, natural languages have both; music has sound but not sense, myth has sense but not sound.

This scheme has a prima facie plausibility, but like so many of Lévi-Strauss's examples of transformations among myths, which (thanks to his eclectic ethnography) come out with such formal perfection that they seem Procrustean, it does not bear close examination. Myths as actually recounted by tribal narrators to tribal audiences are, as we have seen, full of sound and gesture; the sense of "sense" in which mathematics and music have none is arbitrarily narrow. But it is suggestive as a development of the original Saussurean insight that two previously existing differential systems, conceptual and phonic, are required for the emergence of language; the mistake comes in thinking that anything can be generated structurally out of the absence of one of these, when the obvious question is what *other* dimension than sound or sense (as these enter into language) is required for the intelligibility of music or mathematics or myth. It seems likely in fact that the mental apparatus that produces, as just two possibilities among many, the conceptual and phonic systems is rich enough to sustain an indefinite multiplicity of such systems, even though these may share a relatively small number of basic structures.

One theme that emerges strongly in Lévi-Strauss's work on mythology is a moralistic one, which contrasts the recognition and respect accorded to nature by the primitive with our own tendency to slight and exploit it. "A well-ordered humanism does not commence with oneself, but puts the world before life, life before man, the respect for others before *amour-propre*; and even a residence of one or two million years on this earth, since in any case it will come to an end, cannot provide an excuse to any species, even our own, for appropriating it like a thing and behaving in it with neither shame nor discretion" (1968:422). The implicit claim in this rather pious non sequitur is that mythological treatments of nature do not fall into such an error. Myths for the primitive—and for us too if we humbly recognize our own for what they are—constitute a coherent and structured system in terms of which reality can be apprehended and, with suitable modesty, manipulated. But it is not so much a question of accurately representing a truth that brings mastery over nature as of the construction, in the domain of the intelligible, of a system whose complexity will match that of nature. And it is a proper concern of structuralism to show that the objects it studies have this dual character of systematic interrelation and of adequacy to the appropriate features of the world.

## 39. Relations in society

IN SPITE OF the foregoing argument that myths reflect prelinguistic features of nature and society it obviously cannot be denied that they are themselves constructions in language. What about structural features whose *expression* is nonlinguistic? We should be prepared to find that some of them (although not, as Barthes held, all of them) will still be *accompanied* by linguistic expressions; but it is not only language that distinguishes monogamy from polygamy or slaves from citizens. The question that has to be faced is whether nonlinguistic differences can be treated by a structural anthropology that borrows its methods from structural linguistics. We encountered Chomsky's reservations on this point at the end of the last chapter. In chapter 3 the relation of mutual learning between Jakobson and Lévi-Strauss was described—but Georges Mounin has criticized the latter as a dangerous amateur, a "linguist's apprentice" with linguistics in the role of an imperfectly mastered sorcery.

In fact this whole issue seems to me a false problem. My response to Chomsky's demurrer—in effect that it was a pity to grudge people their attempts at the flattery of imitation—actually conceded too much: anthropology does not need the example of linguistics. This follows from the relative positions of structuralism, semiotics, and linguistics worked out earlier in this chapter. We can examine the structural relations of signiferous systems without even going through semiotics, and a fortiori without going through linguistics. However we do need a family of systems for transformational purposes. Structural anthropology, like any structural study, requires a comparative basis; it became possible when the reports of travelers, that people in other parts of the world indulged in strange practices as judged from the point of view of the Christian West, came to be received with detachment rather than as excuses for condemning or annihilating or exploiting the barbarians. And Western civilization began perhaps to move toward its own maturity—a step whose accomplishment is still far off—when it ceased to regard anything non-Western as barbarian: "the barbarian," as Lévi-Strauss remarks, "is first of all the man who believes there are barbarians" (1961:15).

If anthropologists use other societies as mirrors in which to view the distortions of their own, then Montaigne and Montesquieu and Dr. Johnson and Swift are among the ancestors of the discipline. How is it possible, asks Montesquieu, to be a Persian? or in other words, to be a Parisian? According to Lévi-Strauss one becomes an ethnologist because of discontent with one's own society, but it might be just out of curiosity about alternatives. The laws or rules that determine our own behavior in social relations are thrown into relief, indeed perhaps recognized for the first time as what they are, by their contrast with the laws or rules that govern the behavior of our near or distant cousins in other societies. Most of us have become tolerant of differences in this respect, even at home; in social life as in language sympathetic exposure to the strange tends to loosen the rigidity of the familiar, and in fact the general direction in recent times and in developed countries has been away from strong contrasts and toward a kind of social eclecticism.

Against this leveling, fundamentalism fights a holding action that it is too early to call rearguard. The passion of the fundamentalist for details of correct behavior in dress, diet, manners, religious practice, and so on, is an indication of the areas in which unconscious structures are at work. When people become irrationally angry about divergences from some norm—length of hair, sexual preference, grammatical or even orthographic correctness—one can be fairly certain of having touched something fundamental. Collingwood made a similar observation in another context: if you keep challenging people's presuppositions, he said in effect, you can tell you have struck metaphysics when they lose their temper (1939:31). The touchy issues in social behavior tend to be those that involve the most basic oppositions there are, those that according to Durkheim and Mauss constitute the prelogical and prelinguistic ground of logic and language: the opposition between the sexes, or that between order and disorder, sacred and profane.

Of course this hypersensitivity shows itself only when the structure is strained; as long as the relations in question are normally satisfied it functions smoothly and imperceptibly. One might therefore be tempted to define structures that are interesting from the structuralist point of view as sets of *constraints* rather than simply as sets of relations. However relations function as constraints only if (a) they do not hold but somebody thinks they should or (b) they hold but somebody wishes they didn't. And while the hypersensitivity argument shows that desires often come into play in structured situations, nothing indicates that they need to do so in order for the structure to be what it is. One might say that there has to be awareness of a norm, but that this need not be invoked unless the norm is violated.

This however brings up an ambiguity about social structure that has a long history, going back at least to Montesquieu. Is social structure governed by law or by rule? Does it rest on nature or on culture? For Montesquieu law itself is sometimes what it is natural for human beings to do and sometimes what it is socially or politically prescribed that they should do. It is to Montesquieu that we owe not only the conception of ourselves as strange but the idea of society as a total system, "according to which all the features of social life are united into a coherent whole . . . . He sought to show that the laws of a society are connected with the political constitution, the economic life, the religion, the climate, the size of the population, the manners and customs, and what he called the general spirit (*esprit général*)—what later writers have called the 'ethos' of the society" (Radcliffe-Brown 1952:5).

The ancestor of Radcliffe-Brown's structuralism is sometimes taken to be Montesquieu, that of Lévi-Strauss's Rousseau. But in spite of the contrast between these two structuralisms implicitly drawn in chapter 2, their differences are methodological rather than substantial. Radcliffe-Brown anticipated my explicit definition of structure as a *set of relations* (1952:180); where he differed from Lévi-Strauss was in his emphasis on particular cases. This might be taken as an ethnographic virtue. But he too saw that theory would have to go beyond this level. "In the study of social structure," he says, "the concrete reality with which we are concerned is the set of actually existing relations, at a give moment of time, which link together certain human beings. It is on this that we can make direct observations. But it is not this that we attempt to describe in its particularity. . . . What we need for scientific purposes is an account of the form of the structure" (1952:192). His idea here is however more local than Lévi-Strauss's—what he seems to have in mind is the fact that the structure survives even though the terms of the relations (the individual elements of the social system) are constantly changing. He arrives therefore at the diachronic stability of a synchronic structure without taking the step to cross-cultural structural transformations.

Rousseau might be said to be more melodramatic than Montesquieu, rather as Lévi-Strauss is more melodramatic than Radcliffe-Brown. Lévi-Strauss has a sentimental affinity for Rousseau and writes eulogistically about him; both have a somewhat romantic view of the nobility of the savage, of those so-called primitives whose "modest tenacity," in Lévi-Strauss's words, "still offers us a means of assigning to human facts their true dimensions . . . . those Indians of the tropics and their counterparts throughout the world who have taught me their humble knowledge (in which is contained, nevertheless, the essence of the knowledge which my colleagues have charged me to transmit to others)" (1967a:52–53). But Rousseau too confronts Montesquieu's dichotomy, posing "almost in modern terms . . . . the central problem of anthropology, which is that of the passage from nature to culture" (Lévi-Strauss 1962:142). For Rousseau, significantly enough, it is the state of society in which kinship relations dominate that represents the ideal transition between the brutality of nature on the one hand and the corruption of society on the other.

The question that Montesquieu and Rousseau provoke is whether a knowledge of human nature, if there is such a thing, allows us to draw any conclusions about human society. Unlike Hobbes and Locke, who pose the same question in more abstract terms, both Montesquieu in *De l'Esprit des lois* and Rousseau in the *Discours sur l'origine de l'inégalité* approach it more like social scientists than like philosophers. However two related difficulties confront any attempt to draw conclusions at this level: we know human nature only in society, and no society is a pure case of evolution from nature to culture. "Any conceivable tendency of human society to pursue a fixed sequence of stages," says Lowie in *Primitive Society*, "must be completely veiled by the incessant tendency to borrowing and thus becomes an unknowable noumenon that is scientifically worthless." He quotes Maitland's *Domesday Book and Beyond*: "the rapidly progressing groups have been just those which have not been independent, but have appropriated alien ideas and have thus been enabled, for anything we can tell, to leap from stage A to stage X without passing through any intermediate stages. Our Anglo-Saxon ancestors did not arrive at the alphabet, or at the Nicene Creed, by traversing a long series of 'stages'; they leapt to the one and to the other." And Lowie continues: "accordingly the conditions for the operation of social laws among independent peoples nowhere exist" (1920:435).

## 40. Individuals and idiosyncrasies

A FURTHER SYSTEMATIC difficulty arises when we consider that societies are composed of very complex individuals. This is a large topic and belongs in another book—I am myself convinced that every social structure is distributive, and therefore mediated by radical idiosyncrasy at every point, but the arguments for that view require separate development. Without going quite as far as this, Evans-Pritchard expresses great skepticism about generalizations even as limited as Radcliffe-Brown's, and questions whether there are such things as sociological laws at all. "We have to deal," he says, "with values, sentiments, purposes, will, reason, choice, as well as with historical circumstances. It is true that some social processes may take place without conscious direction or even awareness, e.g. languages (this may be why the scientific study of language, both with regard to history and structure, is more exact than that of other social activities) . . . . That there are limiting principles in social organization no one would deny, but within these limits there is nothing inevitable about human institutions. Men have continuous choice in the direction of their affairs, and if a decision is found to be disadvantageous it is not beyond their wit to make a second to correct the first" (1965:33–34). The issue here is not so much the ultimately law-governed character of events, human or otherwise, as the availability of intelligible formulations of the laws in question at the level of the phenomena to be explained. Intelligibility, as we shall see, is a matter of approximation and of optimum complexity, and there is no point in trying to explain social events in terms of the laws of neurophysiology.

There are, of course, as Buckle and then Durkheim realized, statistical laws that, paradoxically enough, govern apparently idiosyncratic events such as suicide. This led Durkheim to speak of "total social facts" that obey their own laws at the group level. This however implies a radical separation of the properties of the individual from those of the group and blocks any inference between them, so that the strategy of inferring the structure of mind from the structures of its products is thwarted, unless one is prepared to allege something like a collective mind. What is implausible about this is that such a mind could not be said to exercise any of the functions (such as purpose, intention, feeling, and so on) that require a *subject*, since there is no evidence that the collectivity can be a subject in this sense (and if it were nothing would guarantee that its feelings and intentions were anything like ours).

Some social facts, it is true, can be predicted from general considerations without regard to individual peculiarities, much as for example the temperature range of domestic thermostats or the size of seats in buses can (within limits) be predicted. "Certain sorts of patterns and certain sorts of relationships among patterns recur from society to society, for the simple reason that the orientational requirements they serve are genuinely human. The problems, being existential, are universal; their solutions, being human, are diverse" (Geertz 1966:5). But these do not seem terribly interesting; if that is all Lévi-Strauss's deep structure amounts to one feels that Radcliffe-Brown was not missing so much. A social theory that treats individuals as units with no *interior* structure, after the manner for example of Talcott Parsons's theory of action, may be structuralist in its way but do nothing to illuminate the nature-culture connection. According to Parsons, "the focus of interest for the theory of action is not in the internal equilibrating processes of the organism as a system, but in the equilibrating processes involved in its relations to an environment or situation in which other organisms are of crucial significance. *It is this relational system that is the system of action*, not the organism as a system" (1952:542). This is all nature at a higher order of complexity, as in the case of ants; one is reminded of Sartre's remark: "We thought we were dealing with sociologists; our mistake: they were entomologists" (1968:91).

The crucial issue here is the "crucial significance" of the citation from Parsons: significance to whom? The intelligibility that arises from structure, as those terms are used in this book, is intelligibility to the human subjects who produce and consume the social and linguistic objects that signiferous structures make possible. If attention focuses on the relations into which an object enters (the structure to which it belongs) rather than to the relations among its own elements (the structure it is), that is because the former help to constitute *it* as what it is, not so much because they constitute a higher-order object, although they certainly do this. To conclude that I as a social being am *helplessly* determined by larger social forces is to suppose that society is just a superorganism with its own quasi-biological laws and its own means of reproduction. This is the tradition of Spencer and the social Darwinists. But it won't work, and for a reason that Lévi-Strauss indicates in passing when he remarks in *Anthroplogie structurale I* that while a horse gives birth to another horse, an ax does not give rise to another ax (1958:7).

Social relations, like tool designs, are internalized in individuals and then transmitted externally to other individuals. They pass through us— through me to the extent that I embody and transmit them—and can be made intelligible to us in the process. I might, it is true, transmit them blindly, by mere imitation, and indeed this is what happens for the most part, not only in language but in manners, morality, religion, and politics as well. With the help of structuralist studies I may enter into full awareness of my role as user and transmitter and play it *intentionally*, which is what in the end distinguishes nature from culture. (To cultivate is to want and mean things to grow, and to do what is necessary—originally, as the etymology of the term reveals, to supplicate and propitiate the gods—to ensure that this happens.) Even so the likelihood that I will have an interest in altering what I transmit (assuming that, once conscious of what is going on, I would wish to do this only for the better) is marginal, especially in the case of language, whose inertia derives from the fact that almost any change will in the first instance result in a *loss* of intelligibility, because I will not be able to communicate the change in question to most of the other users of the language, let alone impose it upon them.

This is no doubt why Esperanto and other such experiments have been such consistent failures. But as Lowie suggests in the passage quoted above, once individuals see the advantage of a new social relationship (especially if it is supported by an appropriate technological development) they will seize upon it and incorporate it forthwith into the structures they use and inhabit. Something like this has been happening in recent times with transportation, communications, contraception, medication, and the like. These changes do not happen unconsciously, although they may happen without a great deal of reflection; in every case they are effected by individual choices. That it would be desirable for individuals to understand the implications of these choices seems beyond dispute. The intelligibility that the structuralist point of view can supply could be of some service here. In particular, as we shall see later, it is in the negative correlate of Lowie's process—the refusal to pass on even what has been internally transmitted—that the strategy of *de*construction, one of the livelier products of structuralism, comes into play.

## 41. The human family

WE SAW EARLIER how Lewis H. Morgan's interest in the kinship terminology of the Iroquois and Ojibwa led him to a kind of proto-structuralism and set an example for Lévi-Strauss. Morgan's conjecture that kinship terminologies constituted a system led him to extend his inquiries, by fieldwork and questionnaire, into other parts of the world, and eventually to the publication under the aegis of the Smithsonian Institution of his great study, already cited: *Systems of Consanguinity and Affinity of the Human Family*. The conclusion of these researches, set out in the preface to that book, was not only that kinship systems are what I have called signiferous systems, in the double sense of containing and transmitting, but that they represent a tremendous achievement of our primitive ancestors:

> In the systems of relationship of the great families of mankind some of the oldest memorials of human thought and experience are deposited and preserved. They have been handed down as transmitted systems, through the channels of the blood, from the earliest ages of man's existence upon the earth . . . . it seems probable that the progress of mankind was greater in degree, and in the extent of its range, in the ages of barbarism than it has been since in the ages of civilization; and that it was a harder, more doubtful, and more intense struggle to reach the threshold of the latter, than it has been since to reach its present status. Civilization must be regarded as the fruit, the final reward, of the vast and varied experience of mankind in the barbarous ages. (Morgan 1871:vi–vii)

"The channels of the blood" can be forgiven in view of the fact that at the time Mendel's first paper on hybridization had only just been published in a provincial Austrian journal and would go unrecognized for another thirty years. As to "intelligence and knowledge," Morgan's point seems to be to distinguish kinship structures from features of human society purely natural in origin. Some systems, for example the Roman, he takes to be more obviously contrived by human deliberation than others (1871:27).

Morgan distinguishes two main kinds of kinship system, which he calls classificatory and descriptive. In the former an individual's relatives are divided into large classes, all the members of which are designated by the same term; in the latter individuals are singled out by "an augmentation or combination of the primary terms of relationship" (1871:12), for example, father, mother, brother, sister, and so on. The move from classificatory to descriptive reflects an increasing complexity in the notion of property and an increasing interest on the part of the state in the protection of individual interests. The individual becomes, in other words, a term of a set of specific relations and not merely a member of a class; he or she acquires what we might now call structural identity.

As we saw earlier, Morgan does refer informally to something he calls "the structure of the system," so that Lévi-Strauss's remark that (in contradistinction to Spencer, in whom we find "the word but not the thing") in Morgan we find "the thing but not the word" (Bastide 1962:143) seems misplaced. Be that as it may, how well Morgan understood "the thing" is shown by his remarkable insight, also cited in chapter 4, into its stability over time: "the system, in virtue of its organic structure, has survived for ages the causes in which it originated, and is now in every respect an artificial system, because it is contrary to the nature of descents as they actually exist in the present state of Indian society" (1871:508). Just as in the case of language we have to distinguish between possible Cratylist origins and current arbitrariness, so in the case of kinship systems. In Morgan's view, for example, incest is a necessary stage in the formation of the consanguineous family, "although it is difficult to conceive of the extremity of a barbarism, which such a custom presupposes" (1871:vi–vii), while the incest prohibition is one of the marks, for Lévi-Strauss, of the transition from nature to culture.

Morgan's studies set a precedent for scope but hardly for rigor. The quality of the information on which his analyses were based was extremely uneven, his generalizations were sometimes Procrustean, and the speculative hypothesis in terms of which he saw the unity of the system was a product as much of his own prejudices as of the evidence. But the scope in itself was important: to view the multiplicity of kinship patterns as products and variants of a basic human structure, but at the same time to do justice to that multiplicity, was a theoretical achievement; to bring together and to take account of such a wealth of cross-cultural material was a methodological one. The whole was a monument to inductive method, having the merit of most such monuments (including Bacon's own), namely that its chief principle was not inductive. For the amassing of evidence never yields the hypothesis, which always comes from a structural insight that organizes the evidence that has been amassed.

The amassing of evidence is nevertheless essential. Bacon's views on this point were essentially correct, and the fact that the development of scientific method took another course was an accidental consequence of the further fact that in the physical sciences a great deal of the evidence comes, as it were, already amassed, or at any rate amassable in fairly obvious places. There is not, that is to say, much doubt as to what it is in the course of people's ordinary experience that is being explained, and the rectification of experience that theory provides does not involve a radical change of perspective, not at least until inquiry moves beyond the flat region of daily experience to phenomena too fast or too small or too remote to be accommodated there. In the social sciences, on the other hand, the character of the phenomena whose description constitutes the evidence may itself be in question. The natural history (or "butterfly-collecting") stage of inquiry is therefore prolonged, and a too hasty "indulgence of the understanding," to use an expression of Bacon's—given that the understanding has an incorrigible taste for generalization and formalization—has to be avoided.

Gladys Reichard's painstaking collection of thirty-five hundred Navaho genealogies has already been alluded to in this connection. What she discovered about Navaho mythology was that it functions as an ordering principle not only for kinship relations but for the most trivial features of common experience. The Navaho seem to totalize, just as Lévi-Strauss says all primitives do. "May it not be then, that these insignificant details about pets and the few localized animal-named clans in the myth are an attempt to include in their legend all of the phenomena with which they have come in contact?" (Reichard 1969:33). And this totalization has a special form in connection with family relations; as we saw in chapter 4, the Navaho always know where they stand within their own clan, but for completeness they have invented a term for the "unknown clan," a term which "is used by outsiders in speaking of a family whose clan-name or affiliation is not well-known."

It is worth repeating from this passage Reichard's formula for the certainty of family relations within the clan. "The members of the family themselves will always know—at least they will have settled upon—their own clan membership and all that goes with it" (1969:15). *"At least they will have settled upon"*—this phrase may well be taken as a motto and a warning. In another context Carol Chomsky has shown that it is characteristic of young children to think they understand what is said to them even when this is not the case: ". . . we find that children do in fact assign an interpretation to the structures that we present to them. They do not, as they see it, fail to understand our sentences. They understand them, but they understand them wrongly" (1969:2). And one might conjecture that the mind requires for its stability not only a structure into which everything will fit—such as is provided on one level by a language capable of naming every object and expressing every relation, on another by a mythology or a social order, and so on—but also a subjective certainty in the assignment of elements to their places in whatever system is chosen to embody this structure, primordially, as Durkheim and Mauss suggest, the kinship system. Such a view would explain a great deal about human behavior. But accepting it would also have self-referential consequences. It would cast doubt upon all our certainties, even those that appeared to have the strictest logical or empirical warrant, because we could never be sure whether they corresponded to objective truths or merely to psychological necessities. Fortunately the two are not mutually exclusive.

## 42. The exchange of gifts

ONE OF THE social phenomena that resist explanation in functional terms, and whose structure seems less than intelligible on the surface, is the potlatch ceremony formerly practiced by certain North American Indian tribes. (Similar ritual exchanges are recorded elsewhere, for example among the early Scandinavians; a more formalistic and less extravagant version is found in the kula ring of the Trobriand Islands.) A potlatch was a ceremonially structured distribution of gifts, which might take place on any one of a number of special occasions—a boy's coming of age, a ritual change of name, a betrothal, a wedding. It might take as long as two years to prepare, and might strain the resources of the giver and of his family or tribe as well. In due time the giver might become a receiver, but by then the stakes would have been raised and the new hosts would have to outmatch his offerings. If it had not been for its extravagant and progressive aspects (not only were gifts often given to people who would never be in a position to reciprocate, but some of the most valuable objects involved were ostentatiously destroyed), the potlatch might have been thought to serve the purpose of keeping goods in circulation, but even so the form seemed unnecessarily complex for a function already adequately fulfilled by ordinary trade. There was in other words something gratuitous and arbitrary about the whole proceeding.

This phenomenon attracted the attention of one of Lévi-Strauss's immediate predecessors, the French anthropologist Marcel Mauss, nephew and collaborator of Durkheim. Mauss was impressed by the fact that other social institutions besides language are marked by the arbitrariness of the link between symbol and referent:

> . . . if it is true that form, in language, is fundamentally distinct from the substance of thought, is even relatively independent of it, then one must add that here is no characteristic peculiar to language, but a characteristic diagnostic of most social phenomena of the morphologi-

cal type, of nearly all the workings of collective consciousness. . . . Most
can be unfailingly recognized by this arbitrary, symbolic nature, as
being selected, so to speak, for no reasons other than historical. The
form of rites and customs, those of money or of aesthetic representations,
are wholly as dependent, one might say, on collective wills and habit
and have as little of necessity as those which clothe language. In any
case one is always dealing with a social phenomenon when there is
arbitrariness of symbolism, just as much as when there is constraint
exercised by such symbolism, once established. (Hymes 1964:125)

"Collective consciousness" here is Durkheim's term, and is problematic. In
an earlier section I discussed the distributive theory of the collective, in terms
of which I would wish to say here "shared consciousness" or something of
that sort, or perhaps "common" in the sense that properties held by *each*
member of some set may be said to be "in common" although there is
nothing essentially collective about them.

   This problem is similar to that posed by Saussure's location of *langue* in
the collectivity, but it is rather more difficult, since it is at least clear that
each individual speaks, even if each does it according to a general standard,
whereas there seem to be some social manifestations that require a "plural
subject" in order to be done at all, and some that can be represented at one
level as an individual act and at another as a contribution to a group act, not
statistically (as in Buckle's suicide studies) but operationally. A solution is
brought nearer by Sartre's analysis of group behavior in his *Critique de la
raison dialectique*, in which he points out that each member of a group can act
individually with the strength of the whole; in a more complex situation one
might say that each, thanks to the others, effects the complex result for which
the whole is required. The second violin plays the symphony in virtue of the
fact that the cello, the oboe, and so on do so too.

   However this takes the argument away from the point at issue—and the
orchestra may not be the best example, because its players follow scores
written by an individual composer (although it does illustrate the relation, to
which we shall return more than once, between arbitrariness and constraint,
or in the language of another author chance and necessity, in that the free
agency of the second violin lasts only as long as he or she plays *that* symphony
and not something else, as in Saussure's "stacked deck"). Mauss sought in
his *Essay on the Gift* to understand the necessity under the arbitrariness of
potlatch practices, and he approached the problem by way of an analysis of
basic group interactions. What can happen, he asked himself, when two
groups not previously acquainted first encounter each other? This creates a
situation of polarity in which only extremes are possible—"there is no middle
ground: trust one another entirely, or mistrust one another entirely"

(1950:277). Distrust can express itself in two ways, by avoidance or by combat (flight or fight), but trust necessarily involves dealings between the parties, in short some kind of *exchange*.

In working out his general theory of exchange Mauss found as little room for individual choice in the system of prestations as linguists have found in the system of grammar.

> For it is groups, and not individuals, which carry on exchange, make contracts, and are bound by obligations; the persons represented in the contracts are moral persons—clans, tribes, and families; the groups, or the chiefs as intermediaries for the groups, confront and oppose each other. Further, what they exchange is not exclusively goods and wealth, real and personal property, and things of economic value. They exchange rather courtesies, entertainments, rituals, military assistance, women, children, dances, and feasts . . . . Finally, although the presta-tions and counter-prestations take place under a voluntary guise they are in essence strictly obligatory, and their sanction is private or open warfare. We propose to call this the system of *total prestations*. (1954:3)

The structure of this system of exchange is obviously a signiferous one for those who participate in it. But by parity of argument it may well be that other signiferous structures lead to other total systems of exchange. There is an obvious sense in which something like this holds in the case of language, where if a conversational opening is accepted some form of reciprocity is thereafter required on pain of hostility. Such exchanges constitute elemen-tary relations by means of which individuals are inserted into the structure of society. Not all of them are as dramatic as the potlatch, in which the transition from arbitrariness to constraint was perhaps most clearly marked. The resulting social structure was of great stability, but there was no option for an individual to fail to satisfy the relation the structure prescribed—or, to invert the argument, it was precisely the stability of the structure that was at stake when the individual was called upon to assume the ceremonial role of giver or receiver.

What is to be noticed in this story of exchange, of gifts or language, is that there is in fact nothing in particular that needs to be communicated before the reciprocity of exchange is established. The exchange is governed by no necessity other than that of communication itself—just as two people, meeting for the first time, may have (antecedently) nothing to say to each other but allow the form of their relationship to be dictated by what happens to be said. Hence the utility of neutral topics of conversation like the weather, which permit exchange by providing a communicable content without engaging either party in a serious relationship. The analogy of personal conversation is not wholly satisfactory, but it serves to remind us that the *fact* of exchange is often more important, for social purposes, than its content. Another way of putting this point, in Saussurean terminology, is to say that the signifier precedes the signified: the activity of signifying is entered upon for purposes that have little to do with the specificity of the signs. The situation is perceived to be one in to which meaning enters (it matters to the participants, among other things because it serves to clarify their relationships to one another), and it therefore calls for language or for something equally signiferous. The exchange of gifts need not be called a kind of language; it is a form of social interaction whose structure, like that of language, allows it to be invested with significance.

## 43. The prohibition of incest

EXCHANGE INVOLVES GOING outside one's own group, giving something up to another group, receiving something in return. Its opposite is the selfish hoarding of goods within the group. One vehicle of exchange in the list given by Mauss is women, who are still (in some circles) *given* in marriage: "who giveth this woman to this man?" asks the priest. The opposite of exchange in this case would be incest, the keeping of women in the family. As we have seen, Morgan thought this a necessary step in the development of kinship relations, since at an early stage he supposed there to have been only hostile relations between families, and marriage involves trading across family boundaries. St. Augustine, in *The City of God*, had a similar view, but on different grounds—he saw that Adam and Eve's children would have had to marry each other, a situation that however was to be put behind the race as soon as possible, for reasons not unlike those given centuries later by Lévi-Strauss:

> Therefore, when an abundant population made it possible, men ought to choose for wives women who were not already their sisters; for not only would there then be no necessity for marrying sisters, but, were it done, it would be most abominable. For if the grandchildren of the first pair, being now able to choose their cousins for wives, married their sisters, then it would no longer be only two but three relationships that were held by one man, while each of these relationships ought to have been held by a separate individual, so as to bind together by family affection a larger number. For one man would in that case be both father, and father-in-law, and uncle to his own children (brother and sister now man and wife); and his wife would be mother, aunt, and mother-in-law to them; and they themselves would be not only brother

and sister, and man and wife, but cousins also, being the children of brother and sister. Now, all these relationships, which combined three men into one, would have embraced nine persons had each relationship been held by one individual, so that a man had one person for his sister, another his wife, another his cousin, another his father, another his uncle, another his father-in-law, another his mother, another his aunt, another his mother-in-law; and thus the social bond would not have been tightened to bind a few, but loosened to embrace a larger number of relations.(1950:500–501)

The function of marriage then is to extend the network of social relationships. "Most abominable" is a harsh judgment for failing to do this, but Augustine is only reflecting, as Morgan does, a common judgment about incest. We have seen that passions are often aroused by relations that violate unconscious structural norms. But what is the origin of these norms?

Norms are essentially cultural—nature has laws only by courtesy, there is no moral obligation to follow them, the world just does so. So the emergence of norms is likely to be observed in those domains that straddle nature and culture, as for example Jakobson says language does. Kinship is another such domain, according to Lévi-Strauss. The latter begins his great work on the subject, *Les Structures élémentaires de la parenté* (*The Elementary Structures of Kinship*) with the distinction between nature and culture, or spontaneous and normative, in whose light the facts about the prohibition of incest "are not far removed from a scandal," since it is both universal and regulative, and therefore "presents, without the slightest ambiguity, and inseparably combines, the two characteristics in which we recognize the conflicting features of two mutually exclusive orders" (1969:8). What is required if the sense of scandal is to be removed is to show that the incest prohibition is not anomalous but illustrates, in a limiting form perhaps, some general characteristic of social interaction, and to show this general characteristic to be a natural consequence of some recognized truth about human society.

The phenomena to which Lévi-Strauss addresses himself in *The Elementary Structures of Kinship* are therefore the various restrictions on permissible marriages in different societies. In a large number of primitive societies marriage is exogamous, so that a man must choose his wife from another tribe or village; in cases where it is endogamous a "dual system" frequently operates, according to which the local group is divided into two subgroups or moieties, and a man must choose his wife from the subgroup to which he himself does not belong. In the limit the subgrouping may disappear and a marriage with a cross-cousin (a child of the mother's brother or father's sister) may be prescribed. Lévi-Strauss's hypothesis is that all these arrangements—exogamy among groups or moieties, and cross-cousin marriage—are cognate with the prohibition of incest, and this is lent weight by the fact that the terms for "brother" and "sister" are often general ("classificatory" in Morgan's sense), applying to all the appropriate members of the same group or moiety, or to parallel cousins (children of the father's brother or mother's sister). The spectrum of kinship structures thus displayed ranges from "elementary structures" in which a definite type of marriage—for example, between cross-cousins—is prescribed, to the opposite extreme where no limitation at all is placed on permissible marriages except the prohibition of incest.

If this interpretation can be sustained then the first desideratum has been met: the prohibition of incest belongs to a more general pattern. But what is the explanation of the pattern? Why should there be any restrictions on permissible marriages? To throw light on these problems Lévi-Strauss moves near the end of the book to another level of generality.

> For several very primitive peoples in the Malay Archipelago [he writes] the supreme sin, unleashing storm and tempest, comprises a series of apparently incongruous acts which informants list higgledy-piggledy as follows: marriage between near kin; father and daughter or mother and son sleeping too close to one another; incorrect speech between kin; ill-considered conversation; for children, noisy play, and, for adults, demonstrative happiness shown at social reunions; imitating the calls of certain insects or birds; laughing at one's own face in the mirror; and finally, teasing animals, and in particular, dressing a monkey as a man, and making fun of him. (1949:613)

"What possible connection," asks Lévi-Strauss, "could there be between such a bizarre collection of acts?" The answer, in his own words, is as follows:

> All these prohibitions thus turn out to have a common denominator: they all constitute an *abuse of language*, and they are, on this basis, grouped with the prohibition of incest or of acts that evoke incest. What does this signify if not that women themselves are treated as *signs*, which are abused when they are not put to the use reserved for signs, which is to be *communicated*? (1949:615)

This last is a celebrated formula, but there is something unsatisfactory about it—it isn't that every sign is abused if not used (the occasion might never arise, for example, for me to use the word "gralloch" in conversation), but rather that when a certain kind of communication is called for the requisite sign must be produced, in this case the transfer of the woman from one group to the other, the marriage itself (rather than the woman herself), as opposed to the abusive form of non-communication that her marriage to someone inside her own group would represent.

Certainly the abuse is within a semiological system. How can obligations and prohibitions arise within such systems? We have already seen the association of the significant with what *matters*; confirmation of this association is to be found in the association of the primitive categories of *mana* and *taboo* with the emergence of language. Cassirer suggests that these two categories correspond to the later logical categories of affirmation and negation, what is to be sought after and what is to be rejected. Lévi-Strauss, in his essay on Mauss's work, remarks that language must have come into being "all at once"—any system, once seen as capable of bearing significance, takes on immediately an element of importance and mystery, even though the nature of its potential significance is not yet clear. "At the moment when the whole universe, at one blow, became *significative*, it did not by reason of this also become *known*, even if it is true that the emergence of language was to speed up the rhythm of the development of knowledge" (1966b:XLVII). The signifier and the signified come into being as correlatives of one another, but there is in the first instance an *excess of the signifier*, a sudden proliferation of differences whose significance cannot yet be grasped. This is surely still a familiar experience: we do sometimes become suddenly aware that some complex of situations, some formerly unnoticed pattern of gestures or symptoms, signifies or portends something although we can't say what. Such a generalized sense of the significant or portentous is characteristic of *mana*, which Lévi-Strauss calls a "floating signifier," the more powerful because of the unspecific nature of its signified. Great importance may come to attach to the sign, and great ceremony to its manipulation, precisely because the consequences of its improper use are unknown.

Such circumspection is characteristic of forms of behavior that are unconsciously structured, and is the obverse of the phenomenon noted earlier, the passionate response that is often evoked by the violation of canons of accepted usage—the acute discomfort people may feel at certain grammatical mistakes, or in the presence of speakers of another language or of an unfamiliar dialect or argot of their own, or in a social situation when somebody does not respond, or responds in a non-standard way, to a conversational opening. Exaggerated concern for correctness and exaggerated alarm and horror at deviations from the norm show that an element of fear is involved. And as in the case of language, the behavior of children is instructive; the real distress that can be provoked by an arbitrary change in the arrangement of the nursery furniture or the plot of a story testifies to the immediacy of the link between structure and value. Philosophers rightly deny the logical connection between "is" and "ought," but the customary and psychological connection between them is too obvious to be denied. Every is is a potential ought, because once it has become familiar and reassuring (and therefore right) any contradiction of it becomes strange and threatening (and therefore wrong).

The structures that result from the incest prohibition, as Lévi-Strauss treats them, are once again formal. They have repercussions at the individual level: a man who has no sister to transmit, or cousin to receive, will be at a disadvantage in a society where a premium is put on marriage and bachelor-hood is an object of ignominy. Such an individual will find himself in a marginal or "liminal" position, to use Arnold Van Gennep's term. "In any society it is inevitable that a percentage . . . of individuals find themselves placed, as it were, outside of any system or between two or more irreducible systems" (Lévi-Strauss 1966b)—in other words structuralism cannot give a complete account of the social, because (unlike language) social systems have elements with lives of their own.

Women, for example: the structural aspects of the exchange of women are paralleled by psychological aspects. The reciprocity between groups ensured by the incest prohibition is also the resolution of a dialectical opposition between the woman as owned (by the men of her own family) and desired (by the men of another). "If women in general represent a certain category of signs, destined to a certain kind of communication, each woman preserves a particular value arising from her talent, before and after mar-riage, for taking her part in a duet. In contrast to words, which have wholly become signs, woman has remained at once a sign and a value" (Lévi-Strauss 1969:496). This is Lévi-Strauss at his most tedious, but if it seems also to be patronizing and offensive to feminist sensibilities we should remember that the attitude described is ethnographically entrenched and still current, not only in the practice referred to at the beginning of this section of "giving away the bride" but in other associations between mar-riage and the exchange of gifts: whatever form the gift takes, dowry, bride price, or just wedding presents, it always attaches itself to the woman rather than to the man.

## 44. Structure and sentiment

IT IS STILL reasonable to ask what function the marriage rules serve apart from their satisfying a need for significant structure or a need to communi-cate. (It seems to be striking testimony to the latter need that even when Mauss's condition of the encounter of two separate groups is not met, the tribe should divide in two in order to make exchange and communication possible.) If a similar question is asked about language, several replies may be offered: expression, information storage and retrieval, theory construction, and so on. But the problems that confront the linguist and the ethnologist are not exactly parallel. One of the asymmetries between the cases lies in the fact that the store of things to be communicated is virtually limitless where language is concerned, whereas it is strictly limited for other forms of exchange: in verbal communication words cannot be said to be lost to the speaker, whereas when a woman is given in marriage she is no longer available for purposes of further communication. Another contrast between the two cases is that while the functions of language are intuitively clear, whereas its true elements (phonemes, morphemes, and so on) could be specified only after careful analysis, the reverse appears to be true in kinship studies, where the elements are clear enough (individuals forming couples with prescribed degrees of consanguinity and so forth) although the function of the institution on any level above the personal (the satisfaction of sentiments or appetites) is what is obscure and requires analysis (Lévi-Strauss 1958:44).

Lévi-Strauss provoked some skepticism because of his assignment of the function of communication to a series of apparently voluntary compliances with a social rule, for the observance of which other workers, as we shall see, have put forward other explanations. But there is another way of putting the matter, with a slightly different—and more utilitarian— emphasis, which shifts from the notion of exchange and communication to that of recycling: in this view women are seen as a dynamic component of society whose totality is conserved while its distribution follows a cyclic pattern that contributes to the stability of the system. Lévi-Strauss works out in some detail alternative forms of such "cycles of reciprocity" involving complex kinship structures.

Some of the elementary relations that constitute these structures are clear enough on the terminological level but offer more difficulty when we try to envisage just what they involve for the participants, who presumably (like the tellers and hearers of myths) enter into them affectively, adopt attitudes toward them. Sentiment cannot be the whole story, but it is clear that no marriage custom would survive that systematically went against the sentiments of the members of the society. The evidence about attitudes is not as simply deciphered as the evidence about terminology, because in situations where the degrees of consanguinity are the same quite different attitudes may be found in different cultures between, for example, a man and his mother's brother. To bring coherence out of this situation Lévi-Strauss considers the system illustrated in figure 6.2, which involves relations between four individuals: a man, his sister, her husband, and their son. This group Lévi-Strauss calls the "unit of kinship," (1967:43) and within it he always finds that two

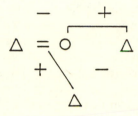

TROBRIAND-MATRILINEAL

CHERKESS-PATRILINEAL

SIUAI-MATRILINEAL

TONGA-PATRILINEAL

LAKE KUBUTU-PATRILINEAL

*Figure 6.2*

relationships among the four salient ones (son-father, husband-wife, sister-brother, and uncle-nephew) can be represented as positive (that is, the members of the pair have warm and informal contacts) while the other two are negative (that is, the contacts are distant and formal). Figure 6.2 in fact shows five variants of the same system drawn from five different ethnographic sources.

These relationships, it is to be noted, are attitudinal and not terminological—the same formal relations of kinship, and the same prescriptions as to marriage, may exist in conjunction with different sets of attitudes, and on the other hand the same attitudes may be found even though the unit of kinship enters into the larger social structure in different ways. Lévi-Strauss identifies this grouping as the elementary unit just because it contains these four salient relations. They do not include the son-mother relation, because the woman enters the picture only through her brother or her husband, her attitudes to whom are always of opposite sign, just as the attitudes of the son toward his father and his uncle are of opposite sign. Lévi-Strauss envisages the possibility of a symmetrical structure with the sexes reversed (a woman, her brother, the brother's wife, and their daughter), but this is "immediately eliminated on empirical grounds. In human society, it is the men who exchange the women, not vice versa" (1967b:45).

When these units are fitted together into a social matrix, the nature of the cycle of reciprocity will depend on the type of cross-cousin marriage involved. The son/nephew may marry either his mother's brother's, or his father's sister's, daughter; these patterns—known respectively as *matrilateral* and *patrilateral*—may accompany conventions according to which the son belongs to his father's or his mother's tribe or moiety (*patrilineal* or *matrilineal* societies). The lineality of the society serves to keep the groups distinct and to protect the *situation* of exchange, while its laterality determines the degree of tightness, as it were, in the kinship structure. One of Lévi-Strauss's main hypotheses is that matrilateral cross-cousin marriage is a better form than patrilateral, because it ensures a more stable social fabric. "Better" here does not mean morally or aesthetically or sentimentally better, but structurally better, assuming that it is a virtue in a social structure to be stable over time. In a patrilateral society the borrowing of a woman in one generation is always paid back in the next, so that the transaction is reciprocal as among elementary units and does not bind them to other parts of the society; Lévi-Strauss calls this a system of restricted exchange. In the matrilateral case, on the other hand, the relationship between units is transitive, so that as generation succeeds generation women are given in one direction, as it were, and received from the other; the accounts balance in the society as a whole, but it may be some time before a cycle of exchange comes back to the original elementary unit, if indeed it ever does. This situation of generalized exchange ensures the interrelatedness, in principle, of all the elementary units. The hypothesis is informally confirmed by the fact that, in societies where cross-cousin marriage is prescribed, the matrilateral form is overwhelmingly more frequent than the patrilateral.

Generalizations and value judgments of this sort about structures seem risky on two counts: they seem to confuse structure and function, and they attribute either mute prescience or collective automatism to acts that seem on the face of it deliberate and free. It is Buckle's suicide problem again. An attack on Lévi-Strauss's theory, focusing precisely on the notion of "better structure," was made along these lines by George Homans and David Schneider in *Marriage, Authority, and Final Causes*. These authors claim that the statistics do not support Lévi-Strauss but rather a thesis of their own, namely, that the matrilateral case occurs in patrilineal societies and the patrilateral in matrilineal ones, because authority over the son/nephew ("ego" in the language of kinship theorists) is vested in the lineal kin-group, so that attitudinal relations on that side will be formal and cold, whereas on the other side they will be informal and warm and thus predispose ego *sentimentally* to prefer the cousin from that side. "As he visits mother's brother often," say Homans and Schneider, discussing the patrilineal/matrilateral case, "ego will see a great deal of the daughter: contact will be established. As he is fond of mother's brother, and as mother's brother and his daughter in the patrilineal complex, the Oedipus complex if you will, are themselves particularly close to one another, he will tend to get fond of the daughter. Their marriage will be sentimentally appropriate; it will cement the relationship" (1955:23). Or, as they say elsewhere, "we would indeed state our general theory loosely as: Where a man finds love in one generation, he will find it in the next" (1955:38).

This last formulation proved altogether too much for Rodney Needham, who devoted a brilliant polemical essay, *Structure and Sentiment* (1962), to a refutation of Homans and Schneider. While Needham's main target was squarely hit he did introduce, according to Lévi-Strauss, a slight distortion in the position of the *Structures élémentaires*, which the preface to the second edition of that work provided an opportunity to correct. Needham makes much of the distinction between *prescriptive* and *preferential* marriage rules; he claims that Lévi-Strauss is really concerned with the former, but that Homans and Schneider make it look as if he were concerned with the latter. Homans and Schneider's account is clearly preferential; not only do they say that ego prefers the cross-cousin on the side opposite to his lineality for the sentimental reasons given above, but they say that Lévi-Strauss says that ego prefers his matrilateral cross-cousin because in some obscure way he realizes that such a choice will be best for his society. Lévi-Strauss cuts through all this by denying that he cares much about the difference between prescriptive and preferential marriage; "in my opinion, they do not connote different social realities, but rather, correspond to slightly differing ways in which man envisages the same reality" (1969:xxxi-xxxii).

## 45. The reality of social structure

THIS REALITY CAN only be society itself as a stable, structured, and signiferous system. It is not envisaged and realized in a conscious or calculating way but is rather what human beings naturally and unconsciously produce. "Society might not have been," says Lévi-Strauss. "If our proposed interpretation is correct, the rules of kinship and marriage are not made necessary by the social state. They are the social state itself, reshaping biological relationships and natural sentiments, forming them into structures implying them as well as others, and compelling them to rise above their original characteristics" (1969:490). Elsewhere he asserts that every society combines many structures, though it is not reducible to them (1958:357). Such structures have been shown to occur on several levels: as oppositions among groups or moieties that set the stage for communication and exchange, as interrelations among elementary units that determine the mode of the exchange and the stability of the group, as a set of personal affiliations or oppositions within the elementary unit, and finally as characteristics of human beings that predispose them to membership in a coherent social order.

Just as in the case of language, the question arises as to the reality of these structures (as opposed to the manifest reality of the elements of the systems that embody them). Lévi-Strauss says that this question "has nothing to do with empirical reality but with concepts built up after it" (1953:525). This is an issue to which I shall return in Part II, but it may be asked at least, if social structures are "built up after" empirical reality, how sound the empirical foundation is in the case at hand. Lévi-Strauss's ethnographic sources are diverse and of mixed value—he seems to accept somewhat indiscriminately second- and even thirdhand testimony from an extraordinary array of documents—but he is clearly aware of this and would be prepared to reject anything shown to conflict with fact. The difficulty, of course—as Duhem was among the earliest to realize—is to know what constitutes conflict with fact. It is clearly the general rather than the specific aspects of social structure that most interest Lévi-Strauss, and the more general a theory is the less likely it is to be brought down by particular counterexamples.

The consequent impression that his structures have an a priori character has been fostered by Lévi-Strauss's willingness to accept Ricoeur's description of his position as "Kantianism without the transcendental subject." But even Kant's a priori structures can be held to have had the status of postulates—the fact that he postulated them as necessary on the basis of a transcendental argument did not make them immune to empirical revision, which indeed modern physics has demanded. Lévi-Strauss himself says explicitly that he has no a priori definition of what is and is not "structurable," but that it is often "the most fluid and fugitive aspects of culture which give access to a structure; whence the passionate and almost maniacal attention which we pay to details" (1958:357). This attention is sometimes selective, but the example he cites of a significant detail in another science suggests that it is just such selective details that count: he points out that natural science often progresses by making a new theoretical structure to accommodate some anomaly previously considered "astructural," as in the case of the precession of the perihelion of Mercury, one of the decisive elements in the abandonment of Newtonian gravitation in favor of general relativity. Of course Lévi-Strauss approaches culture in the expectation of finding structures, but that is a methodological attitude strictly comparable to the expectation of the natural scientist that he or she will find causal correlations.

For Radcliffe-Brown science is "the systematic investigation of the structure of the universe as it is revealed through our senses" (1952:190); as we saw, the aim of the anthropologist for him is to describe the "form of the structure" belonging to a particular culture. Lévi-Strauss is at once more modest and more ambitious. On the one hand, for a given society, he is content to restrict himself to a taxonomy, an establishment of correlations, thus avoiding the awkward necessity of making predictions; on the other he does not hesitate to relate this taxonomy to broad cross-cultural generalities at the unconscious level. The taxonomy constitutes a genuine empirical base, but the theoretical use made of it is unusual—instead of justifying the theory in terms of its usefulness in dealing with similar cases elsewhere, Lévi-Strauss is inclined rather to justify it in terms of the "truths of reason" it embodies.

The basic requirement of Lévi-Strauss's position is that there should exist an autonomous, unconscious, and hidden structure underlying the law-governed, conscious, and apparent one. This underlying structure is like a language, spoken not with words but with the categories of mythology or kinship. One of the problems implicitly posed by the title of this chapter is whether social structures necessarily rest on such a linguistic base; to deny this is after all not to deny their structural reality. It is not a question to be resolved as confidently as the parallel question about language with which the chapter opened. Any resolution is likely in any case to involve some degree of semantic stipulation. What does seem to emerge from the cases we have been examining is that it is reasonable to regard the social as structural, as constituted wholly by the relations into which human beings enter with one another. What mainly differentiates social from linguistic structure is that the terms of those relations in the former are whole individual lives and not arbitrary pairings of sound and sense.

# 7

# Humanistic Structures and Deconstructions

## 46. The humanities and the human sciences

TO RECAPITULATE: THE human organisms that we are live in a world not only of physical objects but of meanings. These attach to what might be called social or conceptual objects: social when their elements (the terms of the relations that constitute them) are people, conceptual when these are ideas (using this term informally). This distinction is not radical, since social objects are not such unless someone has an idea of how their elements are related (so that they are always also conceptual objects), and some conceptual objects have elements that are things as well as ideas—works of art, for example. For that matter words, which for Saussure are conceptual objects (pairings of ideas in the informal sense of the term), are also things, momentary as speech or enduring as written or recorded traces.

Structuralism examines the ways in which relations constitute social and conceptual objects. The relations in question must satisfy two criteria: they must be intelligible, that is, they must embody properties (the most fundamental of which I have called *matching*, a notion to be made more precise in Part II) that when attended to make them recognizably significant; this ensures that the structures to which they belong are signiferous. And they must be seen as necessary or desirable—they must *matter* to those who have to deal with them. Signiferous structures contain and carry meaning potentially; they actually do so only when people attend to the relations that constitute them and invest them with importance, however minimal.

The most ramified and interconnected set of such conceptual relations is linguistic, and it is sometimes taken as paradigmatic for the others. However, we have seen that structures can be signiferous when the relations that constitute them are prelinguistic or independent of language. Notable among these are the relations that human beings enter into with other human beings, especially those near to them—parents, siblings, aunts and uncles, other close associates such as members of the same family or tribe, in general those whom psychiatrists call "significant others." There is of course a language of kinship, but some kinship relations are significant in themselves, before language and more fundamentally than language. Some distant relations may be essentially mediated by language, and many social relations that do not involve kinship are no doubt of this type, but the existence of nonlinguistic signiferous structures has been an essential premise of the argument of the previous chapter.

In the present chapter, however, we shall be mainly concerned with extended structures that the existence of language has made possible. The main functions of language I take to be expression, communication, information storage and retrieval, and theory construction. It is the last that primarily concerns us here; it encompasses not only science but also literature, religion, and (to some degree) ethics and politics and economics—"to some degree" because these last domains include some relations (as they are presently constituted, fewer than we might expect) whose terms are human beings and therefore count as social. (Remember that while social relations are always accompanied by conceptual ones, these are not always or necessarily linguistic.) I call all this "theory construction" to emphasize that the domains in question have in common a *constructed viewpoint*, which may look toward the natural or social world (in science) or toward an imaginary world (in literature) or to a higher or eternal world (in religion). To have a theory is to have such a viewpoint, the *theoroi* in classical times having been specially appointed observers of significant events (the consultation of oracles or the various regional games).

Language lends itself to the construction of theories because it can name objects, attribute properties to them, specify relations among them, and so on, and it can do this iteratively to any desired degree of complexity. It itself is not a theory, although particular languages may make it easier to construct some theories than others (as suggested by the Sapir-Whorf hypothesis). The result of some thousands of years of linguistic activity, whose intensity has grown exponentially in several waves, through oral literature, writing by hand, printing, typing, photographic and xerographic copying, and word processing by computers and computer networks, is a textual domain that dwarfs in extent and complexity all other products of human culture. In this domain the members of literate cultures spend most of their lives.

Among the products of this textual activity in the last couple of millennia are the domains that have come for administrative convenience to be called the natural sciences, the social sciences, and the humanities. In this book I have excluded the natural sciences from the area of structuralist concern, because their structures are obliged to conform to those of nature;

they therefore become as conceptually and mathematically complex as that obligation dictates and throw no special light on the structuring tendencies of human thought. Furthermore, the structures to which natural scientific theories conform consist, we suppose, of relations between material objects (interpreting "material" in an inclusive sense to be further discussed in chapter 12), so that they fall outside the defining principle of structuralism set forth at the beginning of the Introduction. In this exclusion I differ from Piaget (1970), though his failure to observe it seems to me to weaken considerably the value of his treatment of the idea of structure, precisely by making it so general that its specific human significance is lost.

The social sciences are a different matter. I take them, as indicated at the beginning, to deal with objects and events whose causal antecedents include human intentions, so that in principle they will be marked by the structures of those intentions. However two things tend to align them, for some analytic purposes, with the natural sciences: first, the causal consequences of intentions may and very likely will include events that were *not* intended, or even foreseen, so that some features of large-scale social organization may be just as foreign to the interests and understanding of human individuals as the obscurest phenomena of nature; second, nothing guarantees that I will understand the intentions of *other* humans, whose circumstances, experience, language, upbringing, and so on may be wholly alien to me, and whose culture I may therefore be forced to approach much as if it were an exotic fact of nature. It remains true nevertheless that the objects of the social sciences will cease to be such and will fall back into the materiality of their artefactual carriers if some population does not sustain them with the several intentions of its members.

The humanities, however, I take to comprise the study just of those conceptual objects which, as deliberate and conscious products of the creative powers of human beings, have been judged by other human beings to be worthy of attention and preservation, so that they reflect explicit intentions on the part of maker and consumer alike. The same could of course be said of the arts, which accounts for the fact the two categories are regularly linked when contrasted with the sciences—although as remarked earlier I take the arts (other than literature, but even literature in the admittedly perverse sense that language may be just one medium among others for what literature, as one of the arts, wants to do) to be basically independent of language in spite of the fact that they all (including literature) generate ancillary disciplines that are critical or historical, and therefore in either case linguistic. Something "humanistic" belonging to another culture that I am not capable of appreciating as such, because of not understanding its intentional structure as worthy of attention and preservation, I can treat only as an object of the social sciences. The humanities thus involve not only the constitutive and functional intentionality of all objects of the social sciences but what might be called a valorizing intentionality as well; we regard their objects not merely under the aspect of significance but also under that of judgment.

The question whether or not it is appropriate to treat objects of the humanities that we *can* appreciate as such by methods apparently belonging to the social sciences has aroused controversy. The celebrated (or notorious) article of Jakobson and Lévi-Strauss (1962) already referred to in chapter 3 (section 22), which brought all the resources of linguistics they could muster to bear on a sonnet of Baudelaire, is a case in point. As we saw there the poem itself was taken to contain a system of "ordered variants"; unlike myths, which find their place alongside other myths in a system of transformations, poems constitute structures even when considered in isolation; they submit therefore to "vertical" analysis in terms of superposed levels, phonetic, syntactic, and so on, rather than (or in addition, since nothing prevents our treating poems and other literary works in relation to one another as well as in isolation) to "horizontal" analysis in terms of their place among other objects of the same kind. Jakobson and Lévi-Strauss were sharply criticized by Michael Riffaterre (in Ehrmann 1966) for the *indiscriminate* use of linguistic structures in their analysis—it is impossible to tell, he said, which structural features are *poetically* relevant without appealing to actual readers, who in their encounter with the poem are "held up" by features that "force themselves" upon the attention.

This experience of the work will certainly be conditioned by earlier reading, linguistic perspicacity, and so on and will therefore not be the same for all readers. But the way to the poem as a literary object lies, for Riffaterre, not through the social science of linguistics but through the human science (if it can be called that) of criticism, the experimental basis of which is the practice of reading for its own sake. Yet the analysis of Jakobson and Lévi-Strauss does bring something to the reading of Baudelaire's sonnet, and if we take criticism of a work (as I do) to be defined as whatever affects a subsequent reading of it then their analysis belongs to criticism as well as to linguistics. The social science, if I may so put it, becomes a human science on condition that the functional intentionality of the mere observer comes to be supplemented by the valorizing intentionality of the reader as participant in a literary activity.

There is no exact equivalent in English for the French *sciences humaines* or the German *Geisteswissenschaften*. "Humanities" doesn't quite do it, lacking as it does any sense of disciplinary solidity or rigor. What prevents the general adoption of the expression "human sciences" is presumably a phobia that identifies "science" with abstraction, formalism, arrogance, mere materialism, and so on. (Perhaps it takes an early exposure to physics to find it human and beautiful.) But it seems to me that if humanistic study wishes to aim for a form of knowledge—and it surely does this—then there is no reason whatever for the results of this study not to be called the "human sciences." Structuralism provides a working link between the human and the social sciences, in that its methods, tested in the latter, can be adapted to the former without danger of reduction as long as the indispensable supplement of valorization and judgment is forthcoming. This does not mean that all aspects of social science suddenly become relevant to the humanities (though most of them can be made so); nor does it mean that every humanistic interest has to rest on a social-scientific basis (though most of them are suggestive of possible lines of inquiry in the social sciences, especially at a cultural and temporal distance). It does mean that the humanities will be in a position to offer, at least at an introductory level (for nobody can say how far into the field a newcomer will go or how deep his or her experiences will be), intelligible structures of possible experience on which to build an understanding of their various objects and domains.

"Indispensable supplement of valorization and judgment" sounds like an echo of an old controversy. Because the phenomena studied by the social sciences are invested with meaning or sense (in effect what I have been calling intentionality) by those who participate in them, some thinkers, notably Max Weber, claimed that they could not be dealt with adequately unless that sense had been grasped by the social scientist in an empathetic mode of understanding or *Verstehen*, an act of putting oneself in the place of those who originally had the experience of the historical or social episode in question. My point is however somewhat different, and it comes into play not at the boundary between the natural and social sciences but at the somewhat looser boundary between what we are accustomed to calling the social sciences and the humanities, or between the old social sciences and the new human sciences. Just as some objects of the social sciences have to be treated by me as if they were objects of the natural sciences (because I can get at them only statistically, or only etically, not being in a position to understand the intentions of the participants), so some objects of the human sciences may have to be treated by me as if they were objects of the social sciences (because I can get at them only descriptively, not being in a position to assess a judgment of comparative worth). At the same time I know that the former *are* objects of the social, and the latter of the human sciences, and they can be dealt with as such by people who are appropriately situated.

## 47. History as archaeology

THE QUESTION OF the status of history as science—and if science, of what kind— has been from time to time an occasion of administrative as well as of intellectual confusion. It seems at first as if it would not lend itself to structuralist treatment, being apparently an essentially diachronic discipline, and as if the recovery of intentions in historical events would be a hopeless enterprise in view of the pessimism even of convinced historicists like Engels as to the unintentional consequences of intentional actions (see for example his letter of September 1890 to Joseph Bloch: "what each individual wills is obstructed by everyone else, and what emerges is something that no one willed"). And indeed if history were taken to be nothing but a sequential record of past happenings both these difficulties would be formidable.

There is however another way of looking at history, as an essentially synchronic discipline and one readily accessible to structuralist methods. The main practitioner of these methods was Michel Foucault, although as we saw earlier he did not like them to be called structuralist. The book that most explicitly shows them at work is *The Order of Things*, a title that Foucault's publisher claimed he preferred in English to a more literal rendering of *Les Mots et les choses*. To put things in order we must first get our hands on them, and the *past*, the subject matter of history, is by definition no longer available for examination. Fortunately for the investigator, however, words in their written form tend to leave themselves behind as *traces* of the activity that produced them; libraries are full of them, conveniently packaged in books and manuscripts. When Foucault calls his book *An Archaeology of the Human Sciences* he refers to the digging he has done among the shards of our intellectual culture.

The archaeologist, finding a coin here, a pot there, reconstructs cities and civilizations. Foucault, turning over words with immense scholarship and erudition, reconstructs the human sciences, with a few contiguous elements of biological and medical science thrown in. Instead of Babylon or Troy, he gives us Natural History or General Grammar. This archaeological model, which poses as a problem the identity and continuity of the very disciplines being studied (instead of assuming, for example, that there has always been something recognizable as biology), seems to me an important contribution not only to the history of science but to intellectual history in general. The realization that *all historical evidence is contemporary* (just as fossils, mummies, Roman villas exist *now*, not in the past of which they are the remains), while obvious enough once it is pointed out, puts things in a genuinely new light. All history becomes archaeology. We have no past, only the present traces of a past.

Just as the archaeologist uncovers one layer after another, separated by horizons that indicate more or less abrupt changes of circumstance, so Foucault divides the history of the *sciences humaines* into three ages, each marked by an *episteme* or dominant theory of knowledge, separated from one another by discontinuities at the beginning of the seventeenth century and at the end of the nineteenth century. The first is the Renaissance, during which the rule that linked the order of words to the order of things was *Resemblance*: words had a natural affinity for what they named, signs were to be found inscribed in things as though by the hand of God. Language constituted a "fourth natural kingdom," as Saussure puts it; and if language was natural, nature was also a language—the whole world was written, a great Book in which the significance of each episode contributed to an essentially moral interpretation of the universe.

By contrast the rule in the Classical age, which followed, was *Representation*. Language was no longer *part* of the world but a net *thrown over* the world: it criticized, classified, analyzed. The boundary is marked by Don Quixote, who in the first part of Cervantes's book is engaged in a search for resemblance—flocks become armies, windmills become giants—whereas in the second part he is an example of representation, the man about whom the first part was written. But Don Quixote's life is purely exterior. Two hundred years later the Classical age closes, according to Foucault, with the Marquis de Sade, who seeks to reach the limit in the representation of an interior life, the life of Desire. But desire breaks through representation: life asserts itself directly, and is to be confronted without the intermediacy of a language thrown over the world, which protected while it interpreted. In the Modern age that now opens up, the *subject* is as it were naked toward the world, deprived both of the comfort that came from an objective intelligibility in things and of the sense of mastery that came from a confidence in the adequacy of language. Language is now an object in the world, whose significance is no longer intrinsic. As such it is open to manipulation of a kind that was impossible when it was a vehicle for representation: it becomes a material for formalization and for literary construction in styles previously unthinkable.

While in the Classical age the disciplines that Foucault calls General Grammar, Natural History, and the Analysis of Wealth represented linguistic, biological, and economic facts, they did not constitute sciences of man. It remained for the modern age to identify *language, life, and labor* as the objects of linguistics, biology, and economics. And the emergence of this new objectivity poses for the first time a question that had been concealed by the ambiguous status of language in the earlier epochs. Who is it, exactly, that speaks, lives, works? Obviously, in one sense, people; obviously, in another sense, you and me. But neither the radical objectivity of people as things, nor the radical subjectivity of the individual self, seems a satisfactory *general* answer to the question. And so at the beginning of the Modern age Man was invented. "Before the end of the eighteenth century, *man* did not exist. . . . He is a quite recent creature, which the demiurge of knowledge fabricated with its own hands less than two hundred years ago: but he has grown old so quickly that it is only too easy to imagine that he had been waiting for thousands of years in the darkness for that moment of illumination in which he would finally be known. Of course, it is possible to object that general grammar, natural history, and the analysis of wealth were all, in a sense, ways of recognizing the existence of man. . . . But there was no epistemological consciousness of man as such. The Classical *episteme* is articulated along lines that do not isolate, in any way, a specific domain proper to man." And the specific domain that the Modern age did isolate for man is, of course, the domain of the human sciences.

But a difficulty presents itself. It is characteristic of man that he *is not* that which his consciousness presents to him; he *is* his consciousness, not its object, as phenomenology and existentialism have stressed before. In what sense, then, can he be the object of the human sciences? With respect to the world amenable to scientific analysis, man turns out to be *absence*; not physical absence, since people still have bodies, but metaphysical absence, because the subject cannot be located in an objective world. Now if man is absence, the human sciences are an aberration; they need to be redefined to account for the emptiness of their center. The direction of this redefinition must be, according to Foucault, toward the reestablishment of Language as the true human reality, no longer, as in the sixteenth century, because its meaning is given to us objectively, but because our meanings are given subjectively by it. We do not so much speak it as it speaks us; we are spectators of its activity in us, and we have learned from Freud and from writers like Artaud how little, in fact, we have to do with the determination of what it does to us. The postmodern *episteme* that comes to replace the Modern, in its preoccupation with the unconscious and with structure, is one in which, as we saw in chapter 2 (section 14), *man* as an objective category will no longer have a place.

The concept of *episteme* (which for Foucault is a four-syllable Greek word and not a three-syllable French one, as some of his commentators, with the aid of a grave accent, have tried to make it) is central to his conception of the history of ideas, and it is what makes him a structuralist, since the domains through which the history runs can be defined as (sequential) groups of *epistemes* that are structural transformations of one another. An *episteme* is a "configuration" of relations among elements of discourse characteristic of a given age (in the sixteenth century, for example, the forms of resemblance: *convenientia, aemulatio,* analogy, sympathy) (Foucault 1970:25). Foucault's *episteme* reminds one irresistibly of T. S. Kuhn's *paradigm*, and his discontinuities of Kuhn's revolutions, although it is not clear that any easy historical link can be established between the two—Foucault and Kuhn worked in complete independence of each other, or at any rate each disclaimed, in the 1960s, any knowledge of the other (personal communications). (It is worth noting however that a structuralist version of Kuhn's account could be constructed fairly simply, in which a science would be a group of mutually transforming structures and a revolution would be a structural transformation; the underlying structure would turn out to be something like a standard hypothetico-deductive model. A less overtly structuralist form of this suggestion appears in Caws 1967a).

The strategy of history is to show how one reconstructed *episteme* transforms into the next, under what paradigmatic replacements or formal shifts. But the contemporary material on the basis of which the reconstruction is based remains in some sense unaffected by this exercise, which is not the only thing that can be done with it; other arrangements are possible. In the domain of literature, in particular, no a priori order can be imposed on the sequence of a reader's reading. Just as the fossils and mummies exist *now*, not *then*, so all the books are available by reaching for them *today* (or ordering them from the desk at the Bibliothèque Nationale, where Foucault could nearly always be seen at work), no matter what date may be carried on the title page. Foucault speaks of the "existence and co-existence" of literature, whose place is "the space at once real and fantastic of the Library," so that in the end it constitutes a *network* (réseau) more spatial than temporal (Foucault et al. 1968:17–21). The relation of *criticism* is no longer then necessarily a vector from a later to an earlier work but can run in any direction the reader pleases.

The critical relation is constitutive of the structure of the literary domain. But something interesting happens to the concept of structure when this kind of permissiveness enters. If I can traverse the network in any order I like, the particular relations I thus establish or realize will form an idiosyncratic structure shared, perhaps, with no other reader. "Establish or realize"—the terms are not equivalent but conceal a profound difference of conception. "Realize" suggests that there already exists a total structure of the domain, part of which is animated by my reading; "establish" suggests that no such structure preexists my creation of it by the act of reading itself. The contrast of "network" and "structure" seems to me fruitful; one might say that Foucault's network consists of a linked series of micro- (or local) structures but does not necessarily have a macro- (or overall) structure. (This anticipates a theme that will recur in chapter 9 in the form of a contrast between accommodation and necessitation.) A simple reflection that throws a good deal of light on this question is that nobody has read or ever will read all the books.

The change of perspective from overall structure to local structure, from a total picture to a series of partial pictures, is characteristic of Foucault's later work. (It was perhaps because of the apparently megalomaniac pretensions of some structuralists that he wished to disavow any connection with them.) In a way it was a return to earlier principles, a reassertion of the careful prudence of the philosophical historian. For in an earlier work (*Madness and Folly in the Age of Reason*) the structuralist component had been the modest transformation from a social structure in which the leprosarium was the focus of a set of relations of exclusion to a structure in which the asylum played the same role. And after *The Order of Things* and the anomalous *Archaeology of Knowledge* (anomalous because alone among Foucault's works it is almost entirely theoretical, with hardly any empirical content, and is therefore lacking what he does best) the focus is once again on particular local relationships: editors and writers, censors and readers, criminals and jailers, parents and children, and so on. The social world becomes a network, not of discourse, but of power.

Foucault's last work, *The History of Sexuality*, combines the historical periodization of *The Order of Things* with the dispersion of structure characteristic of the network:

> one is dealing with mobile and transitory points of resistance, producing cleavages in a society that shift about, fracturing unities and effecting regroupings, furrowing across individuals themselves, cutting them up and remolding them, marking off irreducible regions in them, their bodies and minds. Just as the network of power relations ends by forming a dense web that passes through apparatuses and institutions, without being exactly localized in them, so too the swarm of points of resistance traverses social stratifications and individual unities. (1978:96)

This view of social structure as locally intricate and complex, built up from scattered points rather than down from some abstract plan, seems more faithful to the facts of the matter than the schematic simplicities of early structuralism; it is not incompatible with historical transformations, since in a (relatively) short period of time—of the order of a generation or two in a society with effective internal communication—the whole tangled pattern may shift, but it resists the temptation to totalize. In view of the consistent failure (acknowledged or unacknowledged) of totalizing historicist programs this appears as a virtue.

At the same time the accompanying view of power as "both intentional and nonsubjective" (1978:94), like the doctrine about our being spoken by language rather than speaking it, seems to me to perpetuate the old structuralist confusion about subjectivity and agency. The ideas that language speaks, power is subjectless but intentional, myths tell themselves, history has purpose, and so forth constitute collectively what I call the "fallacy of misplaced agency." The only agents we have any knowledge of are embodied subjects like ourselves, and to attribute agency to any other entity in the universe, even God himself (though unlike the others that is at least an intelligible attribution), is to extrapolate beyond what we have any warrant for. This does not prevent our speaking of structural relations in society, though as we shall see in chapter 11 the courtesy involved in doing so requires a rather careful caveat.

## 48. Varieties of religious belief

THE DOCTRINE OF Man whose end Foucault announces was developed, I suggested in chapter 2, as a counterpoise to the doctrine of God that has haunted Western thought at least since it became Christianized at the time of Augustine—a doctrine that in pantheistic form goes back to the beginning of culture. As we saw in the Introduction, religion and the intelligible can be thought of as having something in common, namely, their reference to "binding" (from *ligare*). The binding effected by religion may be as it were horizontal or vertical, binding people on the one hand to one another, on the other hand to God. These relations introduce complexities of structure that have been the special concern of Georges Dumézil, who although not part of the visible spearhead of structuralism in the 1960s had (like Lacan) been using an essentially structuralist method independently for some decades.

In one sense the social structures produced by religious bonds require no special method of analysis—they are social structures among others. But religion produces not only institutions and their myths, legends, and sacred texts, it also produces gods, whose names and powers constitute a domain of study in themselves. As Feuerbach observed more than a century ago (echoing, as far as that goes, Xenophanes and Montesquieu) we can draw anthropological conclusions from theological observations, since divine attributes will be hyperbolic extrapolations of human ones; the structure of the pantheon, then, will reflect the structure of the society over which it is supposed to preside. If societies constitute transformational groups, their languages, ceremonies, myths, strategies, and so on being structural variants of one another, their gods are likely to do so too. And in Dumézil we find accordingly a double set of structures, social and theological, that mirror each other across cultural and linguistic boundaries.

Dumézil's main contribution lies in his demonstration that Indo-European religions share with Aryan, Roman, Germanic, and other religions a conception of god as threefold, a trinity not of mystical persons as in Christianity but of divine functions. "These functions are: 1st The administration at once mysterious and regular of the world; 2nd The play of physical vigor, of force, mainly but not uniquely of a warlike sort; 3rd Fecundity, with many consequences and resonances, such as prosperity,

health, long life, tranquillity, sensuality, 'numbers.'" And Dumézil continues: "The sacred poets already correlated these functions with other
triads, notably the topological division of the world into sky (or perhaps
rather 'envelope' of the world), atmosphere, earth" (1952:7). He is at pains
to point out that this structure of the divine function is genuinely synchronic,
in that all the functions seem to coexist in each religion, no one issuing from
the other two, and also that (as in the case of language) the "grammar" of
theology does not seem to admit of a contrast between primitive and
developed cultures but is fully formed in all cases available for study,
allowing of course for variations in the completeness of the structure, and its
details, from culture to culture.

What is especially interesting for our purposes, however, is Dumézil's
insistence that, in contradistinction to what has been said or implied about
language in earlier chapters, the structures of religion were by no means
unconscious on the part of those who lived by them. In the case of Rome, for
example, there was a long-standing conflation of godlike and kinglike functions (the deification of the emperors, from which it is not inconceivable that
early Christianity may have taken a cue, was not as radical a crossing of
category lines for them as it seems to us), and the founding kings echo the
triple functions of the old gods. "But let us first observe—and we cannot insist
on it too strongly," says Dumézil in introducing a late study of the warrior
gods, "that the 'system' formed by the first kings of Rome is not one of our
own findings; the Romans comprehended it, explicated it, admired it as a
system, and saw in it the effect of divine benevolence: we have only had to
take notice of their own sentiment" (1970:6).

The problem posed by this observation has profound repercussions. It
might be called the problem of consciousness of structure. Everyone, whether
primitive or civilized (which only means capable of city dwelling), seems to
be able to use language, recognize kinfolk, listen to stories, and so on without
reflecting on or for that matter knowing anything about the structural
features of language, kinship, or mythology—a reflective awareness of these
features is rare and it is an open question whether it can ever be enjoyed *at the
same time* as their employment in discourse or social interaction. A great deal
of the structure dealt with in this book must therefore be said to be
*un*consciously operative in everyday contexts. As unconscious it will also be
unintelligible. It will be rendered intelligible to the extent that it is brought
into consciousness reflectively and the relations that constitute it specified.
Dumézil maintains that this had already happened among the Romans with
respect to tripartite kingship or divinity. Yet it is clear that for many features
of human experience it has not yet happened or is only just beginning to
happen.

One observation that it may be worth making at once is that the

Romans were very recent. It is usually a mistake to think that there is any virtue in a late arrival on the scene—we have more knowledge and better methods at our disposal, both intellectually and technologically, than our ancestors but our minds are probably no more subtle or complex than theirs were. It has been suggested (Julian Jaynes, 1976) that consciousness itself is relatively recent, having been acquired as a back-formation from observations of the meaningfulness of writing and the apparent autonomy of foreigners, but the term "consciousness" according to this hypothesis seems to be used in a thoroughly Pickwickian sense. If I use language without being conscious of its structure, if in solving problems I seem to hear a god speaking in my head, that does not mean I am unconscious of using language or solving problems, it means only that the productive relations that led to these outcomes were not monitored by me, the outcomes presented themselves as such (as my speech, as the god's speech through me —and who am I to resist the impulse to speak in either case?) and not as consciously contrived. But of course the same is true when I walk or sit at the keyboard of the word processor. These words emerge as the product of a process that I initiate and whose output I carefully filter, but the intermediate relations that lead from the initiation to the output are imperfectly apprehended by me even on reflection after the fact, hardly apprehended at all in the moment of writing.

The interesting point here is that the Romans see their system (reflectively) as an effect of divine benevolence, Jaynes's Mycenaeans see their will or action (unreflectively) as the word of their god. It looks as if structure and divinity are deeply interconnected in the history of Western culture. The Christian identification of God and the Word (that paradigm of structure) in the fourth gospel reinforces this notion. It may come as a surprise if I here invoke the name of Lacan as belonging in this section on religious belief, but Freudian fundamentalism is perhaps no less pious than Christian and there are some unexpected parallels on which I would like to dwell briefly. For Lacan discourse is mediated by the unconscious; the word of the patient emerges from it via the preconscious, bearing whatever analytic freight it may. The unconscious is structured like a language, that is, like a signiferous system—it bears meanings but also conveys them. From whom are its messages to be supposed to come? Lacan's answer to this question is: from the Other.

What seems to be going on in Lacan's theory is something like this: just as Freud supposed that infants sometimes have experiences charged with a sexuality they are too young to understand, which leave material repressed in the unconscious that may emerge disastrously later on (when it can be understood only too well but is refused and displaces itself into neurotic symptoms), so they have linguistic experiences they are too young to understand

that may play a similar pathogenic role. Where do these experiences come
from and how are they stored? In general they come from the Other, the
nameless utterer, who could be anybody and in fact was just anybody whose
utterance fell on the child's ears, but who appears as a transcendent source
that Lacan does not hesitate to equate at times with the Cartesian God
(1978:36). In particular they may come from a quite specific other, the
father; whence the identification of the Other with the Father, whose speech
is law and whose prohibition of the child's desire for the mother (reinforced
by the mother in the Name of the Father, whose Name thus becomes
synonymous with power) represents the installation of an (unconscious)
structure of social order.

The linguistic material that lodges in the unconscious is absorbed by
the child in the form of the signifier; its being beyond his comprehension
means precisely the unavailability of the signified at that stage of his life. The
unconscious, we might say, is a repository of unintelligible signifiers. Its
problem is to find a signified for the signifier, and this is what it does in
dreams and in neurosis. The *correct* signifier would be the "real," whatever
that was at the time of the original experience; *then* it was attached to the
signifier by the Other, but that state is no longer recoverable, and since the
child could not know it anyway the experience for him was mere contingency
or chance, *tyche* in Lacan's adopted Greek. In the search for a signified for a
given signifier another signifier will do quite well, preferably one that has an
innocuous signified of its own, admissible to consciousness, as the true and
frightening signified of the original signifier is not. So we have the dream
work, condensation and displacement, metaphor and metonymy, with all
that implies for the structure of discourse.

The guarantee of the ultimate intelligibility of the whole enterprise—if
such a guarantee is needed—is once again the Other, the structure of whose
language is that of the unconscious and is available to us if only we can
decipher it. "If such a guarantee is needed": it is only if we are uncertain of
our own beliefs and purposes that we need reassurance from without, from
the Other, from the Father, from God (it is only out of a sense of sin that we
are candidates for grace). I shall have occasion in chapter 9 to say more
about our tendency to believe that in the absence of transcendent grounds or
authority our being is without foundation and our projects without meaning;
for the time being I note only that from the naïve structuralism of Dumézil's
Romans, who took intellectual satisfaction in the existence of their gods and
the harmonious arrangement of their world, seems to have evolved a preoccupied dissatisfaction because harmony seems to be lacking and God unat-
tainable. Monotheism is an exacting doctrine; people who grow up in
families where authority is centered in the father seem naturally disposed to
it, but it leads to an all-or-nothing view of religion whose poles are at one

extreme the Absolute and at the other Absence (see *La Structure absolue* of Raymond Abellio, 1965, and *La Struttura assente* of Umberto Eco, 1968).

## 49. The practice of writing

ABELLIO'S "ABSOLUTE STRUCTURE" was a foreseeable extrapolation from Lévi-Strauss's work, on which it was explicitly based; what started as a modest program of local groups and transformations was exaggerated by Lévi-Strauss himself to make it appear on the one hand more unified, and on the other more comprehensive, than the evidence warranted, first by his appeal to a basic structure of Mind, and then by his insistence on stretching his structural analyses to fit the whole world of myth (as well as chopping off some of the myths to fit the analyses). Some of this work was still in the future when Abellio published his book, but the vector was there, and it was a short step to absolute structure, which according to Abellio "in the last analysis, is an Idea which dispenses with words, it is the supreme Idea even" (1965:23).

It was no doubt this sort of megalomania that contributed to the disavowal of structuralism by some writers whose work was nevertheless squarely within the domain as I have come to understand it. Some "poststructuralism" is to be understood as post *that* structuralism, the structuralism of absolutes and centers and origins. Renouncing structuralism for that reason seems to me unfortunate, to concede too much to those who allowed their taste for apotheosis, whether religious or Academic, to color their doctrines. The work of structural analysis has I think to begin with the matching structures, linguistic, literary, anthropological, and so on, in which I find myself involved here and now; it does not have to be built out from some fixed center or up from some fixed origin.

A radically decentered view of a world whose origins are in indefinite regress is still, in my view, compatible with everything that is valuable in structuralism. For it is possible to think of the intelligible not as given, but as *constructed*. A large part of its domain will consist of *texts*, those woven structures (*texere* is "to weave") whose mode of production is writing. This conception of the intelligible as a domain of essentially textual construction, constituting a "network" in Foucault's sense, has a number of implications of which I stress two: first, that the domain includes all texts, not just literary ones but especially, among others, philosophy itself; second, that the reader or critic does not necessarily leave these constructions in their given form but may modify as well as adding to them, in particular by the activity of *deconstruction*. This "modification" is to be understood contextually, in that whatever deconstructive activity we may engage in leaves the original text available in its undeconstructed form for anyone who has not included our own text in his traversal of the network (or for anyone who denies its critical relevance).

Deconstruction is a philosophical enterprise (having obvious affinities with analysis, a point to which I will return in the next section) whose aim is to overcome the ethnocentricity or logocentricity in which Western thought is entangled because of the way in which its intellectual traditions have emerged from the languages and cultures of Europe. Its principal exponent has been Jacques Derrida, who in spite of his affinity with the structuralists of the 1960s was left out of my account of structuralism in France because he emerges from a different tradition, phenomenological rather than linguistic, his points of reference being Hegel, Husserl, and Heidegger, along with Nietzsche and Rousseau. His work has appeared principally in collections of essays (*Writing and Difference, Grammatology, Dissemination*, and *Margins of Philosophy*, among others) as well as in multilingual and multitextual works like *Glas, Spurs*, and *The Postcard*, in which he experiments with non-standard modes of presentation. That these collections should be in the form of *books* does not prevent Derrida from sustaining as a main thesis that the *book* is dead, and that writing must henceforth issue in *texts*.

"The book" stands for a whole tradition, which held that the intelligibility of the world could be encompassed in a book, that the world was in some sense a book. Derrida examines the activity of *écriture* or writing (the English gerund reflects inadequately the combination of process and product conveyed by the French) which mediates the world and the book, and finds that the violence it does to the immediacy of the word disqualifies it from performing the task to which the book pretends. Among other things the book aspires to completeness and to truth, whereas (as Nietzsche pointed out) writing "was not originally subject to the *logos* and to truth" (Derrida 1967:33). The violence of writing is not in itself undesirable—it is an accompaniment of creation, indeed of any action (the force of the word against the world), it is required, as Nietzsche again saw, to provide a dialectical balance for passive contemplation: Dionysus against Apollo, *élan* against structure. But its products are inscribed *in* the world, they do not comprehend the world; the text is a *trace* left by human activity, and its structure will be the clue to the human enterprise.

The idea of the text as trace suggests the possibility of tracing its provenance back to some origin. But the domain of text is not objective in the way in which the domain of ordinary archaeology is, with its real shards and ruins; texts require animation, that is, they inevitably involve the subject, and the subject for Derrida is dynamic from the start—there cannot be said to have been an origin, the earliest manifestations of thought having been already a dialectical exchange between the fixed and the changing, between the closed and the open, between speech and writing, already inscribed in time because of the *deferring* of the dialectical resolution. Duality is always already present, unity is never yet attained. "Deferring" is one of the senses of "*différance*," a variant introduced by Derrida which by replacing the "e" of *différence* by an "a" gives an active sense to what is otherwise a passive relation. (*Différer* has the senses both of "differ" and "defer," which in Middle English meant the same thing; there is thus no straightforward translation that catches both meanings, but nothing prevents us from using "differance" as a neologism in English to correspond to Derrida's neologism in French.)

Difference provides the temporal motive power of thought and is not arrested except by the death of the subject, an event whose significance in Derrida's philosophy echoes Plato rather than Spinoza—the free man thinks of death but refuses it, a *refus de la fin* that mirrors the *refus du commencement*. The denial of the origin implicitly gives primacy to structure over history, since any historical account will eventually have to fall back on structuralist considerations. Suspended as we are between birth and death, surrounded by texts and equipped with the means of writing, what is our situation? We can explore textual and intertextual structures to our hearts' content but we will remain suspended—we cannot hope to enter into the presence of Being, which seems to be the aim of metaphysics, since that presence will always be deferred or displaced with respect to the moment and the situation in which we find ourselves, will always be under the sign of differance. Does this matter, though? If we have language, through which "Being speaks always and everywhere," need we be nostalgic for a "lost native country of thought"?

This question arises at the end of Derrida's essay on differance and is answered, in effect, by the invocation of play, of dance (as in Nietzsche), of hope (as in Heidegger) (Derrida 1982:27). The domain of textuality is surely one in which everybody can find the optimum level of complexity required for equilibrium, and activity in it is a form of play—a thought that echoes all too obviously the later Wittgenstein. Derrida's own playground is the philological axis that links Greek to German, from Plato and Aristotle to Hegel and Heidegger (and more recently Freud); his work is brilliant and fragmentary rather than systematic, but it remains for me in the best sense structuralist, since what it exploits is precisely the multiple layers of matched structure that construct the text and yield to its deconstruction.

## 50. A short course in deconstruction

THE ONE RESPECT in which Derrida sometimes seems to overstep the bounds of philosophical prudence has to do with his apparent acceptance of

Heidegger's concept of philosophical history as Destiny, *Geschick*, according to which Being is *sent* (*schicken*, to send) as it were from the Greeks to us. At the same time this obscure doctrine was probably the occasion for the emergence of the concept of deconstruction in its contemporary form. The indispensable context of deconstruction is structuralism; it is not "poststructuralist" except in the myopia of fashion—indeed as I have been at pains to emphasize nothing is poststructuralist except in this sense, since structuralism is not yet done with. Deconstruction is one of its moments, one of its truths.

Not that this truth could not have been arrived at in any other way—indeed it has been, repeatedly, in the history of philosophy. It is just that it is clearest in this context. So I will begin this last expository section, in spite of the redundancy of the exercise after so much exposition, with a summary restatement of the context. Next I will put deconstruction into this context and show its precursors in some other contexts. After that I will comment on an ambiguity in the notion of deconstruction, and finally I will address the question of whether and in what senses it can be said to constitute a movement in itself, as so many people seem to want to make it—an alternative to other ways of approaching the world.

First, the structuralist context. Structuralism emerged when it was realized that the intelligible world did not have to be constituted in imitation of the material world. The material world consists of things, which enter into relations with one another; the intelligible world, it came to be seen, consists of relations, which may jointly specify things. (There is a sense in which this could be said of the material world too, as grasped by us; pushing this question leads to the debate between materialism and idealism.) The intelligible world depends for its existence on more or less intelligent subjects, and is transmitted from subject to subject, and thus preserved in being, by their in-struction. *Instructio* means among other things equipping or fitting out; instruction is the activity—any activity—that provides the subject with the inner structures it animates. One of these is language. The problem with language is that we never just internalize its structure, we always also at the same time internalize a lot of the structures it traditionally carries: lore, prejudice, metaphysics, politics, morality. Because language is not only an object of instruction but also its prime vehicle, and because these other structures it carries are offered for ready consumption, often in textual form, people have been swallowing them whole, and wholesale, for centuries. The trouble is that many, if not most, of them are erroneous, repressive, or vicious.

So we grow up in an intelligible world already structured, and most of the time we do not notice this. Modern philosophy began, in a sense, with Descartes's realization of the fact. These too-readily-acquired structures are unreliable and need to be taken apart for examination, disarticulated, dismantled. Not necessarily, it should be noticed, destroyed. The way Descartes goes about it is instructive. In the *Discourse on Method* (Part 2) he says:

> . . . . the sciences found in books—in those at least whose reasonings are only probable and which have no demonstrations, composed as they are of the gradually accumulated opinions of many individuals—do not approach so near to truth as the simple reasoning which a man of common sense can quite naturally carry out respecting the things that come immediately before him. . . .(1931:88)

This suggests that there are sciences, namely, those whose reasonings are categorical and that do have demonstrations, that can do better than the man of common sense and from whose errors he does not in consequence stand in such need of liberation; I draw attention to it because I do not take the natural sciences in themselves to be the prime objects of deconstruction as we should practice it, since their structure is explicit anyway, although of course people's conceptions of them and of their powers are proper objects. Descartes goes on to say what he proposes to do with the pronouncements of the bad bookish sciences:

> . . . . as regards all the opinions which up to this time I had embraced, I thought I could not do better than endeavour once for all to sweep them completely away, so that they might later on be replaced, either by others which were better, or by the same, when I had made them conform to the uniformity of a rational scheme. (1931:89)

That is at any rate what Haldane and Ross have him say, but in fact there is something misleading about the translation, and this is relevant to the theme of deconstruction. "Sweeping away" sounds relatively drastic, but Descartes in fact seems to have more respect even for the bad opinions than this—his language suggests handling them with some care. Adam and Tannery have:

> . . . . pour toutes les opinions que i'avois receues iusques alors en ma creance, ie ne pouvois mieux faire que d'entreprendre, une bonne fois, de les en oster, affin d'y en remettre par apres, ou d'autres meilleures, ou bien les mesmes. . . .

*Oster (ôter), remettre*—there is something circumspect about the terms, far from the destructive violence of "sweeping away." It is as if Descartes has his opinions in a box and takes them out one by one for examination until the box is empty and can be restocked with none but tested beliefs. A more adequate translation would be:

> . . . . for all the opinions I had received up to this time into my belief, I could not do better than to undertake, once and for all, to remove them from it, in order afterwards to replace in it either other and better ones, or even the same ones. . . .

Because of this scrupulous carefulness in the handling of beliefs I regard Descartes as an authentic precursor of deconstruction, since I take such careful disarticulation for the purposes of weighing and testing to be exactly the deconstructionist program. But the word "deconstruction" we get from Heidegger via a translational device on the part of Derrida. The strategy I have been discussing in Descartes is taken up by a good many philosophers, among them Heidegger, who in section 6 of *Being and Time* calls for the destruction (*Destruktion*) of the history of ontology. This is how Heidegger puts it (in the translation of Macquarrie and Robinson):

> . . . Dasein . . . falls prey to the tradition of which it has more or less explicitly taken hold. This tradition keeps it from providing its own guidance, whether in inquiring or choosing. . . .When tradition becomes master, it does so in such a way that what it "transmits" is made so inaccessible, proximally and for the most part, that it rather becomes concealed. . . . If the question of Being is to have its own history made transparent, then this hardened tradition must be loosened up, and the concealments which it has brought about must be dissolved. We understand this task as one in which by taking the question of Being as our clue, we are to destroy the traditional content of ancient ontology until we arrive at those primordial experiences in which we achieved our first ways of determining the nature of Being. . . . (1962:42–44)

(To underline the connection of this enterprise with the rest of philosophy I point out that this "loosening up" which Heidegger says we must perform means at bottom nothing other than what philosophers have always called analysis: translate "up-loosening" *strictly* into Greek and you get "*ana-lysis*.") Heidegger's term *Destruktion* is translated by Derrida as "deconstruction" precisely because Derrida too sees that the wantonly destructive sense it would be too easy to attach to the term "destruction"—as opposed to the gentler "up-loosening"—must be avoided.

Deconstruction matters because we inherit structures that if left undeconstructed will mislead, oppress, or entrap us. But its possibility implies the disposition of the structures in question to come apart or disarticulate if suitably probed. As it happens they are mostly carried in texts, and textual structures lend themselves almost eagerly to deconstructive practice. But then any texts, and not only those whose inherited burdens we were unwittingly bearing, can be treated in this way—hence deconstruction not only as liberation from the history of metaphysics but also as a technique of literary criticism. The proposition against which the deconstructive criticism of the Yale school directs itself is that to a given material linguistic structure, the text itself, must correspond any unique or necessary intelligible structure. All candidates for such status are fair game for deconstruction. And they—and the texts themselves—obligingly come apart along their fault lines when the mafiosi attack them with their little hammers.

Is deconstruction then an alternative world-view? I would argue that in my first sense—as the liberation from structures unconsciously or inadvertently acquired from language, history, and tradition, philosophical or otherwise—it is not an alternative but an imperative. We all have to do that, whether or not we become structuralists. But it is a personal matter; Descartes says, shortly after the passage on sweeping opinions away, "My design has never extended beyond trying to reform my own opinion and to build on a foundation which is entirely my own,"and he cannot do that for us, nor can Derrida, nor can anyone. (Note again that it does not involve an automatic rejection of the received doctrine, which if it survives deconstructive criticism may be reconstructed or reintegrated into the structure.) In my second sense, however, as a particular kind of disarticulation of literary (or other) texts, I take it that deconstruction is one mode of criticism among others. For—to give only two reasons—some of the qualities to which criticism addresses itself are available only in texts as constructed; and criticism at least since Barthes has had the option of going off on its own, with only the most cursory reference to the generating text, certainly far less than its deconstruction.

One final word. The large ready-made structures that instruct new generations, that they swallow whole, can be of quite recent origins. There is every indication that the doctrine of deconstruction is in danger of becoming such a structure, itself in need of deconstruction. I insert this remark as a caveat. Even in a short course there must be room for a moment of self-irony.

# Part II

## Structuralism as Philosophy

# 8

# Structure as a Necessary and Sufficient Condition of Intelligibility

## 51. Structuralism and philosophy

I TURN NOW from the mainly expository part of this book to its mainly philosophical part—though as I said in the Introduction the parts are far from watertight, so that many of the philosophical points I shall be developing in the next chapters have been anticipated in passing at relevant junctures in the exposition. The development of structuralism has taken place chiefly outside philosophy, as a debate in the human sciences over content and method. The structuralist position has defined itself against historicism, atomism, mechanism, behaviorism, psychologism, even humanism—in short against any view that invokes either an a priori reduction or an a priori transcendence. The argument has taken different forms in different cases, but in the end it amounts to this: that we have at our disposal only the present moment and things in the world as they are, that our task is to make sense of these from a standpoint within the world, and that any pretense to an Archimidean fulcrum outside the world, or even at a remove from our own standpoint within it, is suspect.

In at least one of its multiple origins structuralism was directly influenced by philosophy: Jakobson and Troubetzkoy took a vivid interest in the work of Husserl. But structuralism differs on at least two counts from phenomenology (its relation to which will be taken up from another point of view in chapter 12). In the first place, although phenomenological analysis might be relevant to the specification of some elements of a structural system (that is, of the terms related by the relations that constitute the structure—it was precisely the phenomenology of spoken language that interested Jakobson and Troubetzkoy), structuralism is concerned more with the relations than with the elements, more with structure than with substance, more with external than with internal structure. In the second place the revolutionary

169

program of phenomenology: *Nicht erklären und zurückführen, sondern aufklären und hinführen*! is at odds with the program of structuralism, which is essentially explanatory (not that that is incompatible with enlightenment). In the order of explanation, the bracketing of received categories, it is perhaps closer to that other motto of phenomenology: *zu den Sachen selbst*! But the facts it accepts as raw material—utterances, inscriptions, episodes of behavior— would seem to the phenomenologist hopelessly unanalyzed.

The character of structuralist explanation, in its philosophical mode, is best reflected in the remark that it is our task to *make sense* of the world, to render it intelligible—or rather, since it is a fact of experience that much of the world as lived in society and explained by the sciences *is* intelligible, to make sense of that intelligibility, to render it intelligible in its turn. The notion of *sense* brings along with it that of *meaning* (and this again introduces, for reasons that are obvious enough but will be discussed later, the notion of *mattering*). There are in consequence philosophical connections with the semiotics or semiology of Peirce and Saussure, and with the theory of meaning in general, construed not only in the narrow sense as the meaning of linguistic expressions but also more broadly as what is socially or even metaphysically meaningful.

Structuralism, we might say, aims on the philosophical level not so much to explain facts as to explain why they make sense or matter to us; not so much to uncover the meaning of life or of the world as to show how we come to think of these things as having or requiring a meaning. It is our tendency to do this that engages us in the frustrating search for origins, principles, foundations, destinies, and the like. If it can be shown how meaning arises in a more restricted setting, and what are the limits of its range, a great many cosmic and agonizing questions may be shown to be empty; and if we come to accept the closure of our world (although not in the sense of confinement or imprisonment, since it remains as it were topologically open—there is always room within it for novelty) and renounce the attempt to get outside it, we may find its systematic internal organization for maximum intelligibility not only challenging but satisfying.

In all this I do not however wish to generate unrealistic expectations of radical theoretical novelty. Lévi-Strauss, in response to a question posed by Ricoeur, once put it like this: "I confess that the philosophy that seems to me to be implied by my researches is extremely down-to-earth. . . . I should not therefore be alarmed if it were shown me that structuralism leads to the restoration of a sort of popular materialism. But furthermore, I know too well that this orientation runs counter to the movement of contemporary philosophical thought to take a defiant attitude about it: I read the signpost and I forbid myself to go forward along the path that it points out to me" (1963:652). The path I have followed is perhaps not exactly the one he declined, but the result is not far from the one he predicted. If the complexities of language and culture do permit of explanation in terms of popular materialism, that is, on the commonsense assumption alone that wherever human beings happen to be there is a familiar stock of local objects interacting causally, then a further explanation of those objects according to more abstract or fundamental principles does not seem urgent.

Ordinary macroscopic objects do of course yield to further analysis on the part of the natural sciences. Lévi-Strauss's conjecture could be interpreted and broadened to mean that a world containing just the material objects we observe and postulate, having just the properties that physics and chemistry and biology say they have, might (given their astronomically large numbers and the aeons during which they have had the opportunity of arranging themselves) turn out to have engendered, in this anomalous corner of the universe, human beings and languages and societies and other complexes whose behavior seems amenable to structuralist explanation without recourse to further hypotheses—to none at any rate not potentially eliminable by logical transformations or more work along already familiar lines. As to the popularity of the materialism, that is mainly a matter of not doing outright violence to common sense, and does not preclude rigor or refinement in the formulation. As a model I can think of nothing better than the "kind of materialism" Stuart Hampshire has attributed to Spinoza (Hampshire 1971:210).

One further hypothesis seems to be required to make all this work, but one that it would seem obtuse not to grant (though some structuralists themselves have managed to be obtuse in just this way) and one that does not really deserve, given the evidence available to each of us, to be called a hypothesis: the assumption of conscious subjectivity on the part of human beings. Strictly speaking, one subjectivity is enough, namely, one's own; the step by analogy to other human beings is natural but not necessary. Also it simplifies matters to attribute agency and purpose to human subjects. These concessions make it possible to assume the significance of the sign, the basic relational concept that serves to link together the human sciences in which structuralism has been mainly practiced. "If the word structuralism corresponds to anything," says François Wahl, "it is to a new style of posing and working out problems in the sciences that deal with the sign: a style that took its departure from Saussurean linguistics" (Ducrot et al. 1968:7).

## 52. Russell and the structure of relations

I BEGIN THE more philosophical part of this book not with my own work but with that of three philosophers who could not possibly have been accused of any taint of structuralism as it was expounded in Part I, all of whom exhibited in their writings a link between two of the elements of my title, namely, structure and intelligibility. By the intelligible I mean what can be understood. In the first instance understanding attaches less to the world itself than to what is said about it; but when in response to an explanation of something in the world it is appropriate to say, "I understand," meaning not the explanation but what is explained (how it works, came about, is put together) it is always the *structure* of the object or event that has become clear, that is, the relations that constitute it or into which it enters.

This connection between structure and intelligibility outside the structuralist movement is to be found in the work of Russell, the early Wittgenstein, and Carnap among others. The basic notion in Russell is that of the "structure of a relation," which is worked out in Russell and Whitehead's *Principia Mathematica* but set forth more approachably in Russell's *Introduction to Mathematical Philosophy*. The structural definition of a relation is extensional, in terms of the things related rather than of the properties of the relation considered independently of those things; such a method has become standard in mathematical logic, in which relations are specified as sets of ordered pairs.

In Russell's words, "For mathematical purposes (though not for those of pure philosophy) the only thing of importance about a relation is the cases in which it holds, not its intrinsic nature" (1919:60). He introduces the idea of the "map" of a relation, which consists of a set of points, representing the terms of the relation, linked by arrows which indicate between which terms and in which senses the relation holds. The map of a relation between the five points $a$, $b$, $c$, $d$, and $e$, such that the elements are linked among themselves in the order $ab$, $ac$, $ad$, $bc$, $ce$, $dc$ and $de$, would look like figure 8.1. The structure of a relation is then "what is revealed by its map." Carnap calls these maps "arrow diagrams" and remarks correctly that the diagram contains nothing that its "pair list" does not contain (1967:22); strictly speaking the map "reveals" nothing that was not already required to be known in order to draw it, but it is clearly of heuristic value in emphasizing the extensional nature of the concept and the way in which the elementary relations are inserted into the complex whole: the map is of a single relation, and the fact that $ab$ is a component of *this* structure, an entry in *this* pair list, characterizes and in the limit defines the relation between $a$ and $b$ alone.

What $a$ and $b$ are is not specified; mathematics, as Carnap somewhere remarks, is purely structural and need not distinguish one entity from another. In fact the pair list looks very much like a specification of permissible transformations in group theory, the domain of mathematics in which the notion of structure plays its most obvious role. Empirical science, on the other hand, does need to distinguish entities from one another. Given,

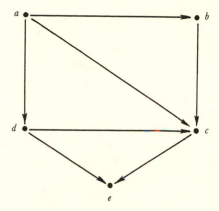

*Figure 8.1*

however, that the relations specified in neutral mathematical terms may be very complex, the possibility arises that if one only knew *all* the relations into which some term entered (or to put it in another way, the one very complex relation to which all the elementary relations of which it was a term belonged) one might thereby have provided a ground of distinction between it and every other entity, without ever naming them in the conventional sense. (The complex mathematical expression of the relation could be regarded as a kind of name.) To know something after all is to know the relations into which it enters; one might say "that among other things," and yet to say what *total* knowledge of something would amount to, *apart* from knowing *all* the relations into which it entered, would be difficult. Again, one might say that some of these relations (being the same color as, being larger than) followed from the properties of the thing known independently (being a certain color, a definite size); but an equally good case might be made for saying that these properties can be attributed only because we can locate the thing in question with respect to other things. All attributes are differential, not only linguistic ones, and it makes as good sense to say that the differences among things determine their properties as that the properties determine the differences.

If this sounds plausible, it is as well to recognize what it entails: from denying that relations have internal properties, so that they must be defined in terms of the things they relate (which appear external to them), we seem to have arrived at the point of denying that things have internal properties, so that they must be defined in terms of the relations that relate them (which again appear external to them). This has the air of circularity and paradox.

The circularity is real, the paradox only apparent. The appearance of paradox is encouraged by the symmetrical construction of the first sentence of this paragraph; there is in fact an asymmetry between the cases, so that things take ontological priority over relations—the relations are as it were defined away, but the things are not, only their properties. Properties, like relations, are means to the *knowledge* of things, but the knowledge they make possible is the knowledge of *what* the things are, not the knowledge *that* they are. The circularity arises because the enterprise of distinguishing among the things in the world has no required or even obvious starting point, but begins *in medias res* and with whatever is to hand; if one begins with properties, relations are generated, if with relations, properties. But upon analysis it appears that relations, in the neutral mathematical sense I discussed earlier, take in their turn priority over properties, since they, and not properties, can be defined in terms of the things directly.

Properties are what we give names to (names, that is, other than proper names). Proper names nail down concrete bits of the world, stable over periods of time; they anchor language in particulars. Other names link only to classes, ontologically unsatisfactory entities whose admission generates real paradoxes. One plausible ambition of structuralism as philosophy might be to do away with classes, accounting for the complexity of the world in terms of particulars and structures of particulars. Not that names, even the name "class," need be given up; they are perfectly good particulars, and the various linguistic structures into which they enter could not easily be dispensed with—it is just that they must be kept under nominalistic supervision.

The notion that particulars, or individuals, or things, may *as we know them* be located in the world only by means of the relations into which they enter, which under the preceding analysis of relations is equivalent to saying that they are located only with respect to other particulars or individuals or things, can be informally confirmed by a couple of examples drawn from widely separated fields. In particle physics the question of the nature of the fundamental heavy particles, or baryons, has (or had until recently) two possible answers: either they are made of hypothetical "quarks," which if they exist ought to be observed in large numbers but have so far eluded observation; or, if the quark hypothesis fails, they must be said to be "made of each other," as Murray Gell-Mann puts it. The latter alternative is known as " bootstrap theory," and it is taken seriously by physicists. It suggests that the circular character of the acquisition of knowledge may be inescapable. The idea that philosophy may be circular is at least as old as Hegel; the idea that science may be is more recent, although adumbrations of it can be found in Aristotle and Newton. Circularity however is not to be despised; while in one sense, after going round a circle, one is back where one started, has made no progress, and so on, in another the world is different the second time around, in that the subject who has made the circuit has a different history and knows the relation between his location and other locations on the circle.

The other example has to do with the subjective conviction that knowledge of an individual is complete only when all its relations to other individuals are specified. (It deals also with the other ordinary-language meaning of "relation," which serves to emphasize the link, to be explored later, between mathematical structures and kinship systems.) Radcliffe-Brown reports a custom among some aboriginal tribes in Australia according to which, when a stranger arrives at a camp, he stops a short distance away so that a delegation can come out to him and question him closely about his family. They establish his exact relationship to every person in the camp, and only when this has been done is he admitted and introduced. Lévi-Strauss, who quotes this story in his *Elementary Structures of Kinship*, says that the Australians have the most sophisticated kinship structures in the world, whose analysis requires the resources of advanced mathematics; in *Race and History* he uses this fact as an argument against the view that the primitive mind is inferior to the civilized. The rest of us spend less of our intellectual capital on such matters.

But that capital is limited. Aboriginal tribes are comparatively small, so that within them, given a willingness to devote a major part of the collective attention to the task, the total relation program can perhaps be carried out successfully. What it yields is a complete definite description: $x$ is the brother of $y$, the matrilateral cross-cousin of $z$, and so on, until all the other individuals involved have been enumerated. For practical purposes, as Carnap points out in the *Aufbau*, the enumeration of properties (in terms of which he conducts his analysis at the beginning) continues only as long as necessary for the unique specification of the individual in question; and we may resort to partial ostension also. In one sense ostensive definition, the *pointing out* of something, is already sufficient to specify it uniquely, but this yields only "knowledge by acquaintance," in Russell's language; although he introduced "knowledge by description" originally to cover cases in which we are not acquainted with the thing described, it turns out in fact that definite descriptions, because of their invocation of relations, generally tell us much more about things—not more immediate details, but more that is of interest to us—than we can learn by acquaintance. One might become acquainted with a bald man and never know that he was the present King of France.

## 53. Carnap and structural descriptions

DESCRIPTIONS, FOR CARNAP, are of three types: property descriptions, relation descriptions, and structural descriptions. The first two are self-explanatory; the third is a kind of relation description, but instead of *naming* the relations into which the thing described enters with other things, one says only what *kind* of relations they are: symmetrical, reflexive, transitive, and the like. What interests Carnap in the *Aufbau* is the possibility of a purely structural *definite* description, which would enable one to specify individuals uniquely. This is crucial for his enterprise, since he wishes to construct an account of the world on the basis of a single relation, "recollection of similarity," which within the constructional system is to be characterized only by its formal properties. The extended example of the Eurasian railroad network, in terms of which he illustrates this possibility, is of the greatest interest for structuralism. The relation of connection by railroad is symmetrical, transitive, and reflexive (the map on page 173 would not do as a railroad map, since *a* cannot be reached from *e*); given a map consisting entirely of double arrows, each point of which corresponds to a point on the Eurasian railroad network, would it be possible to assign the correct names to these points solely from a knowledge of their relations to one another? Perhaps not; it might be that two locations were *homotopic* in the restricted domain of railroad connections. In that case one would move to another domain, say that of telephone connections (just as, if on different occasions identical twins were to present themselves at an aboriginal camp, some other characteristics than kinship would have to be invoked to distinguish them).

What if, after exhausting all the geographical relations known to us, two places on the map are still homotopic? We then move to cultural and historical relations and so on until we have used up all the domains of science. If we still cannot distinguish between them, "then they are indistinguishable. . . . They may be subjectively different: I could be in one of these locations, but not in the other. But this would not amount to an objective difference, since there would be in the other place a man just like myself who says, as I do, "I am here and not there." Carnap's conclusion is that "*each scientific statement can in principle be so transformed that it is nothing but a structure statement*. But this transformation is not only possible, it is imperative. For science wants to speak about what is objective, and whatever does not belong to the structure but to the material (i.e. anything that can be pointed out in a concrete ostensive definition) is, in the final analysis, subjective" (1967:29). The trouble is that "the series of experiences is different for each subject," whereas science requires entities having "a structure which is the same for all subjects, even though they are based on such immensely different series of experiences." Construction theory is to show how, from the idiosyncrasy of subjective experience, a common inter-subjective reality is to be generated.

Success in this would amount to identifying the structural constants of the human mind. But the later constructional stages in the *Aufbau* were merely sketched, and although in his preface to the 1961 reissue Carnap says that he still agrees with the "essential features of the method employed" (1967:v), he in fact abandoned very early the attempt to perform the construction on an "autopsychological basis," that is, on elements of the experience of individual subjects, turning under the influence of Neurath to physicalism, in which physical things, with their properties and relations already attached, are taken as primitive. At the same time the comprehensive and systematic character of his work gave way to more local and technical problems of scientific language and of probability. The ultimate goal, of a rational structure of knowledge each element of which would be scientifically justified, was not abandoned, but after the *Aufbau* Carnap followed more closely the principles laid down in the preface to its first edition, according to which each worker was to undertake a limited task within a collective and cumulative enterprise. In this way the emphasis on a total structure was lessened. But the idea that it might be arrived at on a neutral basis, employing none of the presuppositions implied by traditional conceptual frameworks and systems of nomenclature, was at the time an attractive one.

## 54. Wittgenstein on form and structure

IN CARNAP'S LATER work the notion of structure is less central, although it shows up in *Meaning and Necessity* as "intensional structure," a property of designators in terms of which the notion of "intensional isomorphism" is defined (1956:56). This association of the notions of structure and form, which until relatively recently few people were concerned to distinguish from one another (although as we saw in connection with the work of Cassirer in chapter 1 more attention was paid to form, no doubt because of its prominence in Plato and Kant), recalls Wittgenstein's discussion of the subject in the *Tractatus*. This still repays study in spite of the abandonment of the picture theory of meaning. Part of the trouble with picture theories (or mirror theories) may be that they are usually too ambitious; local pictures, small mirrors, may still have much to recommend them.

The aim of the *Tractatus* is of course to discover the limits of what can be said. It turns out that everything can be said about the world defined as the totality of facts, but that nothing can be said about *how* everything can be said about the world. That we say *is* about the world has to be seen, it shows itself (and it shows itself by mirroring the structure of the world — but that is getting ahead of the exposition). "The world is the totality of facts, not of things" (1922:27, 1961:7); things do not make up facts, in the sense of being parts of facts, but by their interconnections with one another they cause facts to be the case. "What is the case . . . is the existence of states of affairs." Here the English translation becomes controversial: Wittgenstein says "*das Beste-*

*hen von Sachverhalten,*" which Ogden renders as "the existence of atomic facts" and Pears and McGuinness as "the existence of states of affairs," neither of which is accurate although Ogden's version is less misleading. "Existence" is philosophically ambiguous, and while there was no reason for Ogden to avoid it the later translators might have looked for an alternative. "State of affairs" is much too general for the notion of an element or unit that Wittgenstein seems to intend by *Sachverhalt.* These apparently minor points are not irrelevant to the eventual meanings of "form" and "structure," since the *Sachverhalten* are what have form and structure in the first instance: "The determinate way in which objects are connected in a state of affairs is the structure of the state of affairs. Its form is the possibility of its structure" (1961:13). Here again the translation (because of its currency I use Pears and McGuinness throughout) says more than the original; Wittgenstein has "*Die Form ist die Möglichkeit der Struktur,*" that is, simply "form is the possibility of structure," so that in fact it is not clear that he intends the *Sachverhalten* to have form, at least not on the level at which objects have form.

Objects (*Gegenstande*) are more or less interchangeable with things; they are what the world is not the totality of, but they are nevertheless indispensable to it. *Sachverhalten* (whose *Bestehen* constitutes the facts of which the world *is* the totality) are defined as "combinations of objects." Once more the translation throws off the sense: *Verbindung* is not adequately rendered "combination," since that suggests that *Sachverhalten* are as it were compound objects, which makes an absurdity of the later claim that "there is no object that we can imagine excluded from the possibility of combining with others." The *Verbindung* in fact seems much closer to the notion of neutral relatedness referred to in the discussion of Carnap, and as if in confirmation of this Wittgenstein goes on to embrace explicitly the total-relation theory outlined there. "If I know an object I also know *all its possible occurrences* in states of affairs" (1961:9, emphasis added). And *this* turns out to be what is meant by form: "The possibility of its occurring in states of affairs is the form of an object" (1961:11). In this light "form is the possibility of structure" becomes perfectly clear, although most commentators seem to have found it extremely obscure.

Structure is the *way* in which objects are connected in a state of affairs ("*wie die Gegenstande im Sachverhalt zusammenhangen*"), and this, in the end, turns out to be what cannot be said. For whatever we say is itself a fact (and here I pass from textual analysis to a freer gloss), having its own structure, which can depict a bit of the world by being isomorphic with it; but this isomorphism cannot be depicted. Wittgenstein conveys it by an example: "A gramophone record, the musical idea, the written notes, and the sound waves, all stand to one another in the same internal relation of depicting that holds between language and the world. They are all constructed according to a common logical plan. (Like the two youths in the fairy-tale, their two horses, and their lilies. They are all in a certain sense one.)" (1961:39) A further ambiguity in the notion of form is apparent here. Wittgenstein does not use the term "isomorphism" — it is part of my gloss — but it is clear that the facts referred to in this passage are thought of as having the same form, indeed he says explicitly that in order for a picture to depict reality it must have a form "in common with reality." But the "form of reality" is hard to interpret according to the definition of "form" given above. Light is thrown on this by his remark that "space, time, and colour (being coloured) are forms of objects" (1961:13), and the suggestion a little later that "being logical"—again, not his own expression, but an interpretation which exploits an implicit parallel with "being coloured"—is a form of *every* object. The "form of reality" then is the possibility of all structures whatever which are logically consistent with one another, just as the form of the various facts (record, musical idea, notes, sound waves) is the possibility of the various structures that can embody it, including the structures of those very facts.

The structures, however, are not identical: two facts can have the same form, but they cannot have the same structure—if this were to happen, they would be the same fact. That Wittgenstein was using the term "structure" in an unfamiliar way is made clear by the puzzled tone of Ramsey's commentary in his critical notice of the *Tractatus*: "It is to be regretted that the above definitions do not make it clear whether two facts can ever have the same structure or the same form: it looks as if two atomic facts [that is, states of affairs in the later translation—Ramsey of course used Ogden's] might well have the same structure, because objects hung together in the same way in each of them. But it seems from remarks later in the book that the structure of the fact is not merely the way in which the objects hang together but depends also on what objects they are, so that two different facts never have the same structure" (1931:271–72). Black makes a similar point in his *Companion*. The distinction between form and structure follows from the radically extensional character of Wittgenstein's enterprise in the *Tractatus*; the world is the totality of facts, each fact independently having its place in this totality, each being a determinate realization of a possibility of relatedness among objects, having therefore its own unique structure.

This becomes even clearer when we move to a consideration of language. For among the facts in the world are propositional signs, and these in their "projective relation to the world" are propositions, that is, perceptible expressions of thoughts, which in their turn are defined as logical pictures of facts. This "projective relation" is an activity on the part of the thinker ("the method of projection is to think out the sense of the proposition"), so that *it* does not appear in the world. The "sense" of the proposition is what it represents; the proposition "contains the form, but not the content, of its sense," that is, once again the *possibility* of the depicted fact, not its actuality. (There can be false propositions.)

Now "what constitutes a propositional sign is that in it its elements (the words) stand in a determinate relation to one another"; it therefore has a structure, and as might have been expected a structure isomorphic to that of its sense. And this structure is the condition of the meaning of the names that enter into the proposition: "only in the nexus of a propositon does a name have meaning." The structuralist theory of meaning adumbrated here is one in which it is asked, of an expression that purports to have meaning, not so much "What is its structure?" as "To what structure does it belong?" The sense of the proposition, and the meaning of the names that occur in it, arise from the circumstance that it and the fact it depicts constitute a pair of parallel structures between which the depicting relation *manifestly* holds. And just as the world is the totality of facts, so "the totality of propositions is language." To each *Sachverhalt* there corresponds an "elementary proposition" that asserts its existence; if facts are what is the case, propositions are assertions of what is the case.

The "general form of a proposition" is given as

$$\overline{p}, \overline{\xi}, N \, \overline{(\xi)} \ (1961{:}119).$$

This means that a particular proposition is to be arrived at by, first, taking the set of all elementary propositions (including those corresponding to possible but not actual facts); second, taking a subset of this set that consists of all those that are values of some propositional function $\xi$ (which selects the merely possible facts); third, negating these (thus leaving only those elementary propositions that correspond to the facts to be asserted). This is what I meant before by a structuralist thesis in exaggerated form: one recognizes in this procedure not only the implicit doctrine of the parallelism of structures, but also the Saussurean (and Humboldtian) doctrine of language as a distributive totality; and yet it seems extravagant to invoke the totality of language in order to assert a single proposition, and the manner of arriving at the proposition seems perversely indirect even if this necessity is admitted. On the last point Wittgenstein has the following disarming comment: "How can logic—all-embracing logic, which mirrors the world—use such peculiar crotchets and contrivances? Only because they are all connected with one another in an infinitely fine network, the great mirror" (1961:99).

And this remark throws light on the other problem as well. It is the total-relation theory once again; while it is possible to make approximate statements with limited and local parallelisms between language and the world (which are, of course, all we have in practice) still in order to *know* an object we must know all its possible relations, in order to know the meaning of a term we must know the proposition in which it occurs, in order to know the proposition we must know all propositions. For each proposition is in a sense about the whole: "A proposition must restrict reality to two alternatives: yes or no. In order to do that, it must describe reality completely." This is not to be taken as a denial—in view of the practical limitations on our capacity and hence the strict impossibility of carrying out such a program—of the possibility of discourse, since that does not in fact *require* knowledge of objects or of meanings, only of the sense of propositions, which shows itself in their structure. "Man possesses the ability to construct languages capable of expressing every sense, without having any idea how each word has meaning or what its meaning is—just as people speak without knowing how the individual sounds are produced."

Propositions are intelligible as wholes; we *see* their sense without necessarily being able to explicate it. From one point of view the theory of language of the *Tractatus* is too restricted in its requirement that this sense should be a fact, but this is not as serious a restriction as it seems, since propositional signs are facts too, so that the sense of a proposition can perfectly well be another proposition. Depicting *reality* (in some non-linguistic sense) is not all that language does, it also depicts other parts of itself. But language is inscribed in reality, and what cannot be depicted by it cannot be part of reality for me. "The world is *my* world: this is manifest in the fact that the limits of *language* (of that language which I alone understand) mean the limits of *my* world" (1961:115). The later Wittgenstein rejected vehemently this "private language" theory, on the grounds that understanding does not involve the inspection, as it were, of some inner state. But the totality of *my* language makes better sense than the totality of language (which will be either inconsistent or empty, depending on the mode of totalization), and although "which I alone understand" is a trifle melodramatic there is clearly a sense in which this totality is idiosyncratic. My world, however, contains among other things other people's language, to the extent that they communicate it to me, and congruence of structure between my propositions and theirs will assure intersubjectivity and the possibility of communication.

I revert now to the claim that structure (in the three associated senses of "having a structure," "occurring in a structure," and "being congruent in structure with . . .") is not just a necessary condition for intelligibility, which might be granted readily enough, but also a sufficient one. This amounts to saying that for any proposition it is enough to see the determinate relation in which its elements stand to one another in order to understand the proposition, that is, to know its sense. No *further* elucidation is required. The proposition shows its sense by means of its structure; "it cannot be given a sense by affirmation." There might it is true be propositions which, having the structure necessary for intelligibility, also had something else that for some people perhaps heightened the feeling of intelligibility, or something of that sort. But this would belong to the domain of the affective, it could not be claimed that in the absence of such feelings the proposition could not be understood. (Such feelings might also be generated by pseudo-propositions whose structure could not be seen or even coherently recovered by analysis; they would not suffice to make such pseudo-propositions intelligible.)

The simple and direct character of the *showing* of the sense of a proposition is emphasized by Wittgenstein's insistence, already alluded to, that "what can be said at all can be said clearly," which together with the well-known final proposition—"What we cannot speak about we must consign to silence" (1961:151)—sums up, as Wittgenstein says in the preface, "the whole sense of the book." The transparency of the intelligible, the ineffability of the mystical: this is Wittgenstein's dichotomy in the *Tractatus*, which he makes not in order to deny the mystical but to prevent our talking nonsense about it. The mystical is not intelligible, it cannot be said, it does not belong to language or to the world; that language can be adequate to the world, in other words that there can be a world and a language adequate to it, apprehended and spoken by a subject who is not himself in the world but is rather its limit—this is what has to be understood rather than spoken. "Feeling the world as a limited whole—it is this that is mystical."

The *Tractatus* itself is, strictly speaking, a piece of nonsense: it appears to try to say what cannot be said. But in fact Wittgenstein's effort is to show something, rather than to say something; to draw attention to the conditions of thought and to appeal to an isomorphism between his thoughts and those of others. "Perhaps this book will be understood only by someone who has himself already had the thoughts that are expressed in it—or at least similar thoughts." The intelligibility of the book becomes a special case of intelligibility in general: things that do not have sense *in themselves* acquire it through their doubling by another structure—my thoughts parallel yours, and we understand each other. There need to be no internal connection between the elements of the structures as long as the external isomorphism holds, since it is that, and not some other more mysterious affinity, which makes the structures mutually intelligible.

# 9
# Meaning in Life, Language, and Philosophy

## 55. Meaning and the signiferous

HOW FAR DOES this intelligibility reach? Is the universe intelligible? Is human life? The search for meaning in life as a whole, or in the universe as a whole, has been a powerful stimulus to philosophical work, whether embarked on out of faith or out of despair. But like the search for the Philosopher's Stone it is a futile enterprise, which has consumed many otherwise productive intellects and still holds out false hope to a distressed world. Not that there is no meaning to be found—on the contrary, it is to be found abundantly in the works of civilization and in the relationships of daily life. But life as such, and the universe as such, cannot properly have any meaning attributed to them. This is not, even so, a reason for calling them absurd— that would be to commit the same error in the opposite direction. They are just not the *sort* of thing to which meaning or lack of it can be meaningfully attributed.

In this section, then, my task is threefold: to justify the claim that meaning is inappropriately attributed to life or the universe; to explain how, if this is the case, so many people have come to devote so much time and effort to the search for this nonexistent meaning; and to offer relief to those who feel that its absence is intolerable. To the first corresponds the question of the nature of meaning and the kinds of thing to which it can be attributed, to the second question of how and where such things may plausibly be looked for, and to the third the question of what human needs are satisfied by meaning and what are the conditions of their satisfaction.

These questions can be answered by a structuralist theory of meaning. I take the recognition of meaning and the cathexis that this involves to be the joint product of two more fundamental processes which I will call respectively *signifying* and *mattering*. Signifying is the defining property of signs and the fundamental mark of the intelligible; mattering is the defining property of value and the fundamental mark of the purposive (or the intentional in an active

183

rather than a merely phenomenological sense). Significance (the potentiality of signifying) can properly be looked for only in *complexes* of signs or of elements that can be read as signs, and for something to function as a sign there must be, as we have seen, a relationship within it between a signifier and a signified (or in a sense looser than the Saussurean a relationship between it and the object of which it is the sign). Significance arises, in other words, within systems of significance, and these always have a double structure. (Recall the conjecture, in chapter 1, that the sense of intelligibility might arise spontaneously out of the matching of structures.)

We may ask whether the systems themselves can properly be regarded as significant, and the answer to this is clearly negative, *if we mean significant in the same sense as complexes of their elements*. They are, rather, what makes significance possible, and that is the force of my use of the term "signiferous" or sign-bearing, in the double sense of yielding significance (as auriferous deposits yield gold) and carrying it (as a crucifer carries the cross). The signiferous system is a condition of significance rather than a case of it. Language as such, for example, does not signify, but it is a signiferous system, since complexes of its elements (words, sentences, texts) can be mined for significance and used by us to convey it. The fact that human beings have language, however, may be significant in a larger context, for example, a theory of cultural evolution. The requirement of duality for signiferous systems can be met in a large variety of ways; the paradigm case, obviously, is the Saussurean matching of concepts and sound images, but a more fundamental one is the matching of praxis with desire in significant action, and the possibilities are almost endless: anticipation and recognition, address and response, and so on. An exhaustive catalogue of signiferous systems and their modes of signifying would be equivalent to an exposition of human history and culture.

When we come to meaning proper the second component, that of mattering, must also be included. The roots of mattering lie in the structure of biological needs, and it is in the intelligent satisfaction of those needs that meaning first comes into play. In the case of the matching of a structure of praxis with a structure of desire the proportion of the purposive to the intelligible is very high; as the immediacy of need lessens, the balance of the two components changes, until at an advanced stage of culture or education a very complex structure of intelligibility may be evoked by almost casual purposes. One of the ways in which the meaningfulness of significant activity is maintained is through an intention to pursue the intelligible for its own sake, and in high civilizations this becomes, in literature, music, art, and other forms of creative activity, the dominant exercise of meaning.

## 56. The delusion of global meaning

IT IS CHARACTERISTIC of signiferous systems on the one hand that they are capable of extension and on the other that they are activated only partially in any episode of meaningful discourse or reflection. And it is characteristic of mattering that the satisfaction of purposes or needs is recurrent—that once a resolution is reached a new episode begins, indeed that human life consists of a series of parallel and overlapping episodes of mattering, and that the absence of an object of concern at some level or other is a pathological condition. These features account for the emergence of the concepts of *universal* significance and *final* satisfaction, which correspond to the putative meaningfulness of life and of the universe as a whole. These concepts, while strictly speaking empty (in that they correspond to no objective content), are very powerful, and once introduced they quickly become dominant. They answer to a human sense of limitation in the face of the infinite, and of despair in the face of death. They are generalizations from particular experiences of signifying and mattering, and result from a natural tendency to such generalization which, in the limited context of inductive reasoning, is a necessary feature of human thought.

It might be argued that there is no harm in the entertainment of these concepts as regulative, since it is admitted that they have stimulated a great deal of philosophical work. But they conceal a danger, and one to which a great part of the human race has succumbed: namely, that once they are available the more limited senses of significance and mattering, from which they have in fact been extrapolated and without which they would have had no force in the first place, come to be seen as dependent on them. The consequences of this shift are double: on the one hand a great deal of zealous and hopeful work goes into the search for the transcendent and the eschatological; on the other, when this search fails and the systems to which it has given rise are discredited by criticism in the light of advancing knowledge, the ground of everyday meaning seems to be destroyed and a "crisis of meaning" (or of value, its affective component) ensues.

The form that this crisis takes varies according to circumstance, but it can be grave if the eschatological and transcendent systems in question have become widespread and constitute conditions of psychological or social stability. The answer to the crisis lies in exposing the idea of meaning, as it applies to life as a whole, or the universe as a whole, for the delusion it is. It is a delusion because it places the appearance of significance where the reality cannot be, namely, in the systems that make significance possible, and because it offers as an object of mattering something that is presupposed by any experience of mattering. The former is inconsistent, the latter only misguided. But exposing delusions is only a reiteration of the crisis if it is not accompanied by positive recommendations, and in a period when in fact global systems of belief, whether in God or his prophets, or progress, or history, or nature, or humanity, do animate the lives and hopes of many people, it can easily be seen as revolutionary and destructive.

It is worth noting, however, that civilization has already survived at least one such trauma, and this may be a source of reassurance as those that have followed it work themselves out. I refer to the abandonment of the medieval view of the centrality of the earth in the physical universe, which was a consequence of the scientific revolution of the sixteenth and seventeenth centuries. It is instructive to see how the new view established itself. The key figure in this history is Galileo, and his critical contribution lay in his mechanics rather than in his astronomy: it was in the exact but modest working out of limited and local structural matchings of experimental observation with mathematical formulation that the foundations were laid for the gradual building up of a more comprehensive science, without succumbing to the lure of absolute totality. If a unified field theory—which would be the equivalent of a systematization of the universe as a whole—is ever arrived at it will be on the basis of this building up and not as a result of extrapolation under metaphysical stress.

The present crisis is no longer scientific but social and political; the question is, what is the counterpart of the Galilean strategy? It is, I think, the adaptation of his notion of local matching to similarly limited episodes of significance and mattering—works of literature, affective relations among individuals, small-scale examples of social organization, scientific theories themselves—as paradigm cases of human achievement that do not require global principles or transcendent guarantees in order to be lived and appreciated as fully meaningful. And this is just what happens in the structuralist work in the social and human sciences with which the first part of this book was concerned. The task of philosophy is to profit from these inquiries while insisting, as I have tried to do here, that the temptation to leap to universal meanings is pernicious although not incorrigible, that such meanings, whether couched in religious or ideological or nationalistic terms, are unnecessary, and that we can achieve all we can hope to achieve without them. It is, in short, to remind the race that its destiny lies and will always lie within the limits of individual human lives and not outside them.

## 57. The life of meaning

THE THEORY THAT meaning arises from the matching of local structural elements of signiferous systems (or of systems that become signiferous by virtue of the disposition of their elements to match when suitably paired) leads to a conjecture that may provide an answer, of a sort, to the problem of the meaning of life. (Of course there is a sense in which any suitably qualified life might be said to have a meaning in the context of a more inclusive system to which it belonged, so that we might reasonably say, for example, that Bach's life was meaningful in the history of music or Fermat's in the history of mathematics, but this seems likely in most cases to be a *post mortem* judgment, and to make it the basis of one's own meaningful activity would seem grandiose.) There is a sense in which the conditions for meaningfulness are built in to the structure of any life that proceeds, as ours largely does, in a linguistic setting; such a life would literally be a life of meaning, an inversion of the formula that promises a far richer yield than any search for the meaning of life.

In the universe of discourse each of us exists as a double syntagma, composed of two parallel, intermittent, usually alternating syntagmata, one of speaking (or writing), the other of hearing (or reading): parallel because they bear as it were a constant relation to each other, accompanying the same body (or the same mind) wherever it goes; intermittent because we cannot be engaged in discursive activity all the time (even though keeping silent, as Heidegger says, is, like hearing, a possibility belonging to discursive speech [1962:204]); usually alternating, because what we say is usually intended for other ears, what we hear usually the product of other voices. (We also hear what we ourselves say, and people have been known under pressure to give meaning to their lives by talking to themselves.) If it were possible, in the case of a single individual, to reproduce this double syntagma in all its detail, this would be not a recounting but a reliving of his life as a discursive being, the limit of "totalization" as Sartre uses the term (1971: I. 7). The concept of totalization is dealt with at length in the *Critique of Dialectical Reason* (1976), but I cite the more recent work on Flaubert because it represents the closest approach yet made to the reconstruction of an individual life. Not that there is nothing more to the individual than his or her syntagma, as we shall see, but it remains the primary route of access and is so recognized, for example, by psychoanalysis (Lacan's "word of the patient").

These lived syntagmata are finite, in that we begin to speak and are ultimately silenced at more or less definite points in time, and heterogeneous, in that the circumstances of their production and absorption are constantly changing. Reading and writing offer, it is true, a partial escape from the first condition, as in recent times do recording devices of other kinds. (I do not wish to dwell on these modes here beyond pointing out that an essential asymmetry, both existential and temporal, enters into them: I always read what somebody has written *after* he writes it, and in his *absence*. Even if he happens to be physically present his presence to me is not the presence of the writing to me nor his presence to it.) What interests me for the moment is the phenomenon of the moment, the episode of communication that our sharing of this particular syntagma represents. Notice that the idea of "communication" does not necessarily entail any passage of content from my thought to yours, only our sharing of *something* in some framework or other. What we are sharing is a bit of discursive speech in the framework of philosophy, and the philosophical questions I wish to raise about it are two: one about its status as discourse, and one about its status as philosophy.

The first question is how, if at all, the exigencies of discourse (or of language in general) limit the possibilities of thought for the individual or of its transmission from one individual to another. To take the second disjunct first, it is clearly necessary, if language is to serve as a channel for transmitting thoughts between A and B, that A and B should speak the same language. But what does it mean for two people to speak the same language? Consider what we know of the acquisition of language. Infants make noises as naturally as they wave their arms and legs; they indulge in what Jakobson calls a "purposeless egocentric soliloquy" (1968a:24) during which they can produce spontaneously all the sounds the human mouth is capable of forming, far more than will ever be needed for an actual language. They do not do this out of any interest in the world but out of a necessity of their animal nature. Then they begin to form words, or rather begin to realize that they are forming words; this discovery appears to overwhelm them, and quite rapidly they lose the ability to produce, at least spontaneously, nearly all the sounds they once produced, including many they will eventually need for their first language. "In place of the phonetic abundance of babbling, the phonemic poverty of the first linguistic stage appears, a kind of deflation which transforms the so-called 'wild sounds' of the babbling period into entities of linguistic value." Jakobson explains this surprising and relatively sudden deflation by pointing out that "arbitrary sound distinctions aimed at meaning. . . require simple, clear and stable phonological oppositions, and they must be capable of becoming impressed on the memory, and of being recognized and reproduced at will" (1968:24). Once the child realizes that it is in the business of aiming at meaning the casual abandon of the babbling period gives way to the much more serious effort of trying to make itself understood, and for this purpose it can at first handle only a few phonemes at a time. These will be a subset of the set of phonemes characteristic of its first language. To the extent that it uses the same phonemes *and aims at the same meanings* as other speakers of the language it may then be said to be speaking the same language.

But how is this second condition to be fulfilled? In everyday practical contexts there is no difficulty about the matter; most expressions will be firmly anchored, semantically or pragmatically, in common objects or habits. But in discourse like this the problem is more acute. What will be acceptable as a solution will depend partly on whether we hold a referential or an intentional view of meaning. Even at a referential level all is not lost—I have already referred to Heidegger and Sartre, who have an objective status (as written syntagmata only, at least for most of us), I am referring to the concrete episode of language use in which we are engaged, and so on. But if we are talking about the transmission of thoughts any checking in referential terms will be extremely difficult. In simple languages, like the one Wittgenstein imagines at the beginning of the *Philosophical Investigations* (1958:3), it is easy enough: there are four terms, "block," "pillar," "slab," and "beam"; A needs, let us say, a slab; being conscious of this need (thinking "slab") he calls out "slab!"; B brings him a beam; the transmission of thought was not successful. But nothing you could say to me after reading these words, supposing us to meet, would tell me as unambiguously as this whether you had understood. Notice that in this case B does not have to say anything in order for it to be clear that he has not understood; as in the case of Heidegger's too-heavy hammer, "from the fact that words are absent, it may not be concluded that interpretation is absent (1962:200)."

Referring, we might say, is a kind of meaning that points at right angles to the syntagmatic axis, so that even a little chopped-off piece of the syntagma standing by itself—the word "slab," for instance—can still refer to its object. That is what makes dictionaries possible. (Translation is a more complicated case of this—a syntagma and its translation are like the sides of a ladder, the rungs like dictionary equivalences, only the rungs are neither regular nor parallel, may or may not have common referents, and so on.) Intending, on the other hand, points along the axis, which is where the vector I referred to at the beginning comes in. Meaning as intention ordinarily accompanies meaning as reference in any live use of the latter (as opposed to labels, signposts, written texts, and so on), but the reverse is not necessarily the case. What corresponds to A's thought of the slab and to B's understanding of it, in intentional discourse that is not referential, is likely to be something fairly complex, with a corresponding risk of slippage between A and B. The question is, though, whether the intermediacy of language offers any hindrance in principle to A's getting the point across. I am inclined to doubt whether it does, but before giving the argument I must settle the prior part of my first question, that of the limits set by language upon thought.

## 58. Meaning in thought and language

THE QUESTION WHETHER language limits thought—as distinct from the transmission of thoughts—is in part a question of priority, in part a question of the reality of a nonlinguistic interior life. (It may have other parts as well.) For Heidegger it is quite clear that language is only one among the items of equipment (*Zeug*) that the world offers to concern: "words are proximally present-at-hand; that is to say, we come across them just as we come across

Things" (1962:201). The child's "aiming at meaning," the λόγος expressing itself, both make use of something ready for the purpose. Language was not invented in order to make speech possible, even though it did in fact make speech possible. Yet there is a sense in which for Heidegger thought has the structure of language from the beginning. "The existential-ontological foundation of language is discourse (*Rede*) . . . discourse is existentially equiprimordial with state-of-mind or understanding. The intelligibility of something has always been articulated, even before there is any appropriative interpretation of it. Discourse is the Articulation of intelligibility" (1962:203). The sequence is from the intelligible to the discursive to the linguistic. There is room for a distinction, however, between the articulation that belongs to the intelligible and the articulation that belongs to the discursive, in that Heidegger uses different verbs to express them (*gliedern* and *artikulieren*); in terms with which I am more comfortable, intelligibility is the defining property of the structure of thought, and only if language is capable of carrying that structure can it be used for the expression of thought, but that does not make the structure of language *identical* with the structure of thought.

Wittgenstein, in the *Tractatus Logico-Philosophicus*, clearly suggests a sense in which the boundaries of thought are more ample than those of language, although his philosophical terminology and Heidegger's lend themselves to a certain mutual misunderstanding. In the Preface to the *Tractatus* he says: "Thus the aim of the book is to set a limit to thought, or rather—not to thought, but to the expression of thoughts: for in order to be able to set a limit to thought, we should have to find both sides of the limit thinkable (i.e. we should be able to think what cannot be thought). It will therefore only be in language that the limit can be set, and what lies on the other side of the limit will simply be nonsense" (*Unsinn*) (1961:3). He clearly means to say that the other side of the limit of language can be thought, although this thought will not have sense. This sounds odd until we realize that "sense" (*Sinn*) for him is something that shows itself only in propositional language, and according to the theory of the *Tractatus* is essentially referential. For Heidegger on the other hand "only Dasein can be meaningful (*sinnvoll*) or meaningless (*sinnlos*) . . . all entities whose kind of Being is of a character other than Dasein's must be conceived as *unmeaning* (*unsinniges*), essentially devoid of any meaning at all" (1962:193), so that for him "sense" must be taken as existential and intentional. This difference once understood, however, agreement does not seem impossible; for Wittgenstein the existential component is simply out of the reach of propositional language, is not in *that* world at all, but is not thereby annihilated: "the limits of my language mean the limits of my world," but "the subject does not belong to the world: rather, it is a limit of the world" (1961:115,117). In the *Philosophical*

*Investigations* he is more ready to entertain the notion of meanings independently of the occasions of their verbal use, but these are still the meanings *of words*, not things that *I* mean. Wittgenstein's focus is on referential language because of the problematic within which he is working, the influence of Russell and Frege, and so on; that he slights the intentional is, in this context, quite understandable. The same could be said, *mutatis mutandis*, for Heidegger's focus on the intentional and his slighting of the referential. Later on, of course, Wittgenstein made up for it, at least to a degree; I do not know if Heidegger did so.

As a last witness on this point I call on the psychologist Hans Furth, who has made a study of the thought processes of deaf children. He concludes that there is a sense in which thought, as objective adaptation, does require the vehicle of language, but that there is also another sense in which thought, as subjective organization, is independent of it. For Furth, the latter sense is prior; if some contingent circumstance prevents the learning of language, that does not necessarily mean that thought may not, in its own way, undergo a certain development, indeed it must already have done so if language is to be learned: "The internal organization of intelligence is not dependent on the language system; on the contrary, comprehension and use of the ready-made language is dependent on the structure of intelligence" (1966:228). Of course in the absence of language the scope of thought is likely to be limited, but the important thing from our point of view is to insist upon the relative independence of the two domains. This means that whatever the limitations of language, a region of thought lying beyond these limitations can always be postulated *at the individual level*, and this is confirmed among other things by our frequent experience of struggling to find words for a thought that has become perfectly clear. And it seems prima facie evident that if the relation between them is as I have maintained, language can place no a priori limitations on thought, even though it may facilitate thought and even at certain levels be indispensable to it. Once thought has as it were made contact with language it can make use of the stability of language, of its order, of its combinatorial possibilities; it can externalize itself in language, criticize itself, remember its former conclusions. None of this suggests any limitation in principle. In so far as thought operates in language, it naturally does so within the limits of language, whatever they are. But what could thought do, without language, that language *prevents* it from doing? "What we cannot think we cannot *say* either," says Wittgenstein (1961:115), but the relationship does not go the other way—in fact he goes on to say "... what the solipsist *means* is quite correct; only it cannot be *said*, but makes itself manifest."

This brings me back to the topic of A's communicating his thought to B—now however perhaps a thought he is unable to express in language

Clearly in some cases at least he *can* get it across; B says, "I see what you mean," and goes on to make a further remark that makes it clear to A that he really has got it. In this case it was obviously not the *language* that A used that meant what he said, and yet he *used* language to mean it. Now language is, once again, what I have called a "signiferous" or significance-bearing system, which not only *yields* meaning but can *carry* meaning from one person to another. *And the referential meaning of the language used for this purpose need have nothing to do, in the limit, with the intentional meaning of the user of it.* There is nothing extraordinary in the notion of a form of encoding that permits, at the other end of the transmission, a decoding and reconstruction of something to which the code itself is not adequate. It is a commonplace that multidimensional objects can be mapped on to line segments, even if when so mapped they do not look like multidimensional objects, or that, over time, transmission channels of limited capacity can be induced to carry messages of much greater complexity than they could carry all at once. Part of the trick in such cases is to send along with the coded message instructions for its decoding. If the code concealed the message completely—if, for example, the communication were communication between two thinkers of *ineffable* thoughts—then we would say that the language had become esoteric. But esoteric communication can perfectly well take place in plain language, and the uninitiated will simply not know what is going on. (There is a well-known story about a convention of humorists who laugh at numbers.)

The relation between language and thought now becomes considerably more complex, and so does the problem of sameness of meaning and hence sameness of language. I need therefore to go back to the point from which I started, namely, to a consideration of the long syntagmata of which this shared syntagma is a part. For just as thought in one sense precedes language (the intentional prelude to speaking or writing—in those cases where it is a prelude, since the situation also occurs in which the thought and the language produce themselves at the same time: "la pensée se fait dans la bouche," as Tristan Tzara is reported to have said), in another sense it *follows* language. When a bit of discourse is completed it leaves behind some trace in the hearer, perhaps only a memory, perhaps some new concept or some new alignment of old concepts, perhaps in rare cases a complete reorientation or restructuring of his system of thought. That system has clearly been constructed, bit by bit, over the whole period of the hearer's life, and is a product among other things of everything he has heard or read, the entire syntagma on the input side. (The input has had other things in it too—seeing and tasting and feeling, and so on—but for present purposes they can be overlooked.) When in time he becomes a speaker, what he says is the product of this complex totality. More or less of it may be involved, of course, in the production of a particular utterance; there is a whole range of cases from casual remarks or almost behavioristic responses at one extreme to considered judgments calling upon our entire intellectual resources at the other. And it is not always easy to tell where on this spectrum a given utterance lies (remember for example Heidegger's discussion of "idle talk") (1962:211ff.).

Of the structure of this system of thought we know surprisingly little. The mind—for it is clearly the structure of the mind that is in question—is what machine theorists call a "black box," that is, an enclosed system whose characteristics can be inferred only from a study of its inputs and outputs. Thus we learn from Chomsky that the system has a kind of proto-structure, a "grammar," from the consideration that, if immersed in a matrix of spoken language, children acquire the ability to form *new* sentences that are syntactically correct. But such structures remain purely inferential if not merely conjectural. I am reminded of a story about Werner Heisenberg (once told in my hearing by Victor Weisskopf), who when puzzling over the status of electrons in the atomic nucleus was sitting in a café across the street from a public bath. Heisenberg is said to have remarked, "They go in dressed, and they come out dressed, but does that mean that they bathe dressed"? So language goes in, and language comes out, but from this it would be unwise to conclude that what is inside has the form of language. What happens, for example, when we read a difficult text several times and finally come to understand it? We are certainly not memorizing the text—it cannot be a question merely of getting its language into our heads. Clearly part of what happens is the establishment of links between what we find in this text and what we have found in previous texts. But this raises a further question, about the effect of the *order* of the syntagma on the input side. We have very little information about this except at the simplest level, for example needing to have read Hegel and Feuerbach before we can make sense of certain things in Marx. But what difference does it make to my philosophical understanding, as compared to yours, that I should have read Wittgenstein before I read Heidegger, while in your case it was the other way round?

Even if such questions cannot be clearly answered it is now possible at least to give some account of how intentional meaning works in cases where the code is inadequate to the message—and in the light of the foregoing I should wish to maintain that, except in contexts of the most exemplary simple-mindedness, this is *always* the case if referential meanings are not also available. Everything depends, in such cases, on the previous content of the syntagmata of the speaker and hearer: if they have enough in common, the meaning *may* be transmitted, if not it *cannot* be. I can hope you are understanding what I write because I believe that over many years we have read many of the same books and articles, or at least similar ones, heard some of the same people or at any rate like-minded people talking about the same or related topics, and so on. We speak the same language and we have also, within limits, had the same experiences.

## 59. The language of philosophy

WE SPEAK THE same language—but what language is it? Here I come to my second question, about the philosophical character of this discourse. The language of philosophy is certainly not our native language, but one we have more or less laboriously learned, beginning from our native language. And yet learning it was not like learning a *second* language, that might have been somebody else's native language, nor did it involve learning a new grammar or even, except perhaps for a few technical terms, a new vocabulary. It was rather learning a manner, a set of linguistic habits characteristic of philosophy. (Even the technical terms are not strictly necessary, indeed in one sense the ability to dispense with *all* such terms may be a characteristic mark of philosophical language.) Can this manner and these habits in fact properly be called a language at all? Well, that depends on how one recognizes a language. There are some interesting phenomenological analogies. Sometimes the deflation spoken of by Jakobson occurs when somebody realizes for the first time that it is *philosophical* meaning he is aiming at—for just as the child does not set out to use words but suddenly becomes aware that he is doing so, so nobody enters upon philosophy deliberately or consciously. Once we were outside its domain; our concerns were not philosophical concerns and our language was not philosophical language. But as soon as we became aware that our language and concerns had become philosophical, we had already been inside for some time. Even for those who are, as it were, led up to philosophy and shown it from the outside, as in formal instruction, the transition to the genuinely philosophical is not experienced but can only be looked back upon as something that must have occurred.

The reason for this is that philosophy, like language, exists integrally or not at all. This is not to say that it all comes into being at once, but that whatever limited philosophical whole comes into being, comes into being "all at once." Acquiring it involves, as I remarked earlier, not an increment in knowledge or competence but a change in modality. The deflation may not last long; beginning philosophers soon realize that philosophy shares another property with language, a direct product of its coming into being "all at once," which is described by Lévi-Strauss as the "excess of the signifier" (1966b:XLIX). Once one linguistic subsystem has been brought under the philosophical modality there seems no limit to what philosophy can attempt; and just as, in the case of language, this leads to the possibility of poetry, so in the case of philosophy it leads to the possibility of metaphysics, in the sense envisaged by Kant when he says: "The light dove, cleaving the air in her free flight, and feeling its resistance, might imagine that her flight would be still easier in empty space. It was thus that Plato left the world of the senses, as setting too narrow limits to the understanding, and ventured out beyond it on the wings of the ideas, in the empty space of the pure understanding" (1933:47). Wittgenstein perhaps has something of the same sort in mind when he speaks of an engine idling, or a wheel's turning when nothing else moves with it (1958:95). And yet, even to accept this comparatively unfriendly description of some of the things philosophers do, we can't spin the wheels just any old way if we expect colleagues to understand us, there is no point in the dove's just going off by itself. The use of language generally presupposes an interpersonal situation, and as Wittgenstein came to see, any such use can have its rules, there can be indefinitely many language games. And philosophy is surely one among these—or rather a whole family of them.

It would be queer to call English a language game, since in it one can at least attempt to make any linguistic move at all. But I think that natural languages and language games share some of the same defining features, so that it is not wholly inappropriate to call the language of philosophy just a language. Philosophical utterance (*parole*) is governed by the conventions of a language (*langue*) just as English utterance is; it is a question of understanding the concept of *langue* in an appropriate way. That is an embarrassing question for some linguists, who find *langue* too metaphysical or transcendent, but if one takes an Aristotelian rather than a Platonic view there need be no difficulty about it. *Langue* is best understood, I think, not as an ontologically mysterious entity but as really exemplified in some set of language uses (*parole*). It is more than the structure of a single utterance, but less than a disembodied objective structure; we build our understanding of *langue* out of a long series of exercises at the level of *parole*, hearing and uttering concrete syntagmata. Mental structures so built can be viewed as so many languages, each providing the grammar of some activity or other, and one recognizes another user of the same language from the fact that this activity is intelligible to him and that his responses are also intelligible. Language then is a function of its *users*, not only speakers and hearers but also readers and writers, since *écriture* in a literate society comes to play a stabilizing (or inhibiting) role. And one will recognize the occasions of the use of a given language from the context, in Wittgenstein's later terms from the form of life in which one is engaged. I can tell from cultural and professional cues when I am supposed to be speaking the language of philosophy, just as I can tell in other circumstances that it would be inappropriate.

I leave aside here the question whether this language is best regarded as a structure or as a set of rules, although I am inclined to think that in this connection my earlier distinction between the two senses of "signiferous" may be helpful—that structures make most sense for static or referential meaning, rules for dynamic or intentional meaning. I leave aside also the question of how on internal evidence—that is, in the absence of professional cues—one might tell of a bit of language use that it was philosophical, although here I suspect that a good deal that passes for philosophy could only be said to belong to *some* special discipline—philology or psychology or linguistics or logic—and would lack the special mark of philosophy, which I take to lie not in any technicality but in a certain critical and self-referential modality.

My main point has been that any discourse of the kind we are practicing must be of extreme complexity, because of the complexities of our separate and contingent discursive (and experiential) histories and the consequent diversity of our minds, and yet that we can hope to communicate with one another, even at a level that looks completely hopeless if we are preoccupied with the limitations of language. But we can never be quite sure that we have succeeded. The ideal community of syntagmata that this would require is out of reach—there is always too little in my experience to make possible a comprehensive understanding of anything you say above the elementary level, always too much to make possible a simple or lucid expression that you could grasp entire. We have always lived too much, or not enough, to bring our worlds into perfect coincidence (that is, I think, one of the features of the temporality of Dasein). What mitigates—often completely—the anguish of this situation is that there can be sufficient overlap to make successful communication all but certain.

# 10

# Mind, Structure, and System

## 60. System building

THE LINK BETWEEN structure and system established stipulatively in chapter 1 suggests that structuralism as philosophy has "systematic" ambitions. Yet the partially overlapping meaning-structures sketched in the foregoing chapter do not seem very systematic; it follows from the view put forward there that even if we manage practical agreement locally we will not be able to trust the matching of our respective structures without recalibrating, as it were, very far from the topical center of our conversation. Two things mitigate this difficulty: first the availability of common discourse in written texts, second the holistic character of language, its "coming into being all at once," and the overall similarity—conjectural it is true—among the mental structures that call it into being. These things however at best extend the scope of the local, they do not reach out to the completeness of system. In this chapter I shall explore the degree to which structuralism has a systematic character by contrasting it with a philosophical position which avowedly has one, namely, idealism.

Systematic philosophy has been generally *dis*avowed as an objective or even as an interest by many professional philosophers whose view of their subject regards it as an activity of analysis rather than of construction. That this disclaimer should have become so common at a time when, in other disciplines, the idea of system was coming more and more into prominence suggests that philosophers and other scholars may somehow have been talking at cross-purposes. The opposition of analytic and constructive modes comes out clearly in the pejorative use of expressions like "system builders," and a glance at the history of the analytic movement makes it clear that the kind of system it sets itself against is typified by the Hegelian system, the System before which Kierkegaard was on the point of kneeling down, flourishing his handkerchief so as not to get his trousers dirty, only to discover that its completion had once again been postponed (1941:98).

That is not, however, the kind of system that systems theorists, structuralists, and the like have in mind when they use the term. They are much

197

less interested in the inclusive or finished character of the whole than in the interlocking and unfinished character of the parts. What makes a set of elements a system is that they function together interdependently; the manner of their interdependence, that is, the set of constraints imposed by each on the others, determines (or is determined by, according to the sense of the analysis) the structure of the system. No element, insofar as it is an element of the system, can be exhaustively described without reference to all the others. In this context there is nothing odd about systematic philosophy's being analytic, or vice versa, but it is no longer a matter of building systems, rather of discovering them. It has turned out in other fields of inquiry, such as linguistics, that the search for systematic interconnections leads to surprising facts about structure, for example, that all natural languages appear to have essentially similar structures; and one of the pivotal hypotheses of the structuralist movement, as we saw in the first part of the book, suggests that the structure of language may be paradigmatic of a whole class of structures, including those of kinship systems, mythologies, bodies of literature, the Freudian unconscious, and so on. This line of thought leads to the conjecture that, since all these forms of systematic organization are the products of human activities that we call mental, the underlying structure of them all may be the structure of mind, that in fact the defining characteristic of mind may be its capacity to produce and recognize such structures.

A philosophical point of view might, of course, be systematic without being structuralist in this strong sense, but the concepts of system and of structure are so closely linked that their separation is more remarkable than their association. It is here that I make contact with the philosophical work of Brand Blanshard. For Blanshard has realized perhaps more clearly than any other recent writer the use and implications of the notion of system in philosophy, and yet the metaphysical outlook in whose service he invokes it is radically different from that of the structuralist movement. In what follows I wish to examine and contrast Blanshard's position and the structuralist one, and in particular to ask whether his evasion of the structuralist consequences of some of his own propositions is deliberate or merely reflects different preoccupations that tend to carry his thought in other channels. For the purposes of this examination I shall concentrate almost exclusively on *The Nature of Thought*, since it is in that work that the foundations of Blanshard's position are laid down and there is little evidence of fundamental change in the later works.

First, then, as to Blanshard's use of system. The two meanings of the term with which this discussion began are both present in his work, but thanks to a distinction of his own they can be separated easily from each other. The distinction is the one he draws between the two ends of knowledge or thought, the transcendent end and the immanent end. "The transcendent end of knowing is the direct revelation in experience of what is also beyond it. . . . The immanent end is to achieve a state of insight that will bring the theoretic impulse to rest" (1939:I.489). It is clear that the transcendent end, pursued with sufficient zeal, will turn out to be systematic in the global, metaphysical sense of the system builders, and indeed Blanshard is avowedly close to Bradley on this point, quoting him at a crucial stage of the argument: "If the reference of my thought, then, is to be released from ambiguity, I must pursue this defining course until, through fixing the relation of the 'what' before me to everything else, I have determined its place in the one real universe. 'In such a Whole each member would be characterized by its own place and function in the system'. . . ." (1939:I.504) Bradley, given the natural speculative reticence of the Anglo-Saxon mind, was comparatively a wilder extremist than Hegel himself, to whom romantic excesses were a familiar part of the intellectual environment. But the immanent end of thought, in any particular case, will be more modest; "ordinary acts of thinking," says Blanshard, are "attempts at realizing in experience a concrete systematic necessity" (1939.II.26), and it is on the limited systematic character of this end that I wish to concentrate.

Before proceeding, however, the legitimacy of this separation must be defended. Blanshard considers the two ends to be intimately bound up with each other: ". . . any attempt on the part of thought to realize its immanent end, however feeble it may be, is also a partial realization of its transcendent end or object" (1939:I.494). The question that must be raised here is the very large one of the acceptability of limited goals for philosophy—not limited goals for some limited exercise of philosophical attention, but limited goals for the enterprise of philosophy in general. And this in turn raises the question of what the goals of philosophy are in the first place. To this no simple and generally satisfactory answer can be given because of the proliferation of activities, professional and otherwise, under the name of philosophy, but in the present context it does not seem inappropriate to revert to the ancient ideal of understanding or even—following Pythagoras and etymology—of wisdom. As it happens Blanshard himself has written a short essay on "Wisdom," in which he distinguishes two components, reflectiveness or the wisdom of means, judgment or the wisdom of ends. Reflectiveness is "the habit of considering events and beliefs in the light of their grounds and consequences" (Edwards 1967:8.323), that is, in their systematic relations to other events and beliefs; judgment is the practical exercise of informed, rectified, and humanized intuition following upon reflection. As to understanding, it is defined in *The Nature of Thought* as apprehending something "as part of a system which is taken to render it necessary" (Blanshard 1939:II.27).

Now apart from the reference to necessity—to which I shall revert later—there is nothing in any of this to suggest a functional role for the transcendent end of thought; its immanent end appears to be quite adequate for philosophical purposes so conceived. "Grounds and consequences" suggests *adjacent* links in a chain of causation or inference; understanding requires *a* system of necessary connections, not *the* system. How then does the notion of systematic *completion*, of a reality *beyond* experience, get injected into philosophy? Here a further distinction is required. One might introduce the notion of a completed system or an ultimate reality as a pure hypothetical, a kind of nonexistent Utopian target, whose function would be to spur thought on to its *maximum* in the way of systematic interrelatedness and adequacy to experience; or one might introduce such a notion as an item of belief, a purported description of something which, while unknowable directly because of the limitations inherent in our condition, still must be considered to exist objectively because without it the order of the world would be inconceivable. Blanshard's theory of knowledge opts uncompromisingly for the second of these alternatives, as is made clear, for example, in his discussion of degrees of truth:

> To think of any object whatever is to think of it in its relations to what is beyond it. There are always some of these relations (it is needless to maintain this at present of all of them) that are so vital to the thing's nature, and therefore to our concept of its nature, that neither could be what it is if cut off from them. Thus our concept can never be adequate till we have embraced these in our thought. And since *we never do grasp them all*, our thought remains inadequate (emphasis added). (1939:II.319)

The notion of essential inadequacy makes sense only in relation to a real objective truth to which our thought cannot attain; it is not that we can always do better, approaching more nearly a virtual limit, but that we never truly succeed, always falling short of an actual standard.

## 61. Local and global systems

IT IS THIS existent ideal that turns Blanshard in the end into a correspondence-theorist rather than the coherence-theorist he claims to be. But that is getting ahead of the argument. We have still to detach the limited notion of system from the global notion by showing how the latter arises out of the former and at what point speculation takes over from argument. It may be helpful to sketch, in the context of a theory of truth, a plausible sequence of steps from a modest analytic concern to the invocation of metaphysical grandeur. Consider the following line of thought: "I know that

$x$" and "I know that '$x$' is true" seem to stand or fall by the same criteria, whatever these may be. This suggests that at the level of knowledge truth adds nothing; like existence it is a reflective supplement, a second-order predicate. What are the rules of its use? In ordinary speech, at least outside courtrooms and classrooms, it has virtually no descriptive use, only a modal one, often although not always intensifying. I tell you that the President is dead; you ask, "Is that really true?" and I reply, "I was only joking" or "I heard it on the radio." To say of an utterance that it is true is to affirm a certain confidence in it on more or less explicit grounds. Note, however, that in the usual way we would enjoy this confidence naturally, we would not call it into question. The question surely arises because of a doubt, or at least a need for reassurance: I intend to take some proposition seriously, to act upon it in a way that may entail consequences for myself and others, which might be grave if it proved false, therefore I take due account of its warrant.

This pragmatic aspect of the question is overwhelming and unavoidable where the *use* of the concept is concerned. It is habitual, however, to distinguish betwen use on the one hand and meaning or nature on the other. What can we learn about the nature of truth from such facts about its use? The most obvious and immediate conclusion is that it must be systematic, that is, that truth and falsity must have something to do with the *interrelatedness* of propositions. The least we can ask of a truth is that it should be such as not to contradict other truths. But how can we possibly be sure of this, since practical compatibility is one thing, essential compatibility quite another? If we try to penetrate to the essence of this noncontradiction, it always hides itself under the practice: if two propositions are shown to be contradictory, one of the two (we do not yet know which) is thereby shown not to be true, but if no contradiction has appeared it is hard to say—apart from inferential relations and so on, if such hold—in what exactly the agreement consists over and above the practical absence of disagreement.

We need, it seems, some objective correlative of truth that will hold its internal relations in place even when they are not displayed in practice. The mutual compatibility—or, as Blanshard would put it, the *coherence*—of the true seems too insubstantial to constitute its essence, so that we come to see it as doubled and sustained by the mutual compatibility of the real. The latter is not only substantial but evident; there it all *is*, coexisting as a harmonious and self-consistent whole—since any contradiction in the fabric of the real would surely betray itself by catastrophic upheavals on a cosmic scale. This is where speculation enters, as is evident from the fact that there can be no conclusive way of deciding between this belief and its opposite, the dialectical view that there *are* contradictions in the real, that we live among natural and historical upheavals, and that these are what provide the dynamics of nature and of history. (This might be called a correspondence-*incoherence* theory.)

How in fact would the existence of a noncontradictory reality help? For Blanshard it serves as the locus of necessity and as the vindication of truth, but again it is not clear that all the necessity we need and all the truth we can acquire might not be just as necessary and true without it. On this point, exceptionally, Blanshard resorts to rhetoric. "It is past belief," he says, "that the fidelity of thought to reality should be rightly measured by coherence if reality itself were not coherent. To say that the nature of things may be *in*coherent, but we shall approach the truth about it precisely so far as our thoughts become coherent, sounds very much like nonsense" (1939:II.267). But here truth has properties that the coherence-theorist cannot allow it without admitting a correspondence theory. "The fidelity of thought *to reality*," "the truth *about it*," are question-begging expressions if the question is of the existence of the coherently real. It would not be past belief, if the nature of things *were* incoherent, that men should consider themselves to be approaching truth precisely so far as their thoughts became coherent—it might on the contrary be thought admirable, an affirmation of the triumph of logos over chaos. It is interesting to note that Blanshard himself entertains the possibility that there might be "surds in nature" (1939:II.264), although he at once goes on to adopt what he calls the "opposite and brighter view" that there are none. Yet to describe this view as "brighter" seems clearly a matter of temperament rather than of argument.

At other times Blanshard seems to suggest that the movement toward systematic completeness is one that, once started, it is *psychologically* impossible to stop.

> There is this peculiarity about the theoretic as opposed, for example, to the aesthetic impulse, that its satisfaction is always and in the nature of the case incomplete. Any partial system, just because partial, must be rejected and transcended; the impulse to expansion will tolerate no arbitrary arrests; its goal is nothing short of a system perfect and all-embracing. The end of the theoretic impulse may thus be said to be system as such, or better perhaps, a system that would include and order all lesser systems. (1939:II.438)

But here again the point seems to be asserted rather than argued. Why not, in fact, be content with a limited system or a set of such systems? The search for total consistency and total completeness has encountered enough obstacles between Zeno and Gödel to make an insistence upon it almost quixotic, and as a matter of practice, by Blanshard's own admission, we always are confined to the partial: "The system we actually work with is always less than *the* whole. . . . And for all of us, except in rare moments, the interest in truth is satisfied by exercise within these limits" (1939:II.271). Ah, but those rare moments! One would not, I agree, wish to deprive anybody of them; it is no doubt good for all of us to have the experience of throwing our tins of tobacco into the air in Trinity Lane; but at the same time it would be rash to see in an occasional dissatisfaction with the limited any grounds for asserting the existence of what lies beyond it as a matter of fact. This caution does not condemn us, as Blanshard fears, to the identification of the end of thought with some *particular* partial system. Its end may still be to get the bits and pieces of our knowledge into the best systematic order it can, but it need not reject partial systems in cases where transcending them proves impossible.

The trouble of course is that the necessity encountered in partial systems can be at best a local necessity, and this for Blanshard is as bad as having no necessity at all. He holds firmly to the view that there is not the slightest play or slack in the system of the world, that the internal necessary connection of events as of propositions is absolutely tight; and this iron rigidity is the only possible model for the necessity at which, in his view, thought always aims. Even at great distances of space and time the whole fabric of the universe reacts to the most insignificant episode, as this passage from *Reason and Analysis* makes clear:

> A sportsman is shooting a gun in Yorkshire; a poet is writing a lyric in Bloomsbury; these events are different and seemingly unrelated. Both men however had ancestors who came over with the Conqueror, and it is safe to say that except for the Conqueror's action, neither would be where he is or doing what he is. . . . Cancel the act of shooting, and you are committed to cancelling with it the sequence of causes that led up to it, including the action of the Conqueror, and if the Conqueror had not so acted, the sequence of causes leading to the poet's penning his lyric would likewise have to be cancelled. (1962:472)

Plato would surely have seen this as a genuine confusion of the intelligible with the sensible, as a lending of mathematical precision to what could at best be gross and approximate; Aristotle, with his guarded formula "always or for the most part," would have found the claim immoderate; and at the other end of the historical scale everything that science has taught us about the fine structure of the universe suggests that long before the causal chain had been traced back to 1066 a point would have been reached at which, given the complex character of the world at any moment, the distribution of its parts would have been compatible with the poet's writing or with his not writing, the sportsman's shooting or his not shooting, or any combination of these possibilities. Without even raising the vexed question of free action— one answer to which at least would go as far as to maintain that up to the very moment of action the outcome might have been different—it can be argued that a model of the world in which causal chains may, in sufficiently crowded regions, be totally absorbed, is at least as plausible as the one Blanshard espouses. This model would not entail a restriction to *local* effects, but range of influence is not the same as efficacy—a burst of radiation that had come in perfect coherence all the way from the Great Nebula in Andromeda might still be completely dissipated in a few centimeters of lead.

## 62. Necessitation and accommodation

THE VIRTUE OF this model is that it permits us, at last, to deal with systems in effective isolation from one another. Here, then, I end the polemical part of this treatment and move on to deal with some features of Blanshard's theory which, once freed from their associations with absolute idealism, seem to point clearly toward some of the theses of structuralism. The main one has, of course, already dominated the discussion, since it is just the preoccupation with system from which we began, now however to be considered not in the negative light of the metaphysical extremes it may lead to, but in the positive light of the analytic clarity it brings to the problems of truth and knowledge. And its principal contribution to this end is the doctrine of coherence itself. What this doctrine recognizes and does justice to is the self-enclosed character of truth; it insists on finding *within* the system of thought the criterion for the admission of new elements and the warrant for the elements already admitted as true. The strength of this view lies in the fact that all attempts on the part of thought to get outside itself—to experience, or utility, or authority, and so on—encounter an insuperable difficulty at the boundary with the other domain. Structuralists are fond of quoting von Humboldt's remark that we can never step outside the circle of our language except into some other circle of language; the general truth that this reflects is simple and obvious once one has grasped it, but it is surprising how many people still seem to think it necessary to look for transcendent grounds of certainty or of significance.

Blanshard himself, as we have seen, also does something like this, only he looks not for a ground but for a goal; and if—as I believe—the achievement of the goal as he represents it is a forlorn hope, at least its abandonment leaves the rest of the system intact, whereas theories that seek external *foundations* can only collapse if these prove chimerical. The boundary difficulty is that if one is operating inside a system of language or thought, nothing external to the system can be intelligible unless it has already been translated into the terms of the system, that is, internalized; there can therefore be no independent test of its value as external. If I understand only English I cannot tell if the interpreter is correctly rendering what the

Russians are saying, and our collective situation is that we can think only thoughts and have no interpreter. In such a situation it is tempting to think of ourselves as "imprisoned within our own structures," as if the condition of being able to think only thoughts were a hindrance to mind (like a swimmer who imagined that he could swim much better if it were not for the water). But in fact this confinement does not prove fatal; we can think about our own thoughts, and by moving to such second- and higher-order levels transcend the limitations of the lower levels. Also there is plenty of exploration to be done in the interior. First of all, even local regions have their own logical geography; we find that there are anisotropic directions and irreversible paths (which we call probabilities and implications). The most elementary exercise of thought involves systematic interrelations. "We have constructed a little system," says Blanshard, "in which we pass from one part to another, and see how a change in one of them produces effects throughout the system" (1939:II.31). We learn not only to respect the pattern of these effects but also to exploit them in the construction of new arguments.

This last remark opens up a subject to which Blanshard devotes a good deal of discussion, namely, the problem of invention. If we are enclosed within the system, how can room be found for any novelty—how can the system expand if there is no matrix into which it can intelligibly do so? Blanshard, as might be expected, invokes an end, namely, the completion of an as yet incomplete structure, and in this he is in the excellent company of some of the early giants of structuralism. Prince Nicolas Troubetzkoy, for example, believed that the development of phonology had a marked teleological component: "While it is determined up to a certain point by general laws of structure—which exclude certain combinations and favor others— the evolution of the phonological system is at any given moment controlled by its *tendency towards an end*. If we do not admit this teleological element, it is impossible to explain phonological evolution" (1933:245). His colleague Roman Jakobson (as we already saw in chapter 1) considered this to be a mark of a general tendency: "Contemporary ideology," he says, "in its various genetically independent manifestations, throws into clearer and clearer relief, instead of mechanical addition a functional system, instead of the unimaginative comparison of similar cases immanent structural laws, and instead of blind chance an evolution tending towards an end" (1962:110). The question is what, if not an ideal system of systems, can structuralism offer as a representation of this end?

Troubetzkoy and Jakobson do not say, and here it seems to me that Blanshard has come closer to the truth of structuralism than the structuralists themselves. His view, interpreted, to be sure, in a much more restricted way than he ultimately intends, is that the thought and the structure are their own ends. "What if, instead of thought's *having* a purpose, it *is* one?" he asks (1939:II.43). Clearly, if it is, it does not need some *other* purpose in addition. In his analysis of invention he writes: "What carries one to the result is . . . the structure of the system. . . . If anyone reaches a wrong result it always turns out, on review, that he had entered into the system imperfectly" (1939:II.139). The structure, then, is *there* in some sense before the act of invention takes place. Blanshard's account of *how* it is there is ingenious and constitutes his defense against the charge of falling back on a correspondence of thought with reality.

> If we want analogies for the relation of our thought to the system that forms its end, we should leave aside such things as mirrors and number systems and their ways of conforming to objects, and think of the relation between seed and flower, or between the sapling and the tree. Does the sapling *correspond* to the tree that emerges from it? If you say it does, we shall agree that a system of thought may correspond to reality. If, as seems far more likely, you say it does not, and that to use "correspondence" of such a relation is confusing, then you are at one with us in considering "correspondence" a misdescription of the relation we have in mind. (1939:II.273)

This is, I think, another example of Blanshard's tendency to go much further than he needs to in search of explanatory principles; such a view, together with the rigid conception of internal necessary connection, has the effect of locking the incompleted structure into a uniquely determined causal-teleological sequence, and this in turn means that there can be only one solution to any problem of invention and that that solution can never be definitive.

A much more plausible position, and one that is compatible with all but the absolutist components of Blanshard's, would posit the existence, relatively to any incomplete and problematic structure, of a large but finite set of what might be called "potentially intelligible structures," namely, those which, if realized in some vocabulary of language or concepts, would be recognized by mind as significant forms of its completion. (The existential quantifier here is to be interpreted after the manner of the intuitionists rather than after the manner of the formalists—there is no Platonic realm in which these structures exist "ready-made.") Given some partial set of systematically interrelated elements, we can at once rule out whole subclasses of these potentially intelligible structures as incompatible with it, so that the structures that potentially complete it must belong to the group that remains after this process of elimination. To take a simple example: if we are asked to complete a diagram consisting of three sides of a square we can rule out at once all solutions in terms of triangles or circles, but there will remain, in addition to the most obvious case, a whole class of irregular polygons having five or more sides, as well as other open and closed figures, with radiating lines, detached or curved segments, and so on. This example, simple as it is, may be worth pursuing for a moment because of what it shows about the acceptability of proposed solutions. In figure 10.1 (a) represents the problem and (b) through (g) represent the solutions. All the solutions "make sense" except (f), but they make sense in different ways: (b) and to a lesser extent (c) are formal solutions; (d) and (e) are empirical solutions, as in a more ambiguous way is (g)—it might be a fat keyhole, a Byzantine arch, or a loaf of bread. (Even [f] may make a kind of sense to an imaginative perceiver; once the apparatus for the conferring of intelligibility is available almost anything can, given sufficient ingenuity, be invested with it.)

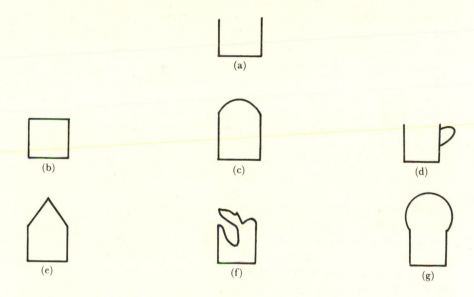

*Figure 10.1*

Now all this will sound like a mixture of formalism, empiricism, and Gestalt psychology, and this is unobjectionable, reflecting as it does the partial truth to which each of these positions has attained; the point that I wish to make, however, is that thought proceeds less by the *invention* than by the *recognition* of intelligible structures, and that the criteria of intelligibility are diverse, depending at any moment on just such a mixture of logic, psychology, and experience. The result of any particular exercise in systematic completion is, then, not so much *implied* as *permitted* by the initial conditions. Here it is possible to underline rather neatly one point of difference between Blanshard's position and what I am representing as the structuralist one. Both agree that the aim of thought is intelligibility, but whereas for Blanshard intelligibility is *necessitation* within a system, for structuralism it is rather *accommodation* within a system. The goal of any particular episode in the life of thought is not, then, some unique and inevitable solution coherent with everything else in the universe, but any one of a number of acceptable solutions coherent with the other elements of its restricted domain.

The striking thing is that in unguarded moments Blanshard talks as if his position were the second rather than the first. We have already seen that he concedes for practical purposes the futility of looking for cosmic wholeness, but a straightforward reading of the early parts of Volume 2 of *The Nature of Thought* produces many other modest and thoroughly acceptable structuralist propositions. "It is evident that thought, even when in the service of action, has an interest or aim of its own. That aim is at understanding the nature of things. And by understanding is meant apprehension in a system" (1939:II.33). "The wholes used in common thought as providing understanding are thus of the widest variety. The one feature they own in common appears to be that they are systems with interdependent parts" (1939:II.34). "That there always is some structure underlying a genuine question and seeking completion in it we may be sure . . . a question is an attempt by a system of ideas to mend a hole in its own fabric" (1939:II. 73,78). But Blanshard does not go on to inquire what the specific structural character of all these systems may be, and by now we can easily explain this omission; if all partial systems are in the end to find their place in one grand system, that fact in itself guarantees their mutual coherence, and there is no need to look for similarities at an analytic level. A corresponding point can be made with respect to the theory of mind: for Blanshard mind is all-embracing, and indeed is in the end equivalent to reality itself, so that its partial manifestations may be structually diverse as long as they are not in contradiction with one another, whereas for the structuralist each system that is a product of mind can be expected to show independently its chief lineaments, and hence to be homologous, under suitable transformations, with all other such systems.

## 63. The multiplicity of mind

THE STRUCTURALIST CONCEPT of mind still needs refinement, I think, and once again Blanshard is helpful in spite of himself. In an attempt to explain how thought can develop even when this means the successive emergence of contradictory beliefs he says: "What the ultimate standard means *in practice* is the system of present knowledge as apprehended by a particular mind. That system changes; hence what coheres with it at one time may not cohere with it at another" (1939:II.272). This suggests a concrete locus for the structure of mind; far from being a Platonic idea it becomes an Aristotelian object, to be encountered seriatim in individuals. Notice that Blanshard is speaking here not just about what some person happens to know, but about "What the *ultimate standard* means in practice" (emphasis shifted). Once more this seems to go far beyond what is needed for the purpose; as a mean between Blanshard's two extremes—the particular and individual and the abstract and universal—the structuralist chooses the historical collective, so that for him the ultimate standard would be those potentialities of mind in general which happen to be *collectively* realized at a given moment of history. And this also makes sense of another view of Blanshard's which, while it sounds radical enough to people brought up on a tradition of first-person empiricism, finds an echo in a good deal of structuralist talk about the unconscious and transindividual aspects of mind. "Since identical laws govern our thinking," says Blanshard, "and an identical end is at work in all of us, since the very existence of universals implies community in our objects, we have argued that the apparent severance between our minds does not in strictness hold and that one identical mind is finding expression through them, (1939:II.180). This "one identical mind" as conceived by the idealist tradition becomes the Absolute, if not God himself; the structuralists, on the other hand, perceive it as a historical product, with all the contingencies that implies, and yet as genuinely surpassing any individual manifestation. The phenomena in which it reveals itself are cultural—language, literature, myth—and it is because all our intellectual activities, philosophical or otherwise, take place inevitably in a cultural matrix that we experience its structural constraints as a kind of necessity. Thus Blanshard remarks: "Inventive thinking, instead of being a tense assertion of the will, seems rather to be a surrender of the will to an order whose structure is quite independent of it, and whose affirmation of it through the mind is very largely so" (1939:II.166); if we distinguish between "mind" and "*my* mind," and interpret "the mind" in this quotation as the latter, that represents very lucidly the structuralist position I have been discussing.

The heteroclitic, contingent, collective entity that mind seems to be according to the structuralist account will no doubt seem paltry in comparison with the ideal purity of Absolute Mind, and the crude coherence of its criteria a poor echo of the refined coherence of Blanshard's theory. Yet as Blanshard himself admits, when it comes to practice the former are realizable and workable as the latter are not. They can stand up under the mixed conditions of the practical application of reason and make intelligible the diversity of mental life as it is encountered in actual populations located at and sometimes isolated in particular regions of space and time.

Still the suggestion of an "independent order" remains unsatisfactory, as indeed does the idea of mind as collective. The leading structuralists of the 1960s may have decentered the world, but their account remained metaphysical: structure was immanent in things, historically rooted yet without assignable origins, something in terms of which surface manifestations could be explained but which was itself essentially inexplicable except, precisely, by the invocation of the human mind in some general sense, certainly transindividual though otherwise not independently specified. We would do better, I suspect, to take seriously the hint about the "particular mind" and ask what that would really follow from a *radical* particularity or idiosyncrasy of mental functioning.

According to this view individual minds would not be manifestations of anything more general except in the sense that they would have to have been formed (how exactly we don't yet know, but this is a merely empirical ignorance and not one of principle) on a common neurophysiological basis genetically determined—"common" in the sense that each organism replicates more or less faithfully the neurophysiology of all the others. The questions that this assumption poses include what it means to be a member of a species and how reliable inductive inferences are from an inspection of one member to a conclusion about another, but I shall assume these to be unproblematic for my purposes. Just as each body has to go through its own embryological and developmental history, resulting in an individual who is approximately like, and at the same time profoundly different from, every other, so a fortiori (given the much greater range of the determining variables) each mind will emerge into consciousness with its own potentialities of intention and representation and will proceed to realize its world idiosyncratically.

My language here needs clarification and what it claims needs defense. I make a number of assumptions that are controversial though I think plausible. I assume first that the emergence of mental attributes is continuous with that of bodily ones, that mind in other words just is a function of a suitably complex organism and is susceptible of as much variation among cases as any complex function is, of more variation perhaps because of its far greater complexity as compared to any nonmental function. One way of putting the first part of this point is to say that there are two mind-body problems, only one of which is problematic: the mind-live body problem and the mind-dead body problem. The latter is a problem because we don't yet wholly understand how mental life depends on merely physical conditions, but the former isn't because mental life comes along with bodily life once the latter is granted—perceiving, thinking, remembering, and so on are just some of the things a live human body naturally does.

I assume further that what is properly called "mind" is conscious; the term derives from a root meaning "to think," and our term "think" derives from a root meaning "to seem." "Think" is as near as English gets to an example of a deponent verb, one that has "put aside" (*ponere* "to put") a passive sense in favor of an active one; the old locution "methinks," whose passive sense is preserved in the equivalent expression "it seems to me," was replaced by "I think," which would be equivalent (if we had such an expression) to "I seem it to me." To think of something is to bring it before the mind—not before the mind's eye, as though there were some interior doubling of *vision*, but just before the mind. (To *see* something is to have it brought before the mind by means of the real eye, which is the only eye the mind has. The theory of perception adumbrated here needs separate development, to be sure, but not in a book on structuralism.)

This "bringing before" involves the polarity of consciousness, the mind before which the thought content is brought and the content itself which is brought before it; mere unconscious processing will not count as an activity of mind properly speaking, even though by courtesy we call it mental as opposed to physical activity (but it is physical and is the sort of thing machines regularly do). The anecdote, recounted earlier in connection with language, of Heisenberg's observation of swimmers going into the bathhouse and emerging from it, fully dressed, and his wondering whether they swam dressed, is once again relevant here—that the conscious apprehension of questions and of the more or less ready answers to them should be an activity of mind says nothing about how the connection between them was established or whether it also was an activity of mind. Of course if my earlier distinction is adopted these distinctions really don't matter much, nor does it really matter that people's minds regularly get credit for some of the things their bodies do.

I assume finally that intention and representation are also among the activities of mind. *Intention*, by which I mean here the exercise of intentionality in the phenomenological sense, is the holding (holding in as it were toward the subjective pole, holding out as an object) of the thought content for the mind's *attention*: intention one might say is a vector, attention a scalar, property of mind. Representation is a special case of intention, in which what is so held is taken to bear a relation of isomorphism (in some sense to be specified) to some state of affairs. It seems to me quite possible to have complex intentional contents that are not representations, and this is a point of some importance in view of the frequent assumption that intelligibility requires a *representational* system as carrier (as for example in Jerry Fodor's *The Language of Thought*, where he says, "Computation presupposes a medium of computation: a representational system," 1975:27).

## 64. Apposition and mental structure

THE CONTENTS OF thought held out intentionally for the mind's attention (or the subject's attention—when thinking, the subject *is* his or her mind, which does not rule out being a body or desire or something else at other times) are normally complex, which implies that if coherent they have a structure, which in turn requires that there should be specifiable relations among their elements. The questions that now arise are how the mind intends this complexity, how it acquires it in the representational case (or in the case of intentional contents that are learned rather than thought for the first time), and how much complexity it can manage. I invoke in answering the first question a concept that on an earlier occasion I adapted from English grammar for another purpose (to explain the abilities of logicians—see Caws 1975:491), namely, that of "apposition." Apposition is the putting and holding of two things together, originally in its grammatical use two terms used syntactically in parallel (in "Zeus, the god of thunder, sat brooding on Olympus" the expressions "Zeus" and "the god of thunder" are in apposition) but in my adaptation just any two thought contents, linguistic or otherwise—a name and a face, a word in one language and its translation in another, an expression and its opposite, and so forth. I take apposition to be a fundamental power of mind that has, in mental terms, no more basic explanation, although it will no doubt sooner or later have one in neurophysiological terms.

It is clearly just this power of apposition that enables us to learn linguistic signs defined in Saussurean terms. The concept and the sound-image are both psychological, their (initially arbitrary) association creates the sign—but who effects the creation? And who sustains the association once it has been effected? No candidate is available except the very subject in (or, to speak consistently with the foregoing account, before) whose mind the sign is intentionally held. In the biblical account of Adam's naming of things one would have to imagine a process of sign creation; most of our language is acquired through sign learning, with the occasional exception of those situations in which we play Adam with respect to pets, boats, and the like. But when we learn the name for something nothing puts the elements of the sign together for us, we have to do it, even though the kind of encouragement we get to do so ("Doggie! doggie!" some kindly adult says, pointing at a picture) would make refusal perverse. Yet perversity is possible, as in a slightly different but usefully exemplary context Lewis Carroll showed in his classic fable, "What the Tortoise Said to Achilles." Drawing a deductive conclusion also requires the exercise of our power of apposition, as in the end do all operations of the mind—it is the elementary structure of mind, and in terms of it whatever complex mental structures we acquire (or whatever mental structure, since there will be a sense in which all of them articulate into one, however bizarre its profile or inconsistent its parts) are assembled and perpetuated.

The power of apposition is in fact the explanatory principle of *bricolage* (and also, one might say in passing, of surrealism). There is no a priori limitation on what can be seen as "going together," whether teeth and wood-peckers' beaks, or umbrellas and sewing machines on operating tables, or chair legs and cornices. Among the marks of postmodern culture are, as I see it, on the one hand willingness to recognize (what has always been true) that contemporary literature and art are an outgrowth from and to a greater or lesser degree a rearrangement of elements of earlier literature and art, of a kind that might well be (but outside structuralist circles usually isn't) called *bricolage*, and on the other an unwillingness to rule out, by means of restrictive canons, any kind of borrowing or juxtaposition of available elements, from whatever language, culture, or tradition.

The mental structure belonging to each individual is built up slowly during the course of experience. The relations that constitute it are determined in three different ways: some are inherited biologically as part of the innate structure of the brain, some are established by individual experience, and some are acquired from a transmitted culture. Of the last the most important group constitute the individual's native language. The contributions from the first two of these sources have presumably been fairly constant over the last several hundred thousand years, and by themselves do not lead to a mental structure of any great complexity or interest by comparison to those made possible by externalization in language or other signiferous systems and transmission from one generation to the next. For these grow cumulatively more complex; the structural capacity of mind turns out to be very much greater than is ordinarily needed for survival in the natural world, and this fact has permitted the construction over time of mythological, social, theoretical, political, literary, and other structures, most of them depending on and being codified in language, the general purpose structure whose existence in a developed form seems to be the specific mark of the human. It is the study of language that has drawn attention most vividly to the structural character of mind: each language constitutes a different system, since each uses a different set of phonological and lexical elements, but the relations that these systems embody seem to be universal and to be capable of presenting most if not all intelligible distinctions human beings are capable of making.

The reason why the development of mental structure is comparatively slow is that, to use the language of communication theory, the capacity of the input channels (that is, the organs of sense) is very small in comparison to the storage capacity of the system. Nevertheless the availability of the code of language, especially written language, makes possible an efficient and rapid internalization of structures once developed, as well as the external storage of virtually unlimited quantities of information (using this word in its technical sense and not restricting it to factual knowledge). By now, therefore, by far the greater part of what we know comes to us prestructured and in linguistic form. The accessibility of this information is what permits people of ordinary gifts to acquire mental structures that would have been unintelligible to their most brilliant predecessors, and its cumulative and self-generating character accounts for the exponential growth of knowledge in the last few centuries (that is, since the invention of printing).

This growth, however, is in one respect misleading. There are more alternatives than before in the acquisition of mental structures, but these structures themselves are not cumulative or even additive at all. Externally stored information belongs only potentially to mind; it must have belonged to a mind when it was formulated and put into storage (that is, in most cases, written down), but it remains inert unless activated by some individual. And there is little evidence that individuals arrive now at more complex mental structures, on the whole, than has been the case for the last several thousand years. The study of primitive languages suggests a relatively constant mental complexity in all known cultures. There is no phylogeny of mental structure above the level of the innate—everything is ontogeny, every individual recapitulates the intellectual history of the species.

The function of mental structures, apart from their constituting the intentional objects of thought and furnishing the subject with a domain of contented activity, is to mediate between stimulus and response, between experience and action, between hearing and reading or speaking or writing. One might distinguish structures of belief (which control assent and assertion) from structures of behavior (which control action and reaction), although they are obviously interrelated. The need for deconstruction arises when the externalization of knowledge has gone far enough to make it likely that individuals will acquire ready-made structures of belief and behavior uncritically, so that instead of reacting to actual exigencies of the physical and social environment they undertake intellectual or religious or political enterprises that spring from factitious sources in language, tradition, and the like. Such enterprises may be innocent, but they may have undesirable intellectual or social consequences, perpetuating conflicts and contradictions that would not necessarily arise if each individual considered each project of action on its merits.

## 65. Instruction and optimum complexity

THE ACQUISITION OF ready-made structures, whether uncritically or not, is part of what was referred to in chapter 7 (section 50) as "instruction." Instruction (which for the second and last time, and for temporary pedagogic purposes only, I will deconstruct into its parts, thus: *in-struction*) I take to be a central technical concept in any developed structuralism; it is what accounts for the replication of structures from mind to mind. Sometimes this is because the structures in question are laid down genetically in each individual, as some linguists (like Chomsky) take the basic grammar of human language to be; in this case they are transmitted, mixed, and recombined, from one pair of individuals to others related to them by descent, via an interior route, a process that I call *endosomatic* instruction. (I find this expression useful even though barbaric from a purist point of view, consisting as it does of a Latin noun with a Greek adjective—a remark I feel compelled to add because of having once been accused of barbarism for the use of the expression "theoretical structure," by a stern philosopher who however himself regularly spoke of "scientific theory" without seeming too sharply pained by it.) For the most part, however, instructed structures are transmitted via an external route, most often linguistic, from one individual to others not necessarily related to him or her, and without automatic mixture or recombination (although the reception of the full structure is likely to suffer attenuation, through inattention, prejudice, misunderstanding, and so on), a process I call *exosomatic* instruction.

These are not the only ways in which mental structure can be acquired; some instruction—though in the case of literate individuals not as much of it, proportionally, as we might think—proceeds empirically as we learn features of the world directly, some we accomplish ourselves through processes of reflection, or the reworking of structures previously instructed from elsewhere. This latter is one of the most crucial mechanisms for the development and rendering coherent of intelligible objects, which have after all to be assembled by us as wholes on the basis of fragmentary and partial episodes of instruction. It was noted in the last chapter that, when we read a text, it is not usually the *words* we remember, and if we read it more than once it isn't to remember them better—rather the text is the occasion for a work of interior construction that is bound to be idiosyncratic.

The result of this work is a complex intentional object that in the case of the literary text I have elsewhere called the "*lekton*," following and extending a Stoic usage. (If I say, "Cato is walking," I invoke, in addition to the referent Cato, who is walking or not, and the assertion that he is walking, which is true or not, the complex "Cato-walking," which my utterance posits as an object of attention independently of the actual Cato or the truth of assertions about him; it is this latter that is called the *lekton* [see Mates 1961:11], and it clearly has the status of what Brentano and Husserl called the intentional object.) The lekton, in the case of an extended text, can be an object of very great complexity. How great, one might ask? And what relation does its structure bear to the structure of the text?

A version of this last question will return to preoccupy us in the next chapter: Can we speak of "the" structure of any object of the human sciences? At this point it seems safe only to say that the structure of the intentional object in question is genetically related to that of the text, since it was reading the text that produced it, although this production was mediated by various structures, linguistic, psychological, and so on, belonging to the reader, so that the production was not simple. Of course this is what happens in instruction generally: thanks to the intentional and representational powers of the mind I can have a version of physics, of Shakespeare, of structuralism itself, on the basis of listening and reading, and although my version will be my own—I'll know some things better than others, apprehend them differently from other people even though we may be able to agree enough for practical purposes (to echo the conclusion of the previous chapter), endow them with connotations and associations perhaps quite unlike anyone else's—it will bear a family relation to those of other people who belong to the same network of instruction.

Some of these things will depend more than others on my acquiescence: physics doesn't need me but structuralism may, the world being self-sustaining but movements of ideas requiring embodiment in scholars and thinkers; the truths of science are independent of me, the truths of criticism not, or not to the same degree. (There is a point of controversy here about the case of physics, since it has become popular since Nietzsche to say that even in the physical sciences there's no fact of the matter; the resolution of that misunderstanding would take another book, but I will say in passing that, once I've chosen a descriptive language and committed myself to objectivity to the extent that I can get it, there is a sense in which the world tells me what I must say about physics, but that this is never the case with respect to criticism.)

But my powers of intentionality have limits, and this brings me back to the question of complexity. In chapter 8, in a discussion of the total-relation program for the specification of an individual, the complexity of Australian aboriginal kinship structures was remarked upon, and it was suggested indirectly that the relative simplicity of the rest of the aborigines' world was what allowed them to invest so much of their intellectual capital in a preoccupation with kinship relations, intellectual capital being limited. This limitation was of course understood to apply to humans everywhere and not just to aborigines. If there is a limit to the complexity we can handle—and some such conclusion seems to be lent weight by results in linguistics that show at what point, for example, embedded structures become unintelligible—then clearly a demand for a high order of complexity in the structures of one domain may force us to deal with some other domain perfunctorily, by means of relatively simple structures.

What I call the "optimum complexity principle" asserts that for a given individual in a given culture at a given historical and developmental moment there will, as a condition of mental stability, be an optimum level (or range) of complexity in the structures subject to intentional animation at a given moment, and that this optimum will be constant or will change only slowly with time. I say optimum rather than maximum because at the price of stress it may be possible for the individual to intend, for a time at least, more complex structures, and also because it is possible for equilibrium to be upset by too *little* complexity. The concept of optimum complexity was first put forward (by me at any rate) in connection with the matching of theoretical and observed complexity in the scientific understanding of the world (Caws 1963:161), after a consideration of the emergence of perceptual simplicity from the matching of complexities in emitter and receiver. Here I extend it to structure in general as a feature of the intentional content of thought.

At the limits of structural overload and structural poverty the breakdown in equilibrium is easily enough understood—sensory deprivation at the lower end, and sensory overcrowding at the upper, are known to be pathogenic. Between these limits the optimum is not a matter of life and death (figuratively speaking) but a matter of comfort. As the world becomes more complex, more of its detail will be sacrificed to a process of smoothing over; in the hierarchy of systems we will choose to operate at the level closest to our optimum even if the elements on that level represent great complexity on the next level below. That complexity we shall be obliged for the most part to ignore, unless we choose to make a specialty of it—at the expense of something else. Thus it becomes easier to deal with genres than with works, with populations than with individuals, with centuries and cultures than with local events over shorter periods of time.

It has often been remarked how few of the writers or works popular or important in a given field at a given time its practitioners in fact remember after a generation or two; the number of names and titles carried by their continuing conversation remains roughly constant, even when the absolute number of contributions to the field is growing more rapidly than ever. In some fields we are already at the stage of abstracts of abstracts. What drives the optimum complexity principle, of which these phenomena are confirming instances, is the fact that in the end an individual mind has to grasp and intend the structure of the field, and that even exceptional minds do not have capacities much more than an order of magnitude greater than those of their most pedestrian fellows.

There is something at once alarming and reassuring about this—alarming because there are already many things each of us individually will never attend to, already many books that will never be read again, already reams of data *nobody* will ever attend to (although since we can't say which data our future colleagues may *want* to attend to this is no argument against data gathering); reassuring because this limitation will oblige us to rethink the structure of each domain of human knowledge in each generation to preserve both its systematic character and its accessibility to instructed individuals in the next generation. There is of course a risk that a too wide divergence of interests, not to mention beliefs, may lead to practical disaster, as has happened periodically throughout history at the ideological level, which suggests that some thinkers should always be engaged in such rethinking for the domain of human knowledge as a whole.

# 11

# Human Nature and Society

## 66. The distribution of structures

GIVEN THAT EACH individual subject has the intentional power to objectify more or less complex structures, and hence the ability, given suitable instruction, to apprehend the objects of the natural sciences and sustain those of the social sciences, to embody their structure as it were, it remains true nevertheless (1) that no two individuals will embody the structure of the same object in the same way, (2) that some individuals will embody more or fewer (and different) structures than others, and hence (3) that some objects will be structurally embodied in smaller numbers of individuals than others. In a given population nearly everyone will embody a common linguistic structure (common in the sense that in principle there is enough overlap between any two cases to make communication possible, although proposition (1) will still hold), most people except those on the margins of society will embody a kinship structure, many people will embody structures of mythology, literature, and so on, and in some privileged societies some may embody technical structures in various disciplines, self-referential psychoanalytic structures, and so on (though in the latter case the population will probably be given by n = 2).

The fact that populations exist that actually share structures as complex as language or as arcane as some of the more technical disciplines is itself remarkable, and it bears witness to a very long process of invention, transmission, diffusion, borrowing, and so on. In order for this process to have been uninterrupted (since an interruption in cultural transmission means starting again from scratch or—but this would be only a partial interruption—from some lower level of evolutionary complexity than obtained at the time the interruption occurred, so that the mere existence of a complex structure implies a history without radical interruption) there must have been continuously in existence over an extended period of time both a contiguous population of sufficient size and a method for externalizing the structure for purposes of transmission. Since the receiver in the process of transmission is always an individual (who becomes "instructed" with the

219

structure in question), the embodiment of the structure is radically distributive—there isn't somewhere where it exists independently of such embodiments.

This conclusion generates some difficulty with the idea of "the" structure of a language or a discipline. In the first place the structure can't be reduced to the written grammar, even the most up-to-date textbook, these being on the one hand merely elements of the practico-inert and on the other, when animated by subjects, only approximations to the corresponding structure embodied even by the most learned individual in the population. In the second place it can't be identified either with the union or with the intersection of its individual embodiments, the first of these being inconsistent and the second nearly empty (except in the case of small populations under very tight discipline—and probably even then). In fact there is something empty about the notion of "the" transcendent structure of any object of the social sciences, since there would be nobody to embody it, any individual being able to embody only his or her version of what it would be if it existed. (Of course if he or she doesn't realize what's going on that version will be taken to be "the" transcendent structure, whose existence will thus seem unproblematic.)

Pushed to its conclusion, this argument would have to maintain that there is no such thing as the English language, or physics, or *Madame Bovary*, or the United States—there are on the one hand sounds and marks, apparatus, books, flags, buildings and lands, and on the other an inconsistent congeries of individual embodiments of intentional structures thanks to which the individuals who embody them can agree—within limits, but usually enough for their mutual purposes—about the meanings of utterances, the truths of science, the qualities of French literature, and the institutional requirements of nations. And this seems to me a correct account of the matter. It is however sometimes difficult for social scientists who are used to dealing with societies, traditions, trends, attitudes, and so on, as if they somehow had independent reality to embrace this view. An alternative way of putting it that may be somewhat more familiar is in terms of *models*.

## 67. Operational and representational models

IF WE ADOPT the definitions of *system* as a set of *entities* mutually interrelated and interdependent, themselves functioning together as an entity at some higher level of organization, and of *structure* as a set of systematic *relations*, concrete if embodied in an actual system, abstract if merely specified but not so embodied, then the notion of a *model* can be defined as follows: an abstract structure is a model if it stands for a homologous concrete structure, a concrete structure is a model if it stands for a homologous concrete structure differently embodied. By "stands for" I mean that features of the model are substituted for features of the structure whose model it is, for purposes of presentation, or instruction, or explanation, or imaginative variation, or computation, or prediction. There need be no preferential direction of the relationship model/modeled: a theory according to one familiar view is a model of the aspects of the world with which it deals, in that we can work out the behavior of those aspects in theory without having to realize them in practice, in the confidence nevertheless that that is how it would happen in practice; but, on the other hand, a perfectly concrete object (an orrery for example) can be a model for a theory, and so can another theory. To make the structural features of the model central reflects the fact that it stands for the relationships among the entities that constitute the system, rather than for the entities themselves. A model of a brick house may be realized in matchsticks or cardboard; its fidelity to the original will be judged not by its bricklike qualities but by the relative distribution of the walls and roof, the enclosed volumes, and so on.

In one sense, of course, there is no such thing as an abstract structure, since as soon as it is specified the structure is automatically embodied, in two ways: in language and as part of the mental structure of the person or persons who perform or take note of the specification. I take the latter sense to be prior, because the existence of language as a functioning system depends on *its* embodiment in mental structures. Mental structures, while they have their own autonomy, have evolved as they have because of their modeling relation to structural features of the physical, biological, and social worlds. They are what enable us to respond in the complex ways we do, to remember, to intend, to reflect, to deliberate. But it would be a mistake to say that mental structures model "real" structures. They are as real as anything they stand for. There is a sense, of course, in which models are habitually contrasted with real things—a model ship with a real ship, for example—but that clearly does not imply that the model is in any way unreal, only that its functions are limited with respect to those of the full-fledged object: it looks like a ship, but it may not float, it won't carry cargo, and so forth. And there is a spectrum of meanings of the term, even if we look only at this particular aspect of it (leaving aside, for example, the whole domain of theoretical models), that goes from scale model through working model up to the cases—mannequins, women's clothes, automobiles, and so on—where the model is a duplicate, functions and all, of the original or prototype, or a paradigmatic specimen of a class of essentially similar objects. In every case the homology of structure and the "standing for" relation, in one guise or another, are to be found.

We tend, nevertheless, to think of theoretical models as belonging in some special domain, as "supraempirical," and this, while harmless enough, can lead to confusion and has I think done so in a recent debate about anthropological method. I wish now, therefore, to take up the question of the relationship between structure and model as it arises in the work of Lévi-Strauss and Leach. The structuralism of Lévi-Strauss, in contrast to that of Radcliffe-Brown, looks for social structure not among the observable social relations that obtain in a given culture, but at a deeper level that is revealed only through an analysis of variations at the observable level. With characteristic exaggeration he says: "The term 'social structure' has nothing to do with empirical reality but with concepts built up after it" (1953:525); "nothing to do with" is obviously too strong, but the point to stress is that structure is not abstracted from the data but belongs to a model constructed as it were, independently, which under one or another transformation can render "immediately intelligible all the observed facts" about various domains of social reality. A model built ad hoc to account just for one set of observed facts would not be particularly interesting, and the strength of Lévi-Strauss's method has, of course, been its insistence on pushing cross-cultural analyses to their practical limits, in accumulating data on kinship or mythology from as many sources as possible, first- or secondhand.

The trouble is that in the text last quoted Lévi-Strauss goes on to describe a structure as a kind of model, rather than a model as a kind of structure. This has the virtue of giving a carefully restricted sense to the term "structure," but the drawback of confusing an otherwise clear terminology; it has led to a good deal of floundering, some of which is analyzed in a helpful article by Nutini (1970). Nutini describes clearly Lévi-Strauss's distinction between mechanical and statistical models, and discusses Leach's interpretation of these as jural rules and statistical norms. His own conclusions as to the relations between the two seem to me essentially correct. What remains obscure is just how the notions of "model" and "structure" are to be interpreted. Nutini's suggestions are on the right track. I think, but he is still unclear about the status of the model itself:

> I have established that models are supraempirical; that is, we are dealing not with entities that merely represent two different levels of abstraction of the same phenomena but with different kinds of entities. Nor are we dealing with models conceived merely as the logical structure (principles, formulas), in order to explain the raw data of experience or, if you wish, social reality. Leach's statement to the effect that models are "logical constructions" in the anthropologist's mind would lead us to believe this, but I agree with Nadel when he says, "I consider social structure, of whatever degree of refinement, to be still the social reality itself, or an aspect of it, not the logic behind it." This

position in no way contradicts the conception of models as supraempirical, for its only implication is to make models and what they are supposed to explain equally "real," which was my original assumption. (1970:103)

But he then goes on to raise a general methodological question: "While it is permissible to speak of models and empirical data as equally real from an epistemological point of view, if they are two different kinds of entities, how can one explain the other? In other words, how can they be interrelated" (1970:103)? The standard answer to this last question is, as he surmises, provided by the philosophy of the physical sciences: from propositions belonging to the model (the theory) and with the aid of various supplementary propositions, consequences are deduced that are formally identical with propositions belonging to the data, and this deductive relationship constitutes explanation according to one of the leading accounts (Hempel and Oppenheim 1950). But that remains on the level of formal logic, and the case at hand offers an opportunity for a different approach.

I begin from the remark of Leach, which Nutini dismisses, to the effect that models are logical constructions in the anthropologist's mind. I would myself prefer to say that they are just constructions in the anthropologist's head, and that they may be logical or not (logic itself being such a construction, whose properties—consistency, deductive articulation, and so on—may or may not be exhibited by the other constructions contained in the same head). But clearly, if the models are to be anywhere—and there is something disconcerting about their being nowhere, or in a hypothetical and problematic mental realm—then the anthropologist's head is the obvious place for them, having the advantage that they are right there when he needs them. We know that there are structures in his head, which I have called mental structures not because they are made of mental substance but because they fulfill mental functions (remember that a structure is not a set of entities but a set of relations), and if these structures in turn have the relations of homology and "standing for" to the social reality with which he deals then they can properly be called models. The advantage of this approach becomes clear when we realize that the anthropologist is not the only one who has a head—the people who make up the society he is studying have them too, and it may be that a consideration of the structures and models that they contain will throw light on the vexed problem of social structure.

Among the mental structures belonging to the members of a given social group, then, will be some that model various features of the physical and social world in which the group lives. It should be remarked at the outset that there is no reason to suppose that any two members of the group have identical or even similar mental structures; the ontogeny of the brain, in fact, makes it virtually certain that they will not. It is to be expected, however, that sets of roughly homologous structures will be found distributed among the heads, which will account for the ability of individuals to talk to one another and make their way around similar obstacles and so on. These structures will have been formed by experience and education, and they will determine the individual's conception of his world as well as his behavior in it. It may be that the same model controls both conception and behavior with respect to some feature of the world, but where the relationship between the individual and the world is not neutral it is quite likely that these two functions will involve different models. I therefore introduce a first distinction between "operational models" and "representational models": the representational model corresponds to the way the individual thinks things are, the operational model to the way he practically responds or acts.

Since every model is a structure, this implies a duality of mental structure. Such a duality is not surprising; indeed the situation of human learning would lead us to expect a plurality of structures, there being no reason to suppose that experience or its reinforcement comes in neat and exactly repeating packages. In other words, even a single mental structure that functions as a model, of spatial location, for example, may in fact consist of a set of partially overlapping or "quasi-homologous" structures, a family of structures built up from diverse experiences in diverse contexts. (What blinds us to this likelihood is that our representation of what happens in learning or thought tends to disregard differences that seem small or unimportant and to assimilate to one another episodes that may in reality be quite idiosyncratic.) If there are obvious reasons why the experience of some state of affairs should occur under two different modalities, then a double family of structures may be generated. Familiar cases of this are provided by psychoanalytic theory, where some kinds of experience are associated with pleasure but also with fear; the corresponding mental structures may be quite different and the subject may not even be aware of the relationship between them, or of the fact that the mental states they produce are connected to the same external events. Characteristically, one of the structures in question functions as a representational model of the events and the other as an operational model—that is, if asked for his opinion about a certain kind of behavior the subject may give a plausible enough reply, but, if put into a situation where this kind of behavior is exhibited or elicited, he may act inconsistently with that reply.

It is obviously tempting, given this illustration, to suppose that the representational model is conscious and the operational model unconscious, and this is in fact not a bad approximation to the actual state of affairs in many cases. But the matter may be more complex: there seems to be no reason a priori why incompatible mental structures may not coexist in the same head consciously, provided they are not invoked at the same time. Total repression is one thing, a mere disinclination to face the implications of inconsistent beliefs quite another. The difficulty may be, not to get someone to become aware of what he thinks or is doing, but to get him to see that the one has any relation to the other. Something of this sort may account for the confusion that behavioral scientists get into when they rely on the accounts of patients, subjects, or informants. As far as that goes, there may exist a framework within which the two models are compatible, even though on the face of it, and judged from the point of view of an outside observer, they are not. If one of them is to be unconscious, however, it will clearly be the operational one, since an unconscious representational model would be a contradiction in terms. And it will also be the operational model that corresponds objectively to the empirical state of affairs, since the lines of causal determination will go from it to the behavior to beliefs about it, and not in the other direction. Even here, however, the distinction is not absolutely clear-cut, since the representational model may be causally limiting, in the sense that behavior stimulated by the operational model that is too obviously out of line with the representational model may be avoided. ( I overlook certain obvious refinements of this scheme, for example the possibility that there might be two different representational models, descriptive and prescriptive, corresponding to the way the individual thinks things are and the way he thinks they are supposed to be. For the purposes of my argument one is enough.)

I am suggesting that it may be helpful to think of events dealt with by the social sciences in terms of the mental structures that determine them (the operational models) and that determine, through reports, one of the sources of our information about them (the representational models). I have called these structures models because of the (partial) homologies that obtain between them and the events in question and because in both cases the "standing for" relation also holds. In the case of the representational model, this is easy enough to see. As to the operational case, while *representational* "standing for" obviously cannot be expected of it, there is a much stronger sense of this relation that amounts to virtual *constitution*: it is in terms of this model that the mind consciously or unconsciously computes the situation and decides among actions, projecting their alternative consequences; to the extent that the actions are effective, the situation tends to behave as if things in fact are as the model assumes, whether or not it is objectively accurate. (The most familiar case of this is the so-called self-fulfilling prophecy.) What concerns me for the moment is the anthropologist's view of all this. It is his mental apparatus that confronts the social system in question and tries to understand it. He has his own mental structures, some of them belonging to a family of such structures having a relation of quasi-homology to the mental structures of other anthropologists; what makes anthropology a science is just the existence of a professional population whose mental structures (their lexical and propositional sets, where the lexical set, in accordance with the principles of structural linguistics, is arbitrary, and the propositional set carries the theoretical weight) have this relationship among themselves. These mental structures will be models (of the empirical situation with which anthropology deals), and they will clearly be representational models, since they will constitute the anthropologist's best conjecture about what the empirical situation is.

## 68. Explanatory models and social structures

THE EXISTENCE OF scientific (as opposed to commonsense) views of how things are seems to justify, however, a special name for those representational models that satisfy criteria of scientific rigor—I will call them "explanatory models." An explanatory model is always one of the scientists' mental structures; it is never "in" the empirical data nor (unless the native or the informant also happens to be an anthropologist as well) in the heads of the members of the social group being examined. The explanatory model has to take account not only of the empirical data but of the relationships that hold between these and the operational and representational models in those heads, and failure to do this will inevitably result in a misunderstanding of the data. Of course, what the data *are* exactly is not clear from this casual discussion and requires further elucidation, in the course of which one of the fundamental confusions in this domain will come to light. The trouble is that the data are really of two kinds: observations, or records of observations made by the scientist in the field, and protocols of his conversations with informants. These form the "empirical reality" with which Lévi-Strauss claims that social structure has "nothing to do." Such data are obviously not the whole story: the complexity of the events, and, for that matter, the complexity and frequent implausibility of the accounts that are given of these events, invite conjecture about a deeper and very likely unconscious set of determinations, whose roots lie in the psychological and social history of the group and which require reconstruction. If this reconstruction could be carried out it would "explain" what is going on.

The confusion arises between two things that may be thought to have happened if the reconstruction succeeds. On the one hand, the result may be thought to be an explanatory model; on the other, it may be thought to be an objective structure embodied unconsciously in the social group. Lévi-Strauss seems to choose the latter alternative, since what he means by "social structure" is just the model that the anthropologist succeeds in establishing by his variational analyses of data from different groups. (That the model should extend beyond a particular group, and perhaps, under transformation, to all groups, is as suggested the feature of Lévi-Strauss's approach that has given it its strongest appeal.) So we are back to the methodological problem with which we began, that is, of distinguishing reasonably between "model" and "structure." And I think that the terminological stipulations made so far are sustained by the analysis, since without them confusion reigns. What Lévi-Strauss often seems to have done is to uncover the operational models at work in the heads of the natives, as in the case of the Bororo, where the representational model is of exogamous moieties, but the operational model is of endogamous hierarchical classes. *At the same time* what he proposes is, in effect, an explanatory model or, at any rate, part of one. But these two things *must not* be identified with each other, because the operational model is a mental structure in the native's head (or the natives' heads) whereas the explanatory model is a mental structure in Lévi-Strauss's head. And the latter will always be the richer of the two, since Lévi-Strauss, but not the native, knows about other societies with homologous structures, can estimate the effect of the difference between operational and representational models on the native's view of the world, and so forth. The anthropologist's job is never *merely* to characterize the operational structure of a single society (although that may be part of his job and he may spend his entire career on that part), but always to build the structure that will explain that structure and relate it to other structures.

The situation so far can be represented diagrammatically (see figure 11.1). The problematic labels are those in parentheses. "Conscious" and "unconscious" have already been dealt with, so the outstanding problem is once more that of social structure. (Some things, of course, are missing from the diagram altogether—I have deliberately represented the gross structural similarity of the native and the anthropologist, who are both, after all, humans, but I have refrained from speculation about the role of the anthropologist's operational models, conscious or unconscious, and have omitted the obvious fact that he belongs to a society too.) I revert, therefore, to the definition of structure as a set of relations, and raise the question of the possible objective existence of a structure that is modeled by the anthropologist's explanatory model, and which is neither the representational nor the operational model found among the mental structures of the natives. What relations exist objectively, a set of which might constitute an objective structure?

A useful distinction in this connection, which helps to clarify the relations between the natural and the social sciences, is one made by Schneider between the order of nature and the order of law (1970:377). In the matter of kinship there are objective relations, meaning, in this context, those attested by the natural sciences independently of the opinions of those

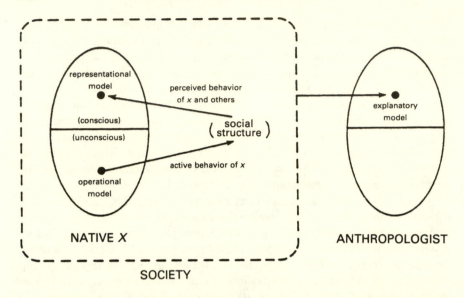

*Figure 11.1*

who enter into them: whatever the Trobrianders may think about the role of the father in procreation, genetics, embryology, and the rest tell us how it all really works. (The philosophically rather casual use of the term "objective" in this chapter is not meant to raise analytical hackles—I do not assume the notion of objectivity to be unproblematic, but I do rely on an unproblematic relative use of the term, according to which, roughly speaking, a view is more objective the more comprehensive the framework within which it is held. My subjective conviction that the stick is bent yields to a (relatively) objective conclusion that it is straight when the framework of my judgment is extended to cover the optics of normal vision, the refractive powers of water, and so on. Scientific theory, as I have pointed out elsewhere (1967:66), has as one of its chief tasks the "rectification of experience," and it does this precisely by enlarging the scope of theoretical understanding. The question of whether it ever arrives at anything like final objectivity is an empty one.) These objective relations always turn out to be essentially causal, and there is good reason to suppose that relations of a causal type are the only natural ones, that is, that the world is causally interconnected in some way independently of our apprehension of this fact, but that all the other relationships we attribute to it reflect our own mental structures. The causal relations we have come to understand are mainly *productive* ones, and this is especially clear in the case of kinship. But what about the others?

In the physical sciences, the noncausal relations are geometrical, or metrical in some other sense (relative weights of elements and so on), or topological or otherwise descriptive; they constitute, as it were, the arbitrary language system within which the propositional (that is, causal) content of the science is expressed. Different geometries therefore transform into one another, different systems of the nomenclature or measurement permit mutual translation. The "facts" of causal relationship, however, are independent of their formulation, or, at any rate, are thought to be so in principle, so that it is worth the effort to reconcile different formulations with one another, look for invariants, and so on. It is assumed that different observers in different places and at different times will find the same causal principles at work and get, *mutatis mutandis*, the same results. But in the behavioral sciences, and especially in kinship studies, the situation is not so simple. It is not a question of establishing causal links; indeed, as Schneider points out, if the relationship between ego and his father, for example, is merely causal and is not also admitted under the framework of law, then it is regarded in America at least as belonging to a "special class" and does not count as a proper kinship relation at all. People (like the Trobrianders studied by Malinowski, among whom presumably the concept of bastardy could have made no sense) may get the causal relationship all wrong and still have an elaborate and perfectly functional kinship system.

But how are the people in such a kinship system *in fact* related? The only answer is that they are related in just the way the system says they are. The legal relations defined by Schneider, of which the marriage relation is a paradigm case, simply do not exist outside the framework of law, broadly interpreted, but within that framework they are real and unambiguous. Here, too, the difference already alluded to between representational and operational models may come into play; relations of duty, of sentiment, of permissible conjugation, may be different in practice from their specifications in indigenous theory. But whereas, in the natural sciences, the final authority in disputed questions is conceded to the empirical data, so that in the end theory has to yield to experience rather than vice versa (even though, through "conventionalist strategems," theory may give experience a good run for its money)—in the social sciences it is often the case that final authority rests with the representational model. In the first instance, it is of course the informant's representational model that becomes part of the empirical data for the investigator. But as we have seen, that does not yield the objective social structure, which is adequately represented neither by the representational nor by the operational models found in the society under scrutiny. It is the scientist's representational (that is, explanatory) model, the theory he constructs to account for the data and their interrelation, that confers objective structure on the system. And the use of "confers" is deliberate, since it would be quite accurate to say that until the explanatory model was constructed the system had no objective structure.

Yet that is not quite the end of the matter. The structure turns out to be "supraempirical," in the sense that it goes beyond what is given in the empirical data, but that does not mean that it is abstract. An abstract structure was said at the beginning to be one that was not embodied; a disclaimer was then entered to the effect that in one sense no structure is abstract. This does not, of course, deprive the term "abstract" of all useful meaning—it is just a reminder that abstraction does not give us entry into some ontologically independent mental or linguistic domain; that it is just one operation among others in the given world of planets and plants and animals, of bodies and brains, an operation that indeed must begin with concrete structures in that world, in order that they may be abstracted *from*. In the definition of the modeling relation, however, it was deliberately stipulated that only one of the terms of the relation could be an abstract structure, and this was because of the difficulty that if no appeal is made to the embodiment in either case the structures become simply the same structure. Abstraction is a relative property—in other words, although every structure, even an abstract one, is embodied in some way or other, in language or in mind (and given a structural rather than a substantial concept of mind the notion of a mental embodiment need not be a contradiction in terms, even though we may not understand the mechanism of such an embodiment), nevertheless for theoretical purposes it may be convenient not to draw attention to the embodiment of the model, in order to concentrate on the properties of the system whose structure is modeled by it; since, after all, it is the understanding of that system that is the goal of the theory.

## 69. Models and mind-dependence

IF, THEREFORE, IN the case of social structure, we allow the operational and representational and explanatory models to be abstract, there must be a structure that they model that is not abstract. We have already seen that it is not satisfactory to suppose that the (abstract) explanatory model models the operational model embodied in the natives' heads, since the structure to which it refers is more inclusive than that model, even though the operational model is a partial model for the structure. It is unsatisfactory for the same reason to suppose that the explanatory model refers to the representational model similarly embodied. The embodiment of the social structure must be sought in the society conceived as a system whose elements are individuals and whose structural relations relate those individuals and not just ideas they have in their heads. Yet have we not claimed, earlier, that the structure is in the anthropologist's head? This is clearly the puzzle with which Nutini grapples when he cites Nadel against Leach: "I consider social structure . . . to be still the social reality itself, or an aspect of it, not the logic behind it " (1970:103). The puzzle can be solved, I think, with a little help from geography and Bishop Berkeley.

Consider the relation "south of," as it applies to Mexico with respect to the United States. Now there is no such relation in nature; it belongs to the representational model of the geographer. Yet once it is specified there can be no doubt that Mexico really is to the south of the United States, in that no other directional relationship of this sort can properly be attributed to it—taking the respective land masses in their entirety it is simply false to say that Mexico is north or east or west of the United States. So the geographical entities in question embody the relationship objectively, even though if nobody had ever thought of directionality in this way there would have been no relationship of this sort to embody. We are driven to this apparently odd conclusion by the consideration that, on the one hand, the representational system determines only the directional grid, not the locations in it of the entities it covers; while on the other, if we assumed the relationship to exist independently of the representational system, we would be committed to the existence of all the relationships that might ever be or have been called for by any representational system now forgotten or yet to be devised. This is a general problem in the theory of relations, and some such position as the one outlined here seems to be required to avoid the postulation of a multiple infinity of instances. In the case under discussion, it means that the society really embodies the relations the explanatory model provides it with, so that the social structure can be thought of as objective and as modeled in various ways by the natives on the one hand and the anthropologist on the other.

What must be remembered is that the social structure, while objectively embodied, is so only as long as it has a representational model. To argue that the structure must be "really there" independently of its representation is to fall into the error of Hylas in Berkeley's *Three Dialogues Between Hylas and Philonous*. In the course of the argument, which concerns the mind-dependent character of physical objects, Philonous the idealist agrees to stake all on one test: if Hylas can conceive of a tree existing "without the mind" (that is, outside it), then Philonous will admit that the thing is possible. Hylas the materialist is delighted—nothing easier, he says, "I do at this present time conceive them existing after that manner" (1954:41). But as Philonous at once points out, he has forgotten his own mind and thus fallen into the trap the question set for him. Now, even in Berkeley, we might feel that this exchange involves a bit of trickery, based on the ambiguity of expression in "conceive of / a tree existing without the mind" as against "conceive of a tree existing / without the mind"; and I certainly do not want to conclude by an affirmation of philosophical idealism. On the other hand, Berkeley was not stupid and there is a serious point to the argument. The point is that, in dealing with mind-dependent entities, one mind is as good as another when it comes to providing a ground of dependence. If trees are dependent on minds, then Hylas's mind cannot be overlooked as a ground of the existence of the tree he is conceiving. The question consistently begged by Berkeley is: what can reasonably be said to be dependent on minds and what not? And as far as we can tell, it is not reasonable to suppose that trees are so. They might, perhaps, be dependent on the mind of God, as Berkeley maintained, but the conjecture is not helpful, since even if true (whatever that would mean), it would still be true that our minds are, again as far as we can tell, dependent on our brains, and that our brains belong to the same order of things as trees; for trees, and brains, to be dependent on *our* minds would involve a logical feat comparable to that of the crocodile that walked up its tail until it came to its head.

But it is by no means unreasonable to suppose that kinship relations depend on minds: ours, or those of other people. Indeed, it might be taken as the crucial mark of distinction between the natural sciences and the social or behavioral sciences that the former deal with mind-independent entities and the latter with mind-dependent ones. This proposition has to be understood in a sufficiently qualified way if it is not to be misleading—it is, again, not a question of asserting separate ontological domains, or of supposing that minds are in the world *in addition to* brains, as something separable from them. The point may be put differently by saying that the causal sequences studied by the social sciences always pass through heads, while those studied by the natural sciences do not, except in the case of specialized sciences such as dentistry or neurophysiology for which the head counts as just another complex physical object. And it is the complexity of the head that makes for one of the gaps between the physical and social sciences, the complexity not so much of its construction as of its behavior. More important still, though, is the fact that the scientist has one and that science is one of the things that goes through it; this leads to a self-referential dimension in the social sciences that is quite lacking in the physical sciences.

Not, of course, that the social scientist can say anything he likes. He has to take account of what other people have done or said, and there are limits to the freedom of interpretation that he can put upon this material. He cannot claim that people are related in any way unless they are in fact related in some way—causally, legally, or otherwise; and he cannot claim that individuals participated in ceremonies or pronounced formulas that they did not in fact participate in or pronounce. But these things constitute the boundary conditions of his work; inside the boundaries he becomes, as the physical scientist does not, a participant in the determination of the structure he studies. And this is because that structure was, in the first place, a product of minds like his own and will continue in being so only if sustained by such minds; by taking it as an object of inquiry he has lent his own being to it; future investigators who seek to understand it can reasonably be expected to take note of his conclusions as an integral part of the data for their own work. A society is, in the last analysis, nothing except what is said and thought about it, by those who observe it as well as by those who compose it. The residue of physical events—the movements and interactions of persons, papers, artifacts, and natural objects—left when this verbal and mental activity has been taken account of is, without it, meaningless.

To summarize: the social structure is not identical with the explanatory model, since the latter is in the scientist's head and the former is out there among the people who belong to the society in question. Nor is it identical with the representational or operational models in the natives' heads, since there are many of them and they actually do things—marry and care for one another, use names of special kinds, live in the same place or in different places, and so on. But the structure is dependent in one way or another on these models, since without them the relations that constitute it would not exist. Priority goes, in the end, to the explanatory model, as the only one that is in a position to reflect all the relevant relations and to get them right.

The foregoing argument gives rise to a double accusation, on the one hand of idealism because of the claim that social structure is mind-dependent, and on the other of ethnocentricity because of the claim that anthropologists sometimes invent the structures of the societies they study. To deal with the latter issue first: in a complex, populous, and advanced society all the relations required by an explanatory model of the social structure might in fact be instantiated. It would then be intelligible to say informally of this structure that it existed "objectively," *was* in some sense the structure of the society (deep or surface as the case might be, depending on which features of the explanatory model were in question). Even so it would be better to speak of the society's *embodying* the structure, rather than saying that it was the objective structure of the society. In the case of fragmented, sparse, and primitive society, however, in which only some relations are instantiated, I do not think we are justified in speaking of objective structure in this way at all. This is the case (and the only case) in which I suggested that social structure, as objective and complete, might be provided by the anthropologist.

The former is more serious and more fundamental. It is however an accusation I willingly embrace. It will have been clear from the tenor of the discussion in chapter 10 that I have profound sympathies for idealism, even of Blanshard's variety, and find its insights invaluable. Its problem is that it reaches too far and claims too much. My idealism is not a form of Idealism, just as for me mind is not a manifestation of Mind; and my idealism applies to only part of the domain of knowledge, not to all of it. I would claim in fact, without scruple, to be *a materialist in the realm of the natural sciences and an idealist in the realm of the social sciences*. I shall return to materialism in the next and final chapter; here I will try to make clearer the ontological features of social structures that make me regard them as mind- (but not Mind-!) dependent.

If there were no human consciousness in it, the world would be as it objectively is, human culture apart. It would contain real relations of the type I call, collectively and approximately, causal. The problem of the natural sciences is to find a way of expressing those relations. The question is whether the relations dealt with by the social sciences have the same sort of objectivity. My claim is that they do not, because such relations (or at any rate an important class of them) are invented and sustained by minds. Not that something sustained by one mind may not be "objective" to another— the trouble starts when we seek the generality of a scientific account.

If this mind dependence is admitted, then the identity of the corresponding heads becomes crucial. There are two cases: natives' heads, and anthropologists' heads. What the natives do and believe and say constitutes the objective domain of anthropological inquiry. What *relations* can be said to exist in that domain, independently of the inquiry? First, the relations that the natives themselves recognize (which correspond to their representational model); second, the relations they embody in their actions (which correspond to their operational model). If these were all the anthropologist ever dealt with he would only uncover what was already there. But this would be mere description, not yet theoretical understanding. In fact the anthropologist introduces theoretical relations, of which these objectively existing relations are special cases, from which they are deviations, and so forth. It is these *other* relations (corresponding to an explanatory model) that constitute the structure "conferred on" the society in question. The case I envisaged is one in which the natives' representational model is "all wrong"; one might, it is true, want to say that their society "has" the objective structure of their operational model, but since their beliefs about what they are doing are *also* part of the objective state of affairs, and in contradiction with their practice, it seems reasonable to appeal to the explanatory model to resolve this objective contradiction.

The parallel cases of geography and language are instructive. The objective existence of the structure of language, one might say, consists in the regularities of action that constitute speech. That there are such regularities it would be foolish to deny, but they are ontologically unsatisfactory for the linguist's purposes. Objective regularities in the domain of the social sciences (unlike those in the domain of the natural sciences) are partial, discontinuous, and subject to change in time. What *actually happens* when people speak a particular language, or behave in ways characteristic of a particular culture, is a series of brief episodes of utterance or action, intelligible to those participating in them but not obviously forming part of any total structure of language or society. In some cases, it is true, the participants may have a *conception* of such a total structure, but this will rarely be identical with the structure postulated by the anthropologist or linguist. What is gained by saying that the structure, of which these episodes are fragmentary and approximate embodiments, really exists before it is postulated?

The natural scientist, in a comparable situation, has everything to gain, since he believes (and with every reason) in an underlying sameness among the elements that form the complexes he deals with, and an underlying constancy in their behavior. An *approximate* surface regularity leads him, therefore, to a search for an *exact* deep regularity, if I may so put it. (The fact that at an even deeper level the whole thing may be statistical does not affect the argument—one level of indistinguishable entities is enough.) But in the social sciences one thing we know for sure, from obvious facts about human ontogeny, is that the elements (that is, human individuals) are quite different from one another, although they may have approximate similarities arising from common circumstances and experiences. The human use of language does not point to an objective, underlying reality of language; indeed, as Saussure correctly perceived, its reality is *exhausted* by its uses. Saussurean *langue*, as opposed to the empirical reality of *parole*, is for him a property of the "collectivity," but he does not specify how it attaches to or inheres in the collectivity. The only satisfactory answer is that it exists distributively, internalized in the heads of the individual members of the collectivity; as they use language, each of them (to adopt my terminology) has an operational model of its grammar, and those who are educated into an awareness of the linguistic rules they follow, or are supposed to follow, acquire a representational model of it too. But both are idiosyncratic, varying from head to head, although with enough overlap to make communication possible; and their logical sum will be inconsistent. "The language" nowhere exists, in any other sense than the original cumulative one, the totality of acts of speech—the nearest we can get to the objective grammar of the language will be in the best theory of some grammarian: an explanatory model again.

What makes this a hard doctrine is the intuitive sense we all have of the language's being *given*, of its being something more than its manifestation in speakers, having an objective and discoverable order. This sense is especially strong in the case of our own language. But on reflection it is evident that our language was *acquired* (on whatever innate foundation) from a miscellaneous collection of individual speakers, and refined later; perhaps, by the study of some standard text. (The existence of standard texts, like the existence of codes of law, helps in the objectification of social reality.) Language passes from individual to individual rather as, once it has been acquired, its products do. Imagine a story that spread through a community by repeated telling, until it had become common property, with the variations characteristic of stories. Nobody would think of asserting that it had objective existence independently of its being told (and yet an outsider, by telling it better, might give it classical form).

The geographical case is more difficult. The trouble is that Mexico and the United States, Pennsylvania and New Jersey, are themselves cultural artifacts. Of course there are objective relations, spatial and causal, between the land masses in question, but the land masses are not segmented, nor the relations *directional*—these require an interested party, Anglo-Saxon or Polynesian, the taking up of a point of view with respect to the land masses. *This* produces the mind-dependent relation that did not formerly exist. Once one has it, it follows that "seaward" and "eastward" are equivalent as applied to the relation between New Jersey and Pennsylvania (but not between Montana and Washington). And because land masses have an objectivity that kinship structures lack, these relations have an independent and testable correlate, which tends to spoil the example.

What it reminds us of, however, is that the intentional and mind-dependent structure of the social sciences is always to some extent projected on to a perceptual and mind-independent structure given by some available features of the world—land-masses, other people's bodies, sounds, marks, and so on. These are independent of our minds in the sense that the states of affairs that occasion our perceptions would be as they are whether or not we had those perceptions (others might have analogous perceptions, or nobody might). Of course this does not mean that we could ever say *how* they are as unperceived (except possibly in terms of abstract or mathematical structure), since to say that would be to offer an account of a possible perception, but that doesn't mean they aren't *any* way, that nothing goes on in the world in the absence of mind. What mind does is to *add* to the world—and add, it must be said, most of the things that are worth having. But again, to belabor a point perhaps (and yet this seems necessary in view of the sort of misunderstanding that surrounds the issue), these additions are mediated by individuals and realized only by them. This is the point I tried to capture in the last chapter by speaking of the multiplicity of mind, and in the beginning of this one by the notion of structure as distributive.

# 12

# Structuralism, Materialism, and Phenomenology

## 70. Singularity and incompleteness in systematic description

I HAVE ARGUED that structuralism is ideally suited to the analysis of the objects of the social sciences, and that its importance derives from this fact. In this last chapter I want to dwell rather more on the deficiencies of structuralism than on its virtues. The argument will proceed in three stages, like a triptych: in the first I shall argue against the reduction of conscious subjectivity, and in the second against the reduction of material objectivity, in favor of a structuralist paradigm that dissolves the one and ignores the other, while in the third I shall argue for a structuralist approach—subject to the limitations that the first two parts impose.

Among the dramatis personae of structuralism one absence has been striking, namely, that of leading philosophers from the Anglo-American mainstream. But what emerges regularly as one of the principal topics of discussion is something that needs to be treated as a technical issue in philosophy, namely, the status of the subject with respect to language. The subject, however, in spite of the fact that each of us is one, has not been a frequent object of professional attention among our more reputable colleagues. Perhaps the best-known remark about it in the standard literature is Wittgenstein's (in the *Tractatus* 5.631–32), some of which was already quoted in chapter 9:

> There is no such thing as the subject that thinks or entertains ideas.
>
> If I wrote a book called *The World as I found it*, I should have to include a report on my body, and should have to say which parts were subordinate to my will, and which were not, etc., this being a method of isolating the subject, or rather of showing that in an important sense there is no subject; for it alone could *not* be mentioned in that book.
>
> The subject does not belong to the world: rather, it is a limit of the world. (1961:117)

And so on (about not seeing the eye and so on). I shall take this passage as a text (in the old homiletic sense).

The book, *The World as I found it*, cannot mention the subject. But its title seems exempt from this restriction. *Someone* has to say, "If I wrote a book"; someone, were this conditional to be satisfied, would have to write it—not just his obedient hand and arm, whose workings would be accounted for in it, but he himself, the observer of the world as he found it, motivated by his intention to give an account of it. The book would be about the world, not, in the first instance, about the subject, or his observations or intentions; Wittgenstein is certainly right on that point. However as the writer got to the end of the book, and looked around to see that nothing had been left out (I note here that he isn't writing "the world as I found it at time *t*," which would pose other problems but not this one), he would find something new in the world, namely, the book, which would therefore have to end with an account of itself, of its title (who might this "I" be?) and of the sentences it contained (though not of their meanings or their adequacy as an account, since these aren't in the world either). Or rather it would *almost* end with that; it would *really* end, of course, with an account of the fact that it mentioned itself. Or at least that would *very nearly* be the end. . . .

I do not mean this merely as a bit of whimsy in the style of Borges or Calvino, but I want to push it a little further. Suppose an observer to whom the writer of the book is invisible, who watches the text unfold, say on a screen (he's at another terminal, somewhere else in the building). What is he to make of this unexpected difficulty about the ending of the book? He might be excused for suspecting the existence of some singularity in the world, at the place where it is being written—something that prevents closure there, something that stands in the way of systematic completion. No matter how hard the writer tries to complete his account of the world as he finds it, there is always one more small step to take—which generates another, and so ad infinitum. This, as you will remember from the *Postscript*, is what amused Kierkegaard so much about Hegel's System:

> I shall be as willing as the next man to fall down in worship before the System, if only I can manage to set eyes on it. . . . . Once or twice I have been on the verge of bending the knee. But at the last moment, when I already had my handkerchief spread on the ground, to avoid soiling my trousers, and I made a trusting appeal to one of the initiated who stood by; "Tell me now sincerely, is it entirely finished, for if so I will kneel down before it, even at the risk of ruining a pair of trousers (for on account of the heavy traffic to and from the system, the road has become quite muddy)"—I always received the same answer: "No, it is not yet quite finished." And so there was another postponement—of the System, and of my homage. (1941:98)

Kierkegaard uses this systematic incompleteness as an excuse for an eventual argument to faith. Our puzzled observer need not go so far—other strategies are available to him. As a natural historian recounting the world as *he* finds it he might note the appearance of discursive singularities, which he might think of metaphorically as eddies of reflexivity, self-referential regresses, loose ends that won't tuck in, and treat them as a natural kind, called, perhaps, "writing subjects." He might think of them as *produced* by the activity of writing, or of representation, or of the production of significance. Pursuing his inquiry into the production of texts in general, he might find that not all texts contain self-referential turns but that all of them can be shown to have systematic connections to other texts, and this might tempt him into a theory of textual production in which the "subject" part drops out, and the "writer" becomes simply a text's way of making another text.

## 71. The persistence of the subject

THE STRUCTURALISTS SUCCUMBED en masse to this temptation—not without subtlety, I might add, since I do not wish to trivialize the position I have been at such pains to expound, but with the effect of thoroughly decentering the subject, or decentering the world in a stronger sense by removing the subject from it. Barthes, for example, in his contribution to *The Languages of Criticism and the Sciences of Man,* proposed that instead of saying, "I have written" (*j'ai écrit*), we should say, " I am written" (*je suis écrit*), although he was careful to point out that that wasn't equivalent to "someone wrote me" (*on m'a écrit*) (Macksey and Donato 1970:143); elsewhere he speaks approvingly of the fact that in Japan it is possible to have "an act of knowledge without a knowing subject." When Ricoeur characterized Lévi-Strauss's position as "Kantianism without the transcendental subject" (1963:618) Lévi-Strauss seemed quite happy with that description (1963:633); in *Tristes Tropiques* he says, "I exist. Certainly not as an individual" (1955:448). One is reminded of Kierkegaard's Hegelians who had "forgotten, in a sort of world-historical absent-mindedness, what it means to be a human being" (1941:109). The odd thing is that they all spoke and reacted just like ordinary human subjects, with intentions and life worlds, so obviously something else was going on. It was the sort of thing that in another context, no doubt, persuaded Derrida to say, at the beginning of a fairly large book, "This then will not have been a book" (1972:9). In part it was a protest against the anthropocentric, logocentric, egocentric tradition of Western metaphysics.

But it is not so easy—nor perhaps so wise—to get rid of the subject, since it plays an essential role. Let me now revert to the book *The World as I found it*. The writer of that book might have spared the observer all the perplexed conjectures just suggested by resorting to a very simple device that has always been recognized as completely effective for purposes of discursive closure. He might have *signed* the book, and dated it: "Ludwig Wittgenstein, Brixen, August 1918" (I imagine *The World as I found it* as being finished at about the same time, and in the same part of the world, as the *Tractatus*). In this way the observer would know that it was an account of the world as seen by an individual, at a time and from a place. The place is important, not of course geographically (though that's not necessarily *always* irrelevant: the note at the end of Marcus Aurelius's first meditation—"among the Quadi at the Granua"—has the effect of a sudden illumination of his Stoicism, and it is by no means a matter of indifference that Boethius, for example, should have been in prison, or Descartes in Holland, or Austin at Oxford) but because it recognizes the *da* in *Dasein*—the subject has to *be somewhere*, and the world can only be described *from* the place where the subject is. The description can be complete in principle *except* that it cannot contain an account of just the features of that place that constitute it as a subjective vantage point. And the obvious way to supplement this defect is for the subject who occupies this vantage point to acknowledge that that is what it is.

The subject in other words is not just a limit of the world, but also its closure against self-referential deflation. Of course it hardly ever has to invoke itself for this purpose, the ideal of a complete account of the world being remote from its normal discursive practice. Most of the time we can just get on with our books about various bits of the world as we find it (science, philosophy, literature, and so on) without worrying about their limitations, which are indeed a condition of getting the work done. But there is nothing wrong with invoking the subject if we feel like it, to remind ourselves that it's *our* world, experienced and valued from our own point of view. In the rhetoric of Quintilian there was a figure called *subiectio*, the suggesting of an answer to one's own question. I am sometimes tempted to think that in full subjectivity we are able to offer ourselves as the answer to our own question, to consider "subject" and "world" as equipollent categories, and that an inability to do this accounts for a lot of the uncertainty suffered by people in existential predicaments. The search for myself in the world is doomed to failure, but it is seen to be unnecessary when I realize that *here I am*, over against my world, which requires me for its existence just as surely as I require it for mine.

However all this begins to sound like therapy and I will leave it for other occasions. What I wish to conclude from this first segment is that while a discursive account of the world need not mention the subject, such an account can only be rendered by a subject and its systematic incompleteness can only be repaired by acknowledging this. What this amounts to is that the only world I can find is one to which I am always already attached by the line-of-sight vector of my attending and intending, so that I am its indispensable complement (or, if what interests me is its completeness, its indispensable supplement). If I were, like Sartre, to feel this as a hapless standing out into the world I would take an existentialist position, but here I will content myself with a phenomenological one, occupying a point of origin of intentionality. This seems to me minimal, inescapable, and irredeemably subjective.

## 72. The stuff of the world

I NOW DRAW attention to another feature of the Wittgensteinian project, namely, that the writing of a book called *The World as I found it* suggests the antecedent existence of the world I found. In the *Tractatus* that world is already given with propositional structure, which stacks the deck in favor of a picture theory of meaning; in his later work, preoccupied as he was with correcting the errors of that theory, Wittgenstein does not seem to have thought much about the independent existence of the world. All this conduces to some thinness in his ontology, and to a relative disinterest in the question why the world should have been as I found it, rather than some other way. Of course *that* can't be mentioned in the book either, since we don't find explanations in the world anymore than we find subjects there.

The second panel of the triptych, then, assumes that the world as I found it wasn't the whole story. This segment belongs to a philosophical tradition that begins with Ionian science, which sought to account for the complexity of appearance in terms of the properties of whatever stuff it may be that the world is made of—a tradition that in spite of the Tao of physics, the Wu Li Masters, and the anthropic principle, has not been abandoned by contemporary physics. Granted that "matter" is a concept belonging to macroscopic experience, it is nevertheless legitimate, if we generalize Bohr's correspondence principle and remember that macroscopic objects *are* agglomerations of microscopic ones, to think of elementary particle stuff as material. It is certainly misleading to think of it as anything else. Elementary particles, it is true, have complex properties, so that complex mathematical expressions have to be invented to describe their behavior; this however does not mean that they are any the less material. Nothing could be more confused than the notion that the world is at bottom "mathematical," mathematics being only the most general device for simulating the properties and behavior of things in the world. When Galileo said in *Il Sagiattore* that the *book* of nature was written in the *language* of mathematics he was not thereby saying that nature was mathematical. This will eventually get us back to Wittgenstein, and on to structuralism, but the task for the moment is to get materialism in place.

By matter I mean, as I have sugggested, whatever it is the world is made of, with whatever properties it has (note for instance that simple location isn't necessarily among them). Unsatisfactory as that is, it will have to do for the moment; I offer it in the spirit of an anecdote recounted somewhere about the biologist Jean Rostand, who, when asked if he thought mind came from matter, replied, "Of course—but I never pretended to know what matter was." To be a materialist is to be, at a certain ontological level, a monist. Some philosophers, like Russell, have tried to avoid biting the materialist bullet by advocating neutral monism, but there seems little point in that; *materia* in Latin just *meant* the stuff of which things were made, whether timber for houses or ships (a sense preserved in the name of the island of Madeira, where particularly sturdy trees were to be found) or living substance for babies (a sense reflected in *mater* and *matrix*, respectively "mother" and "womb"—in the hylomorphic scheme fathers, it was thought, provided the form of the next generation, mothers the matter; this seems in fact to have been the reason why Greek *hyle* translates into Latin *materia*). So if one is going to believe that there is one kind of stuff, and that it isn't purposive or conscious or merely thought, there seems no reason not to call it matter.

### 73. The insistence of materialism

MATERIALISM I TAKE to be the view that matter is, in one sense, all there is in the world—in the sense, that is, that if all matter were destroyed, nothing would be left: no residue of spirit, or of space, or of possibility. Note that the conversion of matter into energy isn't a problem, or even an option, here— the notorious equivalence is between *mass* and energy. If there were only energy then that would be the matter of the world according to the foregoing analysis; if there were only fields, fields would be. There is some danger of confusion at this point, and Gary Zukav, one of the apologists of the non-objective "new physics," runs into it when he says in *The Dancing Wu Li Masters*:. " . . *physical reality is essentially nonsubstantial*. According to quantum field theory, fields alone are real. *They* are the substance of the universe and not 'matter.' Matter (particles) is simply the momentary manifestations of interacting fields. . . ." (1979:219). It is hard to see how reality can be nonsubstantial when fields are the substance of the universe, and I would obviously prefer to say (supposing the position to be accepted), "Fields are the material of the universe and not particles." But even if matter in its particulate sense were "simply the momentary manifestations of interacting fields" we would have to say it's been a long moment. This is not in the least to belittle quantum field theory, but I do mean it as a reminder that theories don't *replace* what they are theories of: the "ultimate goal" of quantum field theory, according to David Gross, "is a complete description of matter and its interactions" (Lerner and Trigg 1981:804). I prefer "matter" to "substance" because of the sugggestion in the latter term of a separation among properties and what upholds or underlies them.

That out of a state from which matter was absent without residue no world could be generated is to be taken simply as evidence that there never was such a state. "Was" can apply only to former states of the world there is. (I assume here that the Big Bang coincides with the beginning of time, though this isn't an argument I want to get into.) As far as we can tell, all the stuff there ever was in the world is still in it, in one form or another, and all of it is in use now, making up things as they are; tenses are necessary because the world's internal relations change, not because there is any other stuff, or any conjectural absence or diminution or augmentation of the stuff there is, to refer to. But to say that matter is the stuff of the world without remainder does not mean that there is nothing else in it, only that there is nothing that could play the role of a remainder. One doesn't have to be a monist all the way up. In Aristotle's words matter (the "material principle" of the Milesians) is "that of which all things that are consist, the first from which they come to be, the last into which they are resolved" (*Metaphysics* 983b8). As it stands this formula does not rule out the contingent permanence, from now on, of something other than matter, since the final resolution back into it might never occur, at least in the case of some privileged things. It clearly does occur in particular cases: material things, even those that in their prime embodied nonmaterial virtues (intelligence, beauty, utility, goodness of other kinds), do habitually decay into material parts that no longer possess these supplementary properties. It has equally clearly not yet occurred in some cases, otherwise the thoughts about it that we now entertain—themselves manifestly not material—could no longer be thought. Optimism about the permanence of the nonmaterial, though, would I think have to count against a philosopher's being called a materialist. I shall take materialism to involve the further claim that material things and their objective relations (an expression to be clarified in what follows) not only could antedate and survive everything else in the world, but did and will do so.

There is a sense, of course, in which any such claim is unphilosophical or at any rate merely metaphysical if made in its universal sense. What else there might be in the world is an open question. But to take my own existential involvement in the world as primordial for my world is reasonable enough, and I can without difficulty distinguish the material things in *the* world from their nonmaterial virtues in *my* world, even if the existence of my world is a necessary condition for my knowledge of the world. My world will not last; the world will. Shifting from the macrocosm to the microcosm makes possible a more meaningful, and more modest, formulation of the materialist claim: I take my body to be a material thing, whose genidentity can be traced back to the formation of its first cell from two parent cells, and forward to the dissolution of its tissues into other things (although not other material, since I take the stuff of the world, under whatever mutations, to be eternal); to be a materialist is to assert that, whatever nonmaterial feelings or values may mark my life, they are not adventitious, and will leave no remainder when my body is at last resolved into its elements. I may leave behind some material traces (what I now write, for example) which may stimulate future subjects to nonmaterial thoughts, but these will have the same temporary status as my own.

The frequent allusions, in the foregoing, to nonmaterial thoughts, feelings, and values, may seem already to have compromised beyond recovery the initial claim to materialism. But everything hinges on the form of dependence of these things on their material conditions. To begin with, we don't know that they occur anywhere in the material universe away from the thin skin of the minuscule planet we inhabit. We know from observations of disease, intoxication, aging, and death that the material conditions for consciousness are complex and precarious; only the very long history of evolution, and of selection against accident and competition, can explain the comparative regularity with which it seems to emerge and persist in human organisms. We know also from historical and anthropological observations that the conditions for the transmission and decoding of cultural traces are just as complex and precarious; only the very large numbers of individuals involved, and their capacity for instructing one another, can explain the comparatively high rate of survival of the works of culture. Culture in its active (as opposed to its practico-inert) form is distributed without remainder among individual consciousnesses, and each individual consciousness, sustained as it is by a material carrier subject to aging and death, will come to an end. (The conjecture that an individual consciousness might be displaced into another sustaining carrier—perhaps the circuits of a computer, or perhaps something as yet unknown to us—I pass over as empty even if potentially reassuring.) The biological survival of the species, unless it should be physically displaced—to another planetary system, for example—we know to be limited in time by the principles of stellar evolution as applied to the sun. So the survival of culture in any recognizable form seems problematic (and for other reasons as well) beyond a few millennia. But the persistence of matter poses no problem at all, and we cannot even formulate an intelligible account of a sequence of events that would involve its denial.

Well, that may be going out on a limb, if for example it should prove that the net mass of the universe is zero and the whole material world virtual, one half of a colossal and accidental case of pair production. I have deliberately allowed the argument to wander toward the cosmological because, just as I was concerned to stress the inescapable presence of the subject, so I want to stress the inescapable objectivity of the material world, and moreover of its overwhelming magnitude, in space and in time. Of course my world remains domestic; the stars in it are mere points, the past a mere memory, or for the most part a mere conjecture, its material a mere postulate. There is a temptation—succumbed to most dramatically by Hegel—to suppose that because, for us, matter itself necessarily exists as a concept or notion (*Begriff*), the latter must have some ontological priority over it. "Matter," he says, ". . . is not an *existent thing*, but is being in the form of a *universal*" (1977:154). There is of course no ultimately compelling argument for the existence of matter apart from our perception and conception of it, but this is just the generalized problem of the ontological argument: a being cannot be inferred from a thought, unless it is the being of a thought. *All* being therefore, except the being of thought, is hypothetical.

But once we have entered the domain opened up by the power of hypothesis (and it must include everything except what Santayana called the "solipsism of the present moment") the ontological priorities all go the other way. If matter exists, and has the properties that science attributes to it, then we can account for the emergence and survival, in this energy-rich pocket of the world, of beings structurally capable of having thoughts; incredible as the fact of our existence would be, if we weren't compelled to believe it by our actually being here, it has been brought well within the bounds of probability by our present knowledge of the age and size of the universe, the distribution of matter in it, and the chemical composition of the biosphere on the one hand and of genetic material on the other. (All the same it is helpful to remember that people do win lotteries.) But if thought alone exists, the contingent features of this knowledge (as apart from the mathematical necessities to which it conforms) become wholly unintelligible. This asymmetry between the two categories provides a trenchant counterargument to the old Argument from Design: all the conscious thought we know is associated with material objects (animals with nervous systems—I leave aside here also the question as to what might be embodied in computers), depends for its very possibility on the maintenance of complex material conditions, and has arisen only in relatively rare cases, very late in evolutionary development—why then should we maintain that these complex material objects and conditions were the products of conscious thought that antedated the very earliest stages of evolutionary development?

What I have been suggesting here is that our whole life, including the life of thought, is embedded inextricably in a context of materiality, and that the attempt to eliminate the material or reduce it to thought runs into insuperable difficulties. This would seem obvious enough if only on the grounds that even if the material of the world were admitted to be thought (whatever that might be taken to mean), *my* thinking about it couldn't be assimilated to the rest of it, for all the reasons rehearsed in the first segment of this chapter, so that for me it would have the status of material as distinct from my thought. In a way this minimal version of the argument is just the inverse of the phenomenological clincher we encountered earlier, except that instead of saying *here I am* I say *there it is*. As far as that goes, Lévi-Strauss himself would raise not the slightest objection to my insistence on the material; after his acceptance of Ricoeur's characterization of structuralism as "Kantianism without the transcendental subject," he remarked: "I confess that the philosophy that seems to me to be implied by my research is the most down-to-earth . . . I would not be alarmed if somebody were to show me that structuralism leads to the restoration of a sort of popular materialism (*matérialisme vulgaire*)" (1963:652).

## 74. The world of relations

LÉVI-STRAUSS HAS some claim to standing as a scientist; most of the other structuralists would, I suspect, have been relatively indifferent to the question of the objectivity of the material world, inhabiting as they did a domain of signs, enunciations, texts, discursive practices, and the like. Why then have I been at such pains to stress the materialist side of the question? The answer is, for that very reason: the absent-mindedness that led Hegel to forget that he was an existing individual is matched by an absent-mindedness (of which Hegel was guilty too, as far as that goes, along with most other philosophers) that leads people to forget that they are material bodies. Both are forms of forgetting what it means to be a human being. Only an embodied subject, and one furthermore having at its disposal the requisite material complexity (namely some thirty billion neurons suitably arranged and interconnected), can engage in discursive or reflective or imaginative or any other mental activity. I say, "at its disposal," not, obviously, in the sense that the subject could say to itself, "I think I'll fire this neuron," but in the sense that for example reading *is* activating the neural apparatus of the eye and brain, even if the reader doesn't know how it's done. (In a similar way the circuitry of my word processor is at my disposal, and I couldn't engage in this particular form of textual production without it.)

This business of having a brain is so obvious that to insist on it is almost embarrassing, and of course for the ordinary practice of life it is quite proper to forget it, as it is proper to forget the fact that one is a body and a phenomenological subject while engaged in daily pursuits to which preoccupation with them would be extraneous. But in theoretical reflection on matters that involve or depend on them it is not proper to forget these things. The point is quite general, and it is central to my argument. Not only the structuralists, but other philosophers, as well as mathematicians and historians and economists and literary critics and so on, are continually referring to entities—explanations and moral rules and theorems and constitutions and interest rates and genres—that have no existence in the material world, and attributing to them properties and conditions as if they were perfectly objective and freely accessible to other people, when in fact they are personal (though socially learned) constructions on the part of individual subjects with brains, whose apparent objectivity is due to a complex process of replication, involving a long history of experiences and intentions, carried in brains and mediated by other material objects.

And yet most of our life—all of our intellectual life, which I take it for my readers means most of our life—consists in attending to and manipulating just these entities. It is what you are doing now, although to the naïve observer a reader might appear to be doing nothing at all. (I remember once being in the library of Beaubourg in Paris, which is a public place, at a table with other serious readers, all immobile, as you probably are now, when a little girl who happened to be passing tugged on her mother's arm, pointed at us, and said in a voice of genuine perplexity, "Maman, qu'est-ce qu'ils *font?*"—what are they *doing?*) We are living in a world sustained by sheer intentionality, each moreover in his or her own world; all we can be more or less sure that these worlds have in common, apart from a perceptual representation of the page (which is "in common" in the sense that, ignoring sensory aberrations, each representation would prove to be a perspectival transformation of each of the others) is the syntagmatic sequence of the text.

Because these intellectual concerns—which include language and literature and art and culture and law and society and in short everything that falls between the subjectivity of the transcendental ego and the objectivity of the material world—dominate our lives I reserve for them the central panel of my triptych, with which indeed the rest of this book has been wholly concerned. Their ontological status has always been problematic for philosophy—whenever, that is, it has been allowed to become so, for one can quite well do philosophy all one's life and not give it a thought—and has led to various more or less radical proposals, the most misguided and extravagant being Popper's invention of a whole world, which he calls the third world or World III, to contain them (1973:107ff). A slighter and more whimsical proposal was made in passing a generation earlier by Gaston Bachelard, who remarked that if the phenomenon is what appears to the subject, and the noumenon is what there objectively, even if inaccessibly, is, we need a new category which he called the "bibliomenon" to denote the kind of being that things have in books (1951:6). And of course books are the paradigm case of the mediating material conditions of the discursive life. So, having disposed of Wittgenstein's "I" and of the world he found, we are left with the book *The World as I found it*. What sort of thing is it? It is manifestly something linguistic, and that poses the problem of language and brings us finally back to structuralism.

Let me revert to the Saussurean idea of "differences without positive terms." While on the one hand the color of the grass and the color of the poppy are positive terms of the perceptual (and hence the conceptual) difference between them, and the sound "red" and the sound "green" are similarly positive terms of the perceptual (and hence the conceptual) difference between *them*, the association of the color of the poppy with the sound "red" into the linguistic sign "red" is not in itself a positive term of any difference but only acquires its linguistic value in the light of the further association of the color of the grass with the sound "green," and of all the other associations that make up the repertoire of linguistic signs. The poppy couldn't have looked grass-colored, nor could "red" have sounded like "green," but if the contingencies of language formation had come out differently nothing would have stood in the way of our *calling* grass "red" and poppies "green."

The linguistic sign is arbitrary; linguistic forms are invented, and they are capable of undergoing transformations into one another. Generalizing these insights into the farthest reaches of the human sciences has been the business of structuralism. But we need to ask *how* the association of the sound "red" with the color of the poppy gets established and maintained. Who does it? The answer to that must clearly be: everyone who speaks English. Why? Perhaps originally not for any terribly profound reason (structuralists aren't usually Cratylists, although as we've seen it wouldn't make a whole lot of difference if they were), but later on because it was a condition of their being understood, of learning not to get killed at traffic lights, and so on. But how? That is no doubt where the thirty billion neurons come in, although we don't need to know in detail for philosophical purposes. Subjects in their capacity as agents have a talent for apposition, for putting one and one together and remembering that they have done so, or for noticing that things usually go together and remembering that—naming pets, registering likes and dislikes, learning people's names, remembering what plums taste like, and so on—in short for making and learning *relations*.

Saussure, as we have seen, was careful to insist that the linguistic sign is not a relation between a sound and an object but between the conceptualization of a sound (the "sound-image") and the concept of an object. This is because the sign is not something we find in the world but something we bring into in being ourselves. (I may learn the sign from someone else but I have to appropriate and sustain it.) Concepts are things the subject can as it were manipulate intentionally. In the same way the entities that enter into other relations that the subject learns or establishes must have intentional status. Some intentional relations have their origin in perception and correspond, we suppose, to relations that actually hold in the material world, relations that I call quasi-causal. Others, even some of those that are learned (from other people), and especially of course those that are established by the subject in question, do not correspond to anything in the material world, even though they may be learned *via* relations embodied in material objects, such as books, and these I call "mind-dependent" relations. The intentional world of the subject is a ramified structure of relations which as learning and thinking proceed arrives at a very high order of complexity. ("Structure," to go back to the definition at the beginning of the book, just means a more or less complex set of relations.) The education of human individuals, especially in advanced civilizations, involves the rapid internalization of large preformed elements of such a structure; I have called this "instruction" (that is, the construction of something inner) and noted in chapter 7 that because it happens for the most part uncritically the freeing of the subject from misleading structures dogmatically acquired calls for a process of "deconstruction."

The most general insight of structuralism, to recapitulate and summarize, is that *the elements of the human world are constituted out of the relations into which they enter*, in other words by their place in an intentional structure. This goes for kinship, mythology, literature, language, and all the other products of social practice, and it seems to me completely correct. If we think of ourselves, our biological individuality is assured by purely material considerations, and the quasi-causal relations into which our bodies enter are subsequent to our being what we physically are, even though some of them are essential to its continuance. But our social individuality was produced and is sustained only by the relations into which we have come to enter. I am a professor only if the university exists and recognizes me as such, I can pay my debts (or be indebted) only if my credit or my cash are recognized as authentic, I am a father only because there exist other people who are recognized (by themselves among others) as my children.

This proposition could be demonstrated in a thousand ways, but I will recall here only one earlier example, from the domain of kinship, that throws it into sharp relief. Because occupying a place in a kinship structure is a matter of being related in definite ways to other people who occupy neighboring places in it, individuation in such a structure requires that there be a unique set of relations for each person; parentage and birth order will generally serve. As we saw in section 18 there is one familiar situation that strains this requirement, namely, the birth of twins. Now it is characteristic of structuralism that, although it finds similar structures everywhere, it finds them differently embodied, which is why it has work to do (thus the decimal monetary system of dollars and cents played the same structural role in the complex of selling and buying, lending and borrowing, and so on, as the duodecimal system of pounds, shillings, and pence; structural variety is—or was—the spice of life). When structures break down, therefore, one can expect them to do so in different ways. So it transpires that twins, who threaten the structure, have to be dealt with somehow, but the threat is met differently in different cultures; they may as we saw be put to death, or given to the king (thus removing them from the domain of normal relations altogether), or be subjected to an elaborate ritual of differentiation in which each is *given* a unique set of relations.


## 75. Subjectivity and structural materialism

WHAT TENDS TO conceal from us the truth that the being of cultural entities is relational is the fact that so many of them are carried by the material systems of what Sartre called the "practico-inert" (1976:67), in writing and other artifacts like money and costumes and machines and buildings. These things are realizations of human projects, collaborative and cumulative, but each element of every one of them was contrived and put in place by the intentional agency of an individual subject or subjects. Of course the subjects in question may not have meant the whole to come out as it did, and the modifications they made may have been incidental to their purposes at the time. But no other mechanism is available in terms of which the development of language, technology, morals, or philosophy itself can be explained. This reflection confirms our original working distinction between the domains of the natural and of the social sciences, namely, that the former explain events whose causal antecedents do *not*, and the latter events whose causal antecedents *do*, include human intentionalities at some point along the way.

The survival and functioning of the works of language and culture require a population of instructed individuals whose intentional worlds from time to time incorporate them. The important thing to realize is that *each* individual is capable of internalizing and intending *as a whole* any social structure in which he or she operates, and that in some cases this regularly happens. Thus each of us knows a whole English language (I don't for obvious reasons say *the* whole English language, which exists nowhere, not even in the most fully developed manual of grammar or the most exhaustive dictionary), most of us have a whole conception of the families and universities of which we are members, and so on. In some complex cases (the national economy, the tax structure) we are likely to participate with less than total comprehension—and to that degree run the risk of alienation.

What enables us to carry the burden of complexity that contemporary social and professional life demands is, once more, the material equipment with which we are furnished—which, in a sense to be specified, we are—supplemented by the devices for the externalization of structure that human practice has developed, together with the fact that for any given case we don't have to do it all the time, or all at once. We can call in, as it were, by remembering it or looking it up, the appropriate bit of structure, whether it's the bylaws of the department or the meaning of *ousia* in Plato or the original Hempelian schema for scientific explanation, and make it the object first of our attention and then of our intentional activity, applying it to cases, testing its implications, making it the object of "free imaginative variation" after the manner of the phenomenologists. We do this sort of thing most of the time; we are doing it now. It is what the subjects that we are are currently "absorbed in," to use a familiar expression. And this seems to me right; I am wholly identified, now, with this argument, I don't have reserves of subjectivity somewhere that are busy with other things. I'm not always that absorbed, and you may not be now, but at any moment, between what I'm concentrating on and what is in the back of my mind, my subjectivity is wholly accounted for. So I want to say: I am this body, with all its apparatus, including the thirty billion neurons; and in this moment my subjectivity is the animation of a philosophical discourse.

*The subject is the animation of structure. The structure it animates is materially embodied.* I hope to have shown in outline at least the sorts of consideration that lead me to accept this conclusion. It will be seen that all three panels of my triptych are required, that no two of them would suffice—structure and material without subjectivity would yield a world of inanimate things; subjectivity and material without structure would yield, I suppose, something like catatonic schizophrenia, if anything; subjectivity and structure without *any* material is inconceivable, although without the material of an objective world it would yield something like a world of dreams, whose order, if it had one, would be inexplicable. It might justly be said that this represents very little advance over Hume's bundle-of-perception theory of the self, or Freud's theory of the ego as "the totality of psi-cathexes at any given time" (1954:384). Evidently the position I take here is in that empiricist tradition. But we are now in a much better position than Hume was (though not in a very much better position than Freud was) to see how the details work out; if it should prove nevertheless that Hume's basic insight was sound, it would not be the first time in the subsequent history of philosophy that such an admission had to be made.

The main thrust of what I have been saying is this: if we want to have clear and correct ideas about ourselves, the world we live in, and the meaningful activities in which we engage, we cannot afford to be blinkered or

partisan in philosophy. There have been many phenomenologists and existentialists who have simply ignored the fact that we are material bodies in a
material world; there have been many materialists and positivists who have
simply dismissed any concern with intentional subjectivity; more recently,
many structuralists have supposed that a world of significance and discourse
could somehow sustain itself without paying attention to either. Nothing
prevents anyone from clinging to such partial perspectives, or from doing
good and serious work within them—which is just as well, since otherwise
the profession would be in a worse state than it is. As far as that goes,
forgetting such general concerns may, as I remarked in passing earlier, be a
condition for fruitful concentration on particular problems. But that ought
not to make us think that the other domains don't matter, or to expect that
some one movement of ideas is going to manage to get everything in, and I
believe it is not only a good but a necessary thing occasionally to think
diverse movements together.

There is nevertheless an order of precedence, as it were, among these
various convictions; if as an intentional subject (for whom phenomenology is
therefore *methodologically* inescapable) I have to choose whether to call my
philosophical position a materialist structuralism or a structural materialism, I must opt for the latter. There is as I see it no viable alternative to the
assumption that everything I have dealt with in this book, subjectivity,
significance, society, and the rest, has somehow been generated out of
whatever stuff the universe contains. It is a striking fact that the conditions
for the formation of these things do not obtain, as far as we know, in most
parts of the universe, have obtained here only for a comparatively short time,
will probably not always obtain, and (anthropic speculations to the contrary
notwithstanding) might never have obtained at all. Subjectivity is not only
arbitrary, as we saw in chapter 9, it is also entirely contingent. There need
have been no subjectivity, and hence no significance and no value. That
these things do exist, however ephemerally, is surely a reason for gratitude,
however impersonal.

# Postscript on Poststructuralism

## 76. Macaulay's anchor

ALTHOUGH PART I of this book dealt with historical aspects of what was called, in its time, the structuralist movement, it must have been obvious throughout that my chief intention in writing it has not been to capture a cultural phenomenon that occupied a brief period in the third quarter of the twentieth century and was then superseded by something else. It has rather been to disengage and develop and use a view and a method that take their place alongside other views and methods that, once introduced (whether in fifth-century Greece or nineteenth-century Germany), have remained in place on the philosophical scene as permanent contributions to the discipline. From this perspective it makes about as much sense to speak of "poststructuralism" as it does to speak of "postmaterialism," and this explains my reluctance to do so, my relegation of poststructuralism to a postscript.

The prefix "post-" after all means that whatever it is prefixed to is now over; when the postscript is begun the rest of the writing is finished, in the postwar period the war has ended, postnatal care begins when the birth is accomplished. In the case of structuralism its relegation to merely antecedent status provokes, in me at least, a desire to rein in the discussion for a moment and ask two questions: Are we sure we want it to be over? And who says it is?

The second question is the easier to answer. If philosophy is, as some suppose, a conversation, it will like all conversations get boring if every now and then we don't, as the expression goes, "change the subject." One weakness of the conversational approach is that it is not well adapted to sustained reflection; another is that it proceeds one topic at a time, and what that is gets determined by the more loquacious participants in the light of what happens to draw attention to itself. This may be a new star on the intellectual horizon, or a new technical discovery, or even the new availability of some neglected work, perhaps in translation. (It is notable that in France the surge of attention to Hegel and to Nietzsche followed quickly upon the publication of translations of their works; something of the same sort has recently been happening with Wittgenstein there and with Foucault here.)

As Foucault himself pointed out in *L'ordre du discours* (whose translation

253

as *The Discourse on Language* missed its main point, which was the *imposition* of order by discourse), the circulation of ideas is imperceptibly controlled by forms of censorship exerted by editorial boards, by critics, by curriculum committees, by market considerations, by unspoken ideological alliances, and so on. These forces take different forms in different fields, and the march of fashion is therefore unequal. It is mainly in literary discourse that structuralism is seen as supplanted by poststructuralism; a small number of philosophers has followed this lead but much of the profession has yet to catch up, preoccupied as it properly should be with questions of greater antiquity and longer reach, among which structuralism as a relative new-comer has to earn its right to compete for attention.

Even in literary studies poststructuralism occupies a position of awkward uncertainty. "Criticism after structuralism," say Richard Machin and Christopher Norris,

> is unable to produce further and greater structuralisms. There's not much science of the kind favoured by structuralism to be found nowadays. It is as though the literary structuralists represented the culmination and the grand finale of all previous attempts to produce a scientific theory of literature; in this case, no "new structuralism" was possible. Perhaps "fitz-structuralism" more usefully describes what happened next; it hints, among other things, at both the dangerously over-productive parent and the contentiously illegitimate offspring. In the event we have the equally graphic "poststructuralism," a term that seems not to name what we do in the present at all, but rather to re-name structuralism itself, as what we used to do in the past. (1987:1–2)

"What we used to do in the *past*"—but structuralism is barely twenty years old, much less than that in the English-speaking world. It is this haste toward the future that I find perplexing, even a bit unseemly. Immediately before the quoted passage Machin and Norris say that "structuralism offered criticism its last chance to make a science out of theorizing literature." To snatch the chance away so quickly is to prejudice hopelessly the question as to whether someone might have realized this goal. There is again, of course, the hint that it would have to be a grand, all-encompassing theory, or nothing, but to insist on that would be like a child's refusing apples and oranges because it couldn't have the moon. David Lodge's practical advice seems to me far more appropriate to the situation as it has developed over these decades: criticism, he says, has to learn "how to work with structuralism, not only in the sense of applying it when it seems useful to do so, but also in the sense of working *alongside* it, recognising its existence as a fact of intellectual life without being totally dominated by it" (1981:7).

It is hard not to conclude that some at any rate of those who suppose themselves to have emerged into a poststructuralist era never stopped very long to consider what structuralism had amounted and might yet amount to. But if the conversation of the avant-garde suggests that everyone should now be talking about something else, nothing compels the rest of us to succumb to that suggestion. We may feel there is an unfinished agenda, there may be some things we still want to thrash out. One good reason for worrying a bit longer at structuralism seems to me to be the chance it offers—a last chance perhaps?—of finding Macaulay's anchor, of checking before it gets out of control a drift into relativism and pragmatism and thence by reaction into fundamentalism and superstition. This drift seems to me to be already under way to an alarming degree.

I do not wish to overwork the metaphor of the anchor, but it has a useful twist. What first comes to mind is of course a bottom anchor, which would correspond to one form or another of foundationalism, tying everything down to an ultimate origin or ground. It seems clear that this strategy will not work—we are enclosed in appearances, in language and in culture, and are unlikely to find a transcendent warrant for our actions or our beliefs. But there are such things as sea anchors, large floating structures whose function is to keep the vessel oriented and minimize her drifting in heavy seas. This theme of orientation recalls the Introduction, but it is not now a matter of having stars to steer by, rather of keeping on course in spite of upheavals. The historicist prejudice everyone seems to have inherited from Hegel, according to which ideas are always getting *aufgehoben* (and note that the *strictest* translation of *Aufhebung* into English is "upheaval"), is no doubt part of what compelled the conviction that structuralism had to give way to poststructuralism, just to keep up the momentum, so to speak. But I want to say that it is not necessary to accept this restless view, and that the work of clarifying and aligning the structures of the various domains of the human sciences, and deepening their connections with new discoveries in more technical fields, especially the neurosciences, has only just begun.

Foundationalism being abandoned, we are of course (as was remarked in chapter 1, section 6) "freely suspended in space," or in the nautical rather than astronautical image appropriate to the discussion of anchors "freely floating" (on the unconscious perhaps—the Freudian association is hard to resist). What we need is not an umbilical cord to some impossible origin, divine or mystical, or a vector to a similarly impossible transcendent destiny, but stabilizers, gyroscopes, devices for *local* orientation, *limited* structural connections of optimum complexity, serviceable for human needs on a human scale. The discovery of and reflection on structures of language, kinship, history, mythology, literature, and so on, on the one hand and of subjectivity on the other seem to me to be on the way to providing what is needed.

## 77. Synchronicity

EVEN POSTSTRUCTURALISM, on this account, will turn out to require structuralist treatment; if that is what I am engaged in, its structure in relation to mine will be up for analysis if I am to understand my insertion into and my equilibrium in my world. It is one of the distinguishing marks of structuralism in all its manifestations that the systems it deals with are synchronic: thus Barthes' insistence on reading Racine as a contemporary, Foucault's notion of literary works as occupying a spatial (and hence timeless) network through which the critic can make his way in any order he likes, the notion of archaeology, also in Foucault ("le structuraliste malgré lui"), the *presentation* of the mythological corpus in Lévi-Strauss, and so forth. But on reflection it appears that there are at least three different meanings that can be given to "synchronic." Granted that its basic meaning is "together in (or with respect to) time," hence loosely "at the same time," "contemporaneous," still we may have different understandings of the time *at which* this contemporaneity is to hold. The first and most neutral meaning is simply attached to some *date*, say 1611; we may get an idea of the state of the synchronic system of the English language at that time by studying the vocabulary and grammar of the King James Bible, and by comparing it to the synchronic system at some later date, say 1988, be able to specify the diachronic changes that have taken place. It is in this sense that the by now standard opposition between structure and history is to be understood: on the one hand a set of principles, a structure, determining the relations among entities at some point of time in (relative) independence of the manner in which the entities were produced; on the other a set of casual sequences, a history, determining the state of the same entities at the same point of time in (relative) independence of the constraints they exert on one another.

A second meaning of "synchronic" emerges if we suppose that the structural principles themselves remain unchanged over time even though the entities they control also undergo diachronic evolution in structurally undetermined respects. The laws of nature seem to be good examples of this; whatever entities there happen to be will conform rigorously to the structures of geometry, physics, and so on, and the nature of the constraints they exert on one another will be independent of the date at which they happen to be observed. The structures in this case are atemporal; our understanding of them may change through time, but they themselves, we assume, do not. It is an open but important question to what degree atemporal structures of this sort underlie cultural phenomena; both Lévi-Strauss and Chomsky have conjectured that an unchanging structure of mind—unchanging, at any rate, over the sort of time span we have to deal with—may eventually be inferred from the structures of language, mythology, and so on.

If such atemporal structures exist, the world at any moment is the product of their interaction with one another and with the contingent content of being—if being has anything contingent about it. (If not, the world would have to be regarded as the interaction of the structures alone.) Part of the world at that moment will be the formulation or the embodiment of whatever structures there are: in people's minds or brains, in language, in other kinds of concrete extension. And these embodied structures will be "synchronic" in a third and much stronger sense, that is, as coexisting with one another in a particular moment, namely, the moment in which the subject is activating the systems that embody them. For practical purposes that means the present moment. (The expression "present moment" is *token-reflexive*, in that as it is written, uttered, read, and so on, it refers to the moment of its writing, utterance, or reading, not to some abstract moment.) It is through the present moments of subjects, unconscious in some cases (as one might say that the apple is subject to the laws of gravity), conscious in others, that the structures have their entry into the world. And it is immediately obvious that this is just as true of diachronic structures, for example, history, as it is of synchronic ones, for example, language. For it is *now* that I assign the date 1611 to the King James Bible or the date 1871 to the Commune of Paris. Diachronic structures, we are forced to conclude, are just synchronic structures among others, except that they happen to make reference to time.

This explains why the spatialization of time ("length of time") appears so natural to us; it also suggests that the history/structure opposition is less critical than at first it seems. For history is nothing but the present structure of its proper domain, a domain that includes present utterances in the past tense together with a vast collection of present objects, documentary, monumental, artifactual. Of course that domain will be different tomorrow, because today's traces will have been added to it, but that does not mean that the structure of history will have changed. And in a similar way the changing focus of intellectual attention, the fact that yesterday's preoccupation with structuralism has given way to today's with realism or pragmatism, does not mean that the structure of intelligibility has changed.

## 78. The poststructuralist scene

I MAKE HERE no criticism of any of the activities that go to make up the post structuralist agenda; my only reservation is that calling them poststructuralist makes a claim that I take to be unfounded and that I therefore wish to contest. I am, as we have just seen, unavoidably contemporary with what I study, and one of the things I have to do in order to render it intelligible is to grasp the synchronic relations that constitute it, by matching them to linguistic or conceptual relations belonging to my store of such things; the more resourceful the store, the readier the matching and the prompter the achievement of intelligibility. This activity of seeking out and matching, which also locates the object in question with respect to other objects of the same type, and thus provides it (in the ideally complete case) with a double structure, internal when its parts are seen as fitting in with one another, external when it itself is seen as fitting into a more inclusive scheme, *is* structuralist activity, even if the internal fitting is arrived at deconstructively or the external via critical theory.

Poststructuralist activity is therefore perhaps like postprandial activity: one can't always be eating, although tomorrow it will certainly be necessary to do so again. This metaphor might be extended, with help from Hegel and Nietzsche, into the view that even if philosophy arrives *post festum* the recurrent character of intellectual life will ensure its renewed relevance later on, as when people save their old clothes in the expectation that they will become fashionable once more. That however would be to concede too much; even though I began the exposition of the structuralist movement under the sign of fashion I want in closing to keep my distance from it. For when structuralism becomes old, as it will, this will not be as philosophy does in Hegel, painting its grey in grey, but as basic tools or techniques do, becoming familiar and timeless, like knives or hammers, without losing their efficacy or their actuality.

Why then did structuralism arrive so late on the scene? No doubt because thought did not have to confront as a *central* problem the absence of subtance or foundation in the human sciences until a certain relativism was thrust upon it by the geological, biological, anthropological, psychological, and linguistic discoveries of the nineteenth century. That relativism is still an issue (a poststructuralist one!) and there is still a good deal of perplexity about it. My own conviction is that between the poles of subjectivity on the one hand (which is not relative because it cannot be displaced from itself) and materiality on the other (which is not relative because it remains there, under whatever guise—even that of mere appearance—orthogonal to the subject's intentionality, making up the only world it has) the human world will prove to consist of a series of partial structures whose relativity to one another means only that we don't always want either to take the trouble of supplementing them until we arrive at the full formulation of inclusive and mutually transforming structures, or having done this actually to carry out the transformation. Nor do we have to as long as we understand that both are possible. (But that understanding becomes important when actual conflicts arise.)

The poststructuralist scene, then, is just the intellectual scene as it always was, with this difference, that there is now available a method for the understanding and analysis of the objects of the human sciences to which recourse can always be had when other methods prove unsatisfactory, as from time to time they no doubt will. If by poststructuralist we agreed to mean after the *beginning* of structuralism rather than after its end then the designation of our epoch in this way would be benign. But because post-post-structuralism is already looming I prefer to think of the epoch as structuralist, simply, without temporal modalities. Many of the structures analyzed in structuralist writings—myths, musical and literary works, cyclic patterns in "cold" societies—appear as devices for the conquest of time; structuralism, in insisting on the strongly synchronic character of intelligibility, may itself prove, in the domain of the human sciences, to be the first such device that actually works.

# List of Works Cited

This is not a bibliography of structuralism but a working list of references, with all the idiosyncrasy that that implies. Whenever a citation in English is referred to a work in another language the translation is my own.

Abellio, Raymond. 1965. *La Structure absolue.* Paris: Gallimard.

Aron, Raymond. 1969. *D'une Sainte Famille à l'autre, essais sur les marxismes imaginaires.* Paris: NRF/Gallimard.

Augustine, Saint. 1950. *The City of God.* Trans. Marcus Dods. New York: Random House/Modern Library.

Bachelard, Gaston. 1951. *L'Activite rationaliste de la physique contemporaine.* Paris: Presses Universitaires de France.

Barthes, Roland, 1963. *Sur Racine.* Paris: Editions du Seuil.

———— and Martin, André [texte et photos]. 1964. *La Tour Eiffel.* Paris: Delpire (collection "le genie du lieu").

————. 1966. *Critique et vérité.* Paris: Editions du Seuil.

————. 1967. *Système de la mode.* Paris: Editions du Seuil.

————. 1969. "La peinture est-elle un langage?" Review of Jean-Louis Schefer, *Scénographie d'un tableau. La Quinzaine littéraire,* no. 68, 1–15 mars, p. 16.

————. 1971. Interview in *La Quinzaine littéraire,* no. 130, 1–15 décembre, p. 4.

Barthes, Roland. 1982 [1970]. *The Empire of Signs,* trans. Richard Howard. New York: Hill & Wang.

Bastide, R., ed. 1962. *Sens et usage du terme structure dans les sciences humaines et sociales.* The Hague: Mouton and Co.

Benveniste, Emile, 1966. *Problèmes de linguistique générale.* Paris: Gallimard.

Berkeley, George, [1713] 1954. *Three Dialogues Between Hylas and Philonous.* New York: Liberal Arts Press.

Blanshard, Brand. 1939. *The Nature of Thought.* 2 vols. London: George Allen & Unwin Ltd.

————. 1962. *Reason and Analysis.* LaSalle, Illinois: Open Court.

Bloomfield, Leonard, 1933, *Language.* New York: Henry Holt.

Boas, Franz. 1911, *Handbook of American Indian Languages.* Washington, D.C.: Government Printing Office (Smithsonian Institution).

Bourbaki, N. 1966a. *Eléments de mathématique, Fascicule XVII, Théorie des ensembles, chs. 1 et 2.* 3ᵉ éd. Paris: Hermann.

———. 1966b. *Eléments de mathématique, Fascicule XXII, Théorie des ensembles, ch. 4.* 2ᵉ éd. revue et diminuée. Paris: Hermann.

———. 1969 *Eléments d'histoire des mathématiques.* Paris: Hermann.

Bouveresse, Jacques., 1984. *Le Philosophe chez les autophages.* Paris: Editions de Minuit.

Broekman, Jan. 1974. *Structuralism: Moscow—Prague—Paris.* Trans. Jan F. Beekman and Brunhilde Helm. Dordrecht: D. Reidel Publishing Company.

Burke, Kenneth. 1967. *The Philosophy of Literary Form: Studies in Symbolic Action.* 2d ed. Baton Rouge: Louisiana State University Press.

Burnet, John. 1957. *Early Greek Philosophy.* New York: Meridian Books.

Carnap, Rudolf. 1956 [1947]. *Meaning and Necessity: A Study in Semantics and Modal Logic.* Chicago: University of Chicago Press.

Carnap, Rudolf. 1967. *The Logical Structure of the World.* Trans. Rolf A. George. London: Routledge & Kegan Paul.

Cassirer, Ernst. 1944. "The Concept of Groups and the Theory of Perception" (trans. Aron Gurwitsch). *Philosophy and Phenomenological Research* 5, no. 1:1–35.

———. 1945. "Structuralism in Modern Linguistics." *Word* 1, no. 2 (August): 99–120.

———. 1946. *Language and Myth.* trans. Suzanne K. Langer. New York: Harper & Brothers.

———. 1953. *The Philosophy of Symbolic Forms.* Vol. 1, *Language.* Trans. Ralph Manheim. New Haven: Yale University Press.

———. 1955. *The Philosophy of Symbolic Forms.* Vol. 2, *Mythical Thought.* Trans. Ralph Manheim. New Haven: Yale University Press.

———. 1957. *The Philosophy of Symbolic Forms.* Vol. 3, *The Phenomenology of Knowledge.* Trans. Ralph Manheim. New Haven: Yale University Press.

Caws, Peter. 1963. "Science, Computers, and the Complexity of Nature." *Philosophy of Science* 30, no. 2 (April): 158–164.

———. 1965. *The Philosophy of Science: A Systematic Account.* Princeton: Van Nostrand.

———. 1967a. "Aspects of Hempel's Philosophy of Science." *The Review of Metaphysics* 20, no. 4 (June): 690–710.

———. 1967b. *Science and the Theory of Value.* New York: Random House.

———. 1969. "The Structure of Discovery." *Science* 166 (December): 1375–80.

———. 1974. "Parallels and Orthogonals." *Semiotext(e)* 1, Vol. 2 (Fall) [*The Two Saussures*]: 54–65.

———. 1975. "Mach's Principle and the Laws of Logic." In *Minnesota Studies in the Philosophy of Science, volume VI: Induction, Probability, and Confirmation,* edited by Grover Maxwell and Robert M. Anderson, Jr. Minneapolis: University of Minnesota Press.

Charbonnier, Georges. 1961. *Entretiens avec Claude Lévi-Strauss*. Paris: Plon/ Julliard.

Chatelet, François. 1967. "Où en est le structuralisme?" *La Quinzaine littéraire*, no. 31, 1–15 juillet, pp. 18–19.

Chomsky, Carol. 1969. *The Acquisition of Syntax in Children from 5 to 10*. Cambridge: The MIT Press.

Chomsky, Noam. 1957. *Syntactic Structures*. The Hague: Mouton and Co.

———. 1964. *Current Issues in Linguistic Theory*. The Hague: Mouton and Co.

———. 1966. *Topics in the Theory of Generative Grammar*. The Hague: Mouton and Co.

———.1967. "Introduction." In Maurice Gross and André Lentin, *Notions sur les grammaires formelles*. Paris: Gauthier-Villars.

———. 1968. *Language and Mind*. New York: Harcourt, Brace, and World.

———. 1969. "Chomsky parle de la linguistique" [interview by Jean-Marie Benoist]. *La Quinzaine littéraire*, no. 74, 1–15 juin, pp. 18–20.

———. 1980. *Rules and Representations*. New York: Columbia University Press.

Clarke, Simon. 1981. *The Foundations of Structuralism*: *A Critique of Lévi-Strauss and the Structuralist Movement*. Sussex: The Harvester Press.

Collingwood, R. G. 1939. *An Essay on Metaphysics*. Oxford: Oxford University Press.

Culler, Jonathan. 1975. *Structuralist Poetics*: *Structuralism, Linguistics, and the Study of Literature*. Ithaca: Cornell University Press.

Derrida, Jacques. 1967a. *L'Ecriture et la différence*. Paris: Editions du Seuil.

———. 1967b. *De la grammatologie*. Paris: Editions de Minuit.

———. 1972. *La Dissémination*. Paris: Editions du Seuil.

———. 1982. *Margins of Philosophy*. Trans. Alan Bass. Chicago: University of Chicago Press.

Descartes, René [1931] 1955. *The Philosophical Works of Descartes, Rendered into English by Elizabeth Haldane, C.H., LL.D., and G.R.T. Ross, M.A., D.Phil.* New York: Dover.

Dresden, Sem, Lein Geschiere, and Bernard Bray. 1961. *La Notion de structure*. The Hague: Van GoorZonen.

Ducrot, Oswald et al. 1968. *Qu'est-ce que le structuralisme?* Paris: Editions du Seuil.

———. and Tzvetan Todorov. 1972. *Dictionnaire encyclopédique des sciences du langage*. Paris: Editions du Seuil.

Dumézil, Georges. 1952. *Les Dieux des Indo-Européens*. Paris: Presses Universitaires de France.

———. 1970. *The Destiny of the Warrior*. Trans. Alf Hiltebeitel. Chicago:

University of Chicago Press.

Durkheim, Emile, and Marcel Mauss. 1963. *Primitive Classification*. Trans. Rodney Needham. Chicago: University of Chicago Press.

Edwards, Paul, ed. 1967. *The Encyclopedia of Philosophy*. 8 vols. New York: The Macmillan Company and The Free Press.

Ehrmann, Jacques, ed. 1966. *Structuralism*. New Haven: Yale French Studies.

Evans-Pritchard, E. E. 1965. *The Position of Women in Primitive Society and Other Essays in Social Anthropology*. London: Faber & Faber.

Fekete, John. 1984. *Theory and History of Literature*. Vol. II, *The Structural Allegory: Reconstructive Encounters with the New French Thought*. Minneapolis: University of Minnesota Press.

Fodor, Jerry A. 1975. *The Language of Thought*. Cambridge: Harvard University Press.

Foucault, Michel. 1966. *Les Mots et les choses: une archeólogie des sciences humaines*. Paris: NRF/Gallimard. [cf. 1970]

————. 1970. *The Order of Things: An Archaeology of the Human Sciences.*, New York: Pantheon Books. [cf. 1966]

————. 1978. *The History of Sexuality: Volume I: An Introduction*. Trans. Robert Hurley. New York: Pantheon Books.

———— et al. 1968. *Théorie d'ensemble* (Tel Quel). Paris: Editions du Seuil.

Freud, Sigmund. 1954. *The Origins of Psycho-Analysis: Letters to William Fliess, Drafts and Notes: 1887–1902*. Trans. Eric Mosbacher and James Strachey. New York: Basic Books.

Furth, Hans G. 1966. *Thinking Without Language: Psychological Implications of Deafness*. New York: The Free Press.

Geertz, Clifford. *Person, Time, and Conduct in Bali: An Essay in Cultural Analysis*. New Haven: Yale University (Southeast Asia Studies, Cultural Report Series no. 14).

Girard, René. 1972. *La Violence et le sacré*. Paris: Grasset.

Godel, R. 1957. *Les Sources manuscrites du Cours de linguistique générale de Ferdinand de Saussure*. Geneva: Droz.

Goodenough, Ward H., ed. 1964. *Explorations in Cultural Anthropology*. New York: McGraw-Hill.

Hammel, E. A., ed. 1965. *Formal Semantic Analysis* [report of a conference sponsored by the Wenner-Gren Foundation for Anthropological Research]. Washington: *American Anthropological Association*.

Hampshire, Stuart. 1971. *Freedom of Mind and other essays*. Princeton: Princeton University Press.

Harris, Zellig S. 1954. "Distributional Structure." In *Linguistics Today*, edited by André Martinet and Uriel Weinreich. New York: Linguistic Circle of New York. [*Word* 10, 2–3 Aug.–Dec., pp. 142–62].

————. 1968. *Mathematical Structures of Language*. New York: Interscience

Publishers.

Hegel, G. W. F. [1807] 1977. *Phenomenology of Spirit.* Trans. A. V. Miller. Oxford: Clarendon Press.

Heidegger, Martin. [1927] 1962. *Being and Time.* Trans. John Macquarrie and Edward Robinson. London: SCM Press Ltd.

Hempel, C. G., and Paul Oppenheim. 1948. "Studies in the Logic of Explanation." *Philosophy of Science* 15, 2, April 1948, pp. 135–175.

Herdan, Gustav. 1960. *Type-Token Mathematics: A Textbook of Mathematical Linguistics.* The Hague: Mouton and Co.

Hjelmslev, Louis. 1966. *Le Langage.* Trans. Michel Olsen. Paris: Editions de Minuit.

Homans, George C., and David M. Schneider. 1955. *Marriage, Authority, and Final Causes.* Glencoe, Illinois: The Free Press.

Humboldt, Wilhelm von. 1836. *Uber die Kawi-Sprache auf der Insel Java, nebst einer Einleitung über die Verschiedenheit des menschlichen Sprachbaues.* Berlin: Abhandlungen der Königlichen Akademie der Wissenschaften.

Hymes, Dell, ed. 1964. *Language in Culture and Society: A Reader in Linguistics and Anthropology.* New York: Harper & Row.

Jakobson, Roman. 1962. *Selected Writings I: Phonological Studies.* The Hague: Mouton and Co.

———. 1968a. *Child Language, Aphasia, and Phonological Universals.* Trans. A. R. Keiler. The Hague: Mouton and Co.

———. 1968b. "La Langue est le moteur de l'imagination" [interview with Michel Tréguer and François Chatelet]. *La Quinzaine littéraire*, no. 51, 15–31 mai, pp. 18–20.

——— et al. 1952. *Preliminaries to Speech Analysis: The Distinctive Features and Their Correlates.* Cambridge: The MIT Press.

———, and Morris Halle. 1956. *Fundamentals of Language.* The Hague: Mouton and Co.

———, and Lévi-Strauss, Claude. 1962. "'Les Chats' de Charles Baudelaire." *L'Homme* 2, no. 1 (janvier-avril): 5–21.

Jameson, Fredric. 1972. *The Prison-House of Language: A Critical Account of Structuralism and Russian Formalism.* Princeton: Princeton University Press.

Jaynes, Julian. 1976. *The Origin of Consciousness in the Breakdown of the Bicameral Mind.* Boston: Houghton Mifflin.

Kant, Immanuel. [1781] 1933. *Immanuel Kant's Critique of Pure Reason.* 2d impression with corrections. Trans. Norman Kemp Smith. London: Macmillan and Co. Ltd.

Karsz, Saul. 1967. "Après Althusser." *Aletheia*, no. 6 (avril): 232–34.

Kierkegaard, Søren [1846] 1941. *Concluding Unscientific Postscript to the "Philosophical Fragments": An Existential Contribution by Johannes Climacus.* Trans David F. Swenson, Lillian Marvin Swenson, and Walter Lowrie. Princeton: Princeton University Press.

Kubler, George. 1962. *The Shape of Time: Remarks on the History of Things*. New Haven: Yale University Press.

Lacan, Jacques. 1966a. "La science et la vérité." *Cahiers pour l'analyse* 1 (*La Vérité*). Paris: Cercle d'épistémologie de l'Ecole Normale Supérieure.

———. 1966b. *Ecrits*. Paris: Editions du Seuil.

———. 1973. *Le Séminaire, Livre XI: Les quatre concepts fondamentaux de la psychanalyse*. Texte établi par Jacques-Alain Miller. Paris: Editions du Seuil.

———. 1978. *The Four Fundamental Concepts of Psycho-Analysis*. Trans. Alan Sheridan. New York: W.W. Norton and Co.

Langer, Suzanne. 1967. *Mind: An Essay on Human Feeling*. Vol. 1. Baltimore: Johns Hopkins University Press.

———. 1972. *Mind: An Essay on Human Feeling*. Vol. 2. Baltimore: Johns Hopkins University Press.

———. 1982. *Mind: An Essay on Human Feeling*. Vol. 3. Baltimore: Johns Hopkins University Press.

Lerner, Rita G., and George L. Trigg, eds. 1981. *Encyclopedia of Physics*. Reading, Mass.: Addison-Wesley Publishing Company, Inc.

Levin, Sam. 1962. *Linguistic Structures in Poetry*. The Hague: Mouton and Co.

Lévi-Strauss, Claude. 1945. "L'Analyse structurale en linguistique et en anthropologie." *Word* 1, no. 1 (April): pp. 33–53.

———. 1949. *Les Structures élémentaires de la parenté*. Paris: Presses Universitaires de France.

———. 1953. "Social Structure." In *Anthropology Today* [International Symposium on Anthropology, New York, 1952]. Chicago: University of Chicago Press.

———. 1955. *Tristes tropiques*. Paris: Plon.

———. 1958. *Anthropologie structurale*. Paris: Plon.

———. 1961. *Race et histoire, suivi de L'oeuvre de Claude Lévi-Strauss par Jean Pouillon*. Paris: Editions Gonthier.

———. 1963. "Réponses à quelques questions." *Esprit*, nouvelle sèrie 11 (novembre): 628–653.

———. 1964. *Mythologiques*. Vol. 1, *Le Cru et le cuit*. Paris: Plon. [cf. 1969b]

———. 1966a. *Mythologiques*. Vol. 2, *Du Miel aux cendres*. Paris: Plon.

———. 1966b. "Introduction à l'oeuvre de Marcel Mauss." In Marcel Mauss, *Sociologie et anthropologie*. 3ᵉ éd. augmentée. Paris: Presses Universitaires de France.

———. 1966c. *The Savage Mind*. Chicago: University of Chicago Press.

———.1967a. *The Scope of Anthropology*. Trans. Sherry Ortner Paul and Robert A. Paul. London: Jonathan Cape.

———. 1967b. *Structural Anthropology*, trans. Claire Jacobson and Brooke

Grundfest Schoepf. Garden City, N.Y.: Anchor Books.

————. 1968. *Mythologiques*. Vol. 3, *L'Origine des manières de table*. Paris: Plon.

————. 1969a. *The Elementary Structures of Kinship*. Trans. James Herle Bell, John Richard von Sturmer, and Rodney Needham. Boston: Beacon Press.

————. 1969b. *The Raw and the Cooked: Introduction to a Science of Mythology: I*. Trans. John Weightman and Doreen Weightman. New York: Harper & Row. [cf. 1964]

————. 1971. *Mythologiques*. Vol. 4, *L'Homme nu*. Paris: Plon.

Lodge, David. 1981. *Working with Structuralism: Essays and reviews on nineteenth- and twentieth-century literature*. London: Routledge & Kegan Paul.

Lowie, Robert H. 1920. *Primitive Society*. New York: Boni & Liveright.

Machim, Richard, and Christopher Norris, eds. 1987. *Post-Structuralist Readings of English Poetry*. Cambridge: Cambridge University Press.

Macksey, Richard, and Eugenio Donato, eds. 1970. *The Languages of Criticism and the Sciences of Man*. Baltimore: Johns Hopkins University Press.

Marx, Karl. 1965. *Pre-Capitalist Economic Formations*. New York: International Publishers.

Mates, Benson. 1961. *Stoic Logic*. 2d printing. Berkeley and Los Angeles: University of California Press.

de Mauro, Tullio. 1968. "Nous ne connaissons pas Saussure" [interview]. *La Quinzaine littéraire*, no. 51 15–31 mai, pp. 21–23.

Morgan, Lewis H. 1871. *Systems of Consanguinity and Affinity of the Human Family*. Washington D.C.: Smithsonian Institution.

————. 1877. *Ancient Society, or Researches in the Lines of Human Progress from Savagery, through Barbarism to Civilization*. London: Macmillan.

Mounin, Georges. 1968. *Saussure, ou le structuraliste sans le savoir*. Paris: Editions Seghers.

————. 1970. *Introduction à la sémiologie*. Paris: Editions de Minuit.

Murdock, George Peter. 1949. *Social Structure*. New York: The Free Press.

Needham, Rodney. 1962. *Structure and Sentiment: A Test Case in Social Anthropology*. Chicago: University of Chicago Press.

Nutini, Hugo. 1970. "Some Considerations on the Nature of Social Structure and Model-Building: A Critique of Claude Lévi-Strauss and Edmund Leach." In *Claude Lévi-Strauss: The Anthropologist as Hero*, edited by E. Nelson Hayes and Tanya Hayes, Cambridge: The MIT Press. [Originally published in *American Anthropologist* 67, 1965, pp. 707–731.]

Ogden, C. K. 1967. *Opposition: A Linguistic and Psychological Analysis*. Bloomington: Indiana University Press.

————, and Richards, I. A. 1949. *The Meaning of Meaning: A Study of the Influence of Language upon Thought and of the Science of Symbolism*. 10th ed. London: Routledge & Kegan Paul.

Parsons, Talcott. 1952. *The Social System*. London: Tavistock Publications.

Pedersen, Holger. 1962. *The Discovery of Language*. Trans. John Webster Spargo. Bloomington: Indiana University Press.

Peirce, Charles Sanders. 1931. *Collected Papers of Charles Sanders Peirce*. Ed. Charles Hartshorne and Paul Weiss. Vol. 1. Cambridge: Harvard University Press.

————. 1958. *Values in a Universe of Chance: Selected Writings of Charles S. Peirce* (1839–1914). Ed. Philip P. Wiener. Garden City, N.Y.: Doubleday Anchor Books.

Piaget, Jean. 1970. *Structuralism*. Trans. Chaninah Maschler. New York: Basic Books.

Picard, Raymond. 1965. *Nouvelle critique ou nouvelle imposture*. Paris: Pauvert.

Pike, Kenneth L. 1967. *Language in Relation to a Unified Theory of the Structure of Human Behavior*. The Hague: Mouton and Co.

Porset, Charles, ed. 1970. *Varia Linguistica*. Paris: Editions Ducros.

Popper, Karl. [1972] 1973. *Objective Knowledge: An Evolutionary Approach*. Oxford: Clarendon Press.

Pouillon, Jean. 1966. "Présentation: un essai de définition." *Les Temps Modernes*, no. 246 (novembre).

————, and P. Maranda, eds. 1970. *Echanges et communications: mélanges offerts à Claude Lévi-Strauss à l'occasion de son 60éme anniversaire*. 2 vols. The Hague: Mouton and Co.

Radcliffe-Brown, A. R. 1952. *Structure and Function in Primitive Society*. London: Cohen and West.

Ramsey, Frank Plumpton. 1931. *The Foundations of Mathematics and Other Logical Essays*. London: Routledge & Kegan Paul.

Reichard, Gladys. 1928. *Social Life of the Navaho Indians*. New York: Columbia University Press.

Ricoeur, Paul. 1963. "Structure et herméneutique." *Esprit*, nouvelle série 11 (novembre): 596–627.

Riffaterre, Michael. 1971. *Essais de stylistique structurale*. Paris: Flammarion.

Robey, David, ed. 1973. *Structuralism: An Introduction—Wolfson College Lectures 1972*. Oxford: Clarendon Press.

Russell, Bertrand. 1919. *Introduction to Mathematical Philosophy*. London: George Allen & Unwin, Ltd.

Sapir, Edward. 1949. *Language: An Introduction to the Study of Speech*. New York: Harcourt, Brace and Co.

Sartre, Jean-Paul. [1952] 1968. *The Communists and Peace*. Trans. Martha H. Fletcher with John R. Kleinschmidt. New York: George Braziller.

————. [1960] 1976. *Critique of Dialectical Reason*. Trans. Alan Sheridan–Smith. London: NLB.

Saussure, Ferdinand de. [1916] 1959. *Course in General Linguistics*. Ed. Charles Bally and Albert Sechehaye with Albert Reidlinger. Trans. Wade Baskin.

New York: Philosophical Library.

―――. 1967. *Cours de linguistique générale*. Tomes 1 et 2. Ed. crit. par Rudolf Engler. Wiesbaden: Harrassowitz.

―――. 1968. *Cours de Linguistique* générale. Tome 3. Ed. crit. par Rudolf Engler. Wiesbaden: Harrassowitz.

Scheffler, Harold W., and Floyd G. Lounsbury. 1971. *A Study in Structural Semantics: The Siriono Kinship System*. Englewood Cliffs, N. J. Prentice-Hall.

Seung, T. K. 1982. *Structuralism and Hermeneutics*. New York: Columbia University Press.

Shapiro, Harry L., ed. 1960. *Man, Culture, and Society*. New York: Oxford University Press.

Stalin, Josef. 1951. *A propos du marxisme en linguistique*. Paris: Les éditions de la nouvelle critique.

Starobinski, Jean. 1967. "Les Mots sous les mots: textes inédits des cahiers d'anagrammes de Ferdinand de Saussure." In *To Honor Roman Jakobson, Essays on the Occasion of his Seventieth Birthday, 11 October 1966*. The Hague: Mouton and Co.

―――. 1971. *Les Mots sous les mots: les anagrammes de Ferdinand de Saussure*. Paris: Gallimard.

Stent, Gunther S. 1969. *The Coming of the Golden Age*. Garden City, N. Y. Doubleday/Natural History Press.

Terence. 1740. *P. Terentii Carthaginensis Afri Comoediae Sex*. London: D. Midwinter et al.

Thompson, D'Arcy Wentworth. 1961. *On Growth and Form*. Abr. Ed. John Tyler Bonner. Cambridge: Cambridge University Press.

Trubetzkoy, Prince N. 1933. "La Phonologie actuelle." In H. Delacroix et al., *Psychologie du langage*. Paris: Librairie Félix Alcan.

―――― [Troubetzskoy] [1932] 1967. *Principes de phonologie*. Trans. J. Cantineau. Paris: Klincksieck.

Turner, Victor W. 1969. *The Ritual Process: Structure and Anti-Structure*. London: Routledge & Kegan Paul.

Vachek, Joseph, comp. 1964. *A Prague School Reader in Linguistics*. Bloomington: Indiana University Press.

Wellek, René, and Austin Warren. 1949. *Theory of Literature*. New York: Harcourt, Brace and Co.

Wells, Rulon S. 1947. "De Saussure's System of Linguistics." *Word* 3, nos. 1–2 (August): pp. 1–31.

Whorf, Benjamin Lee. 1956. *Language, Thought, and Reality: Selected Writings of Benjamin Lee Whorf*. Ed. John B. Carroll. Cambridge: The Technology Press of the Massachusetts Institute of Technology [published jointly with John Wiley and Sons, Inc., New York, and Chapman and Hall, Ltd., London].

Wittgenstein, Ludwig. 1922. *Tractatus Logico-Philosophicus*. Trans. C. K
Ogden. London: Routledge & Kegan Paul. [cf. 1961]
————. 1958. *Philosophical Investigations*. Trans. G. E. M. Anscombe. 2d ed.
Oxford: Basil Blackwell.
————. 1961. *Tractatus Logico-Philosophicus*. Trans. D. F. Pears and B. F.
McGuinness. London: Routledge & Kegan Paul. [cf. 1922]
Zukav, Gary. 1979. *The Dancing Wu Li Masters: An Overview of the New Physics*.
New York: William Morrow and Company.

# Index

Abellio, Raymond, 159n
Absence, 159
Absolute, 159
Abstract, abstraction, 230
Absurd, 38
Aesthetics, 33
Althusser, Louis, 14, 22, 35–36; *Lire le Capital*, 35; *Pour Marx*, 35
Analysis, analytic, 32, 160, 164
Anaximander, 86
Anthropology, 23, 49ff., 226, 258
Apposition, 212ff.
Archaeology, 149ff., 160, 256
Argument from design, 245
Aristotle, 86, 87, 161, 174, 203, 209, 243; *Metaphysics*, 243
Aron, Raymond, 14
Artaud, Antonin, 152
Atomism, 12, 85, 169
Augustine, Saint, 86, 134, 155; *City of God*, 133
Austin, John, 240

Bach, J.S., 187
Bachelard, Gaston, 247
Bacon, Francis, 128–129
Badiou, Alain, 22
Barthes, Roland, xiv, 2, 37–38, 112, 114, 121, 239, 256; *Critique et vérité*, 35; *Eléments de sémiologie*, 110; *Mythologies*, 115; *Sur Racine*, 35; *Système de la mode*, 21–22, 38, 114; *S/Z*, 115
Bastide, Roger, 43n, 128n
Baudelaire, Charles: "Les Chats," 54, 148
Behaviorism, 1, 12, 46, 96, 104, 169
Benedict, Ruth, 49
Benveniste, Emile, 29, 63, 64n
Bergson, Henri, 12, 30
Berkeley, George: *Three Dialogues Between Hylas and Philonous*, 231–232
Bertalanffy, Ludwig von, 14
Big Bang, 243
biology, 258
Bismarck, Otto, 7
Black, Max: *Companion to Wittgenstein's Tractatus*, 179
Blanshard, Brand, 198ff.; *The Nature of Thought*, 198ff.; *Reason and Analysis*, 203
Bloch, Joseph, 150
Bloomfield, Leonard, 46n, 96
Bohr, Niels, 241
Bootstrap theory, 174
Borges, Jorge Luis, 32–33, 238
Bororo, 227
Boas, Franz: *Handbook of American Indian Languages*, 46, 95
Boethius, 240
Bourbaki, 14ff.
Bouveresse, Jacques, 39n
Bradley, F. H., 199
Brains 6, 232 (see also Neurophysiology)
Braque, Georges, 14
Breton, André, 22
Bricolage, 7, 25, 37, 213
Brockman, Jan, 41n
Buckle, Henry, 125, 131, 140
Burke, Kenneth, 53
Burnet, John, 87n
Bushmen of the Kalahari, 44

Calvino, Italo, 238
Camus, Albert, 38
Carnap, Rudolf, 172, 175ff.; arrow diagrams, 172; *Der Logische Aufbau der Welt*, 175–177; *Meaning and Necessity*, 177; pair list, 172
Carroll, Lewis, 212
Cartesian Cogito, 31, 104
Cassirer, Ernst, 11, 16–18, 28, 43, 61, 75, 136, 177; *Philosophy of Symbolic Forms*, 16–18 (see also Symbolic forms)
Cervantes, Miguel de, *Don Quixote*, 151
Charbonnier, Georges, 24n, 59n
Christianity, 29
Chomsky, Carol, 101, 129
Chomsky, Noam, 41, 46–48, 61–62, 101–105, 107, 121, 193, 256; *Current Issues in Linguistic Theory*, 27
Clarke, Simon, 3n
Classes, 174

Coherence, 201–202, 204;
  coherence-theorist, 200 (see also
  Blanshard)
Collingwood, R.G., 122
Consciousness, 156–7, 234, 244
Correspondence-theorist, 200 (see also
  Blanshard)
Cratylists, 248
Criticism, 34–36, 53ff., 153, 254
Culler, Jonathan: *Structuralist Poetics*, 55,
  111
Cuvier, Georges, 44

Dasein, 164, 190, 196
Decentering, 239
Deconstruction, 21, 159ff., 149
Descartes, René, 5, 22, 103, 107, 162–165,
  240
Derrida, Jacques, 160–161, 164–165, 239;
  *Glas*, 160; *Of Grammatology*, 160; *Margins
  of Philosophy*; *Spurs*, 160; *Writing and
  Difference*, 160
Dewey, John, 4
Diderot, Denis: *Encyclopédie*, 38
Differance, 161
Difference, 73, 77
Distinctive features, 92ff.
Distributional structure, 98ff.
Donato, Eugenio, 239
Double articulation, 89ff.
Dresden, Sem, 12n
Dualities, 67, 79
Ducrot, Oswald, 14n, 84n
Duhem, Pierre, 142
Dumézil, Georges, 155–157
Durkheim, Emile, 125, 131; *Primitive
  Classification*, 42–43, 117, 122, 130

Eco, Umberto, 159n
Eiffel Tower, 38
Ehrmann, Jacques, 50n, 54, 74n, 148n
Empiricism, 207
Engels, Frederic, 150
Engler, Rudolf, 63
Episteme, 152
Esperanto, 126
Ethnology, 31
Etic/emic, *see* Pike, Kenneth
Evans-Pritchard, E. E., 124
Existentialism, 5, 14, 21, 22, 34, 152, 252

Fallacy of misplaced agency, 154
Fekete, John, 4n
Fermat, Pierre de, 187
Feuerbach, Ludwig, 155, 193

Flaubert, Gustave, 187
Fodor, Jerry: *The Language of Thought*, 112,
  211
Formalism, 14, 25, 105ff., 207; spurious,
  106 (see also Russian Formalism)
Foucault, Michel, xiv, 22, 29, 33, 152–55,
  256; *Archaeology of Knowledge*, 154; *The
  History of Sexuality*, 154: *Madness and Folly
  in the Age of Reason*, 154; *Les Mots et les
  choses* (*The Order of Things*), 32–33, 35,
  150, 154; *L'ordre du discours* ("The
  Discourse on Language"), 253–254
Fourier, Charles, 38
Frege, Gottlob, 191
Freud, Sigmund, 14, 22, 30–31, 41, 152,
  157, 161, 198, 251, 255
Functionalism, 13, 23, 26
Fundamentalism, 122
Furth, Hans, 191

Galileo, 186; *Il Sagiattore*, 241
Geertz, Clifford, 51, 125
Gell-Mann, Murray, 174
Genetic structuralism, 34
Geneva, 85
Geology, 258
Geometries, 229
Geschiere, Lein, 12
Gestalt psychologists, 14, 42, 207
Girard, René, 52, 54
Glossematics, 97
Godel, Robert, 63, 64n, 67n, 72n, 79n, 202
Goodenough, Ward, 50n
Goldmann, Lucien, 34; *Correspondance de
  Martin de Barcos, abbé de Saint-Cyran* 34;
  *Le Dieu caché*, 34
Gross, David, 243
Group theory, 14–15, 17, 26–8

Haldane, Elizabeth, and G. R. T. Ross,
  163
Halle, Louis, 92, 94n, 98
Hammel, E. A., 50n
Hampshire, Stuart, 171
Harris, Zellig, 41, 47, 98–99
Hegel, G.W.F., 4, 160–161, 174, 193, 199,
  238, 245–246, 253, 255, 258; Hegelians,
  239; Hegelian system, 197
Heidegger, Martin, 4, 60, 160–162, 187,
  189–191, 193; *Being and Time*, 64
Heisenberg, Werner, 193, 211
Hempel, C. G., 223
Heraclitus, 86
Herdan, Gustav, 98n
Hermeneutics, 1, 21

History, historicism, 64, 69, 149ff., 153–4, 162ff., 169, 186
Hjelmslev, Louis, 97, 100
Hobbes, Thomas, 124
Horalek, Karel, 13
Homans, George: *Marriage, Authority, and Final Causes*, 140–141
Humanism, 29, 32–33, 120, 169; humanity, 36ff., 186
Humanities, human sciences, 1, 33, 145ff.
Humboldt, Wilhelm von, 61–62, 65, 180, 204
Hume, David, 251
Husserl, Edmund, 4, 160, 169, 216
Hymes, Dell, 131n
Hypograms, 81

Ideology, 35
Idealism, idealist(s), 17, 48, 61, 234
Incest, 128, 133, 135, 137
Instruction, 162, 215ff., 249: endosomatic, 215; exosomatic, 215
Intelligibility, 7, 18, 25, 33, 35, 126, 169ff., 208, 259
Interpretant, 70
Ionian science, 241
Isomorphism, 177ff.

Jakobson, Roman, 11–12, 14, 42, 83, 85, 88, 90–93, 94n, 95, 98, 121, 134, 169, 188, 194, 205; analysis of Baudelaire's "Les Chats", 54, 148; notion of distinctive feature, 92; theory of phonology, 105
Jameson, Fredric: *The Prison-House of Language*, 113
Jaynes, Julian, 157n
Johnson, Samuel, 122
Jones, Ernest, 41

Kant, Immanuel, 4, 16, 18, 28, 45, 50, 103, 104, 177, 195, 239
Karcewski, S., 11
Kierkegaard, Soren, 31, 197, 239; *Concluding Unscientific Postscript*, 238
Kinship, kinship systems, 50, 127ff., 216, 229, 249; (see also Lévi-Strauss and Morgan)
Kolakowski, Leszek, 109
Kroeber, Alfred, 49
Kubler, George, 54
Kuhn, Thomas, 4, 152

Lacan, Jacques, xiv, 22, 30–32, 74, 155, 157–158, 187; *Ecrits*, 30; *Le Séminaire*, 30

Langer, Suzanne, 48, 75
Language, 24, 28, 59ff., 62ff., 130ff., 179ff., 249–50; deep structures of, 62, 102; *langage*, 67; *langue*, 64, 66ff., 80, 85, 94, 101, 110–11, 131, 180, 195, 235; learning, 100ff.; private language, 180; surface structures of, 62, 102 (see also Linguistics)
Law, 123
Leach, Edmund, 5, 41, 222–23, 231
Lekton, 215–16
Lerner, Rita, 243
Levin, Samuel, 54
Lévi-Strauss, Claude, xiv, 6, 11, 18, 21–27, 28n, 33, 36–37, 42, 49–50, 52, 54–55, 59, 62, 65n, 105, 109, 111, 120–123, 124n, 127–130, 133, 136–137, 138n, 139, 140–43, 148, 159, 170–171, 239, 246, 256; *Anthropologie structurale*, 126; categories of primitive mentality, 107; excess of the signifier, 194; mythical structures, 25, 31; *Mythologiques*, 50, 115–19; *La pensée sauvage*, 23, 25, 36; *Race et histoire*, 175; *The Raw and the Cooked*, 115–116, 118–119; *Les Structures élémentaires de la parenté*, 11, 134–135, 141, 175; *Tristes Tropiques*, 239
Lie groups, 15
Linguistic Circle of New York, 11, 42
Linguistic community, 76
Linguistics, 3, 29, 45ff., 121, 198, 258; comparative, 42; mathematical, 97; semiotics-linguistics triad, 113; structural, 41, 42, 45–49 (see also Language)
Literature, 25, 34, 53ff., 66, 147f., 249
Locke, John 13, 103, 124
Lodge, David, 254
Logos, 160
Lotringer, Sylvére, 81n
Lounsbury, Floyd, 50; Crow and Omaha kinship, 50
Lowie, Robert, 49n; *Primitive Society*, 124, 126–127
Loyola, Saint Ignatius, 38

Macaulay, Thomas Babington, 4, 253
Machin, Richard, 254
Macksey, Richard, 239
Madeira, 242
Maitland, F.W.: *Doomsday Book and Beyond*, 124
Magic, 24, 120
Malinowski, Bronislaw, 23, 229

Marcus Aurelius, 240
Maranda, Pierre, 50n
Markov chain, 97
Marr, Nikolai, 109–110
Marriage, 133ff.
Martinet, André, 89, 93
Marx, Karl, 14, 35–36, 109, 193; base and superstructure, 109
Marxism, 3, 22; theory of culture, 110
Matching, 145
Materialism, materialist, 5, 170–171, 234, 237ff., 250ff.
Mates, Benson, 60, 216
Mathematics, mathematical, 14, 16, 47, 107, 172–174, 186, 241
Mathesius, Vilem, 65
Mattering, 170, 183
Maupertuis, Pierre-Louis de, 60
Mauro, Tullio de, 64n
Mauss, Marcel, 43, 130–137; *Essay on the Gift*, 26, 131; *Primitive Classification*, 43, 117, 122, 130; theory of exchange, 132–33
Mead, Margaret, 49
Meaning, 16, 38, 99, 117, 112, 170, 183ff.
Mechanism, 12–13, 169
Medawar, Peter, 7
Mendel, Gregor, 127
Metaphor, 158
Metaphysics, 162, 239
Metonymy, 158
Mind, 23, 28, 30, 31, 48, 61, 107, 125, 197ff., 223, 234
Mind-dependent relations, 236
Mirror stage, 31
Möbius strip, 32
Model(s), 220ff.; explanatory, 227; operational, 224–234, representational, 224–234
Montaigne, Michel de, 122
Montesquieu, Charles-Louis de Secondat, baron de, 122–124, 155
Morality, 25, 162
Morgan, Lewis H., 14, 41, 43–45, 50, 60, 95, 109, 135; kinds of kinship system, 128, 133; study of Iroquois and Ojibwa, 43, 127; *Systems of Consanguinity and Affinity of the Human Family*, 43, 81n, 127
Mounin, Georges, 63, 90, 121
Murdock, George, 50, 53
Music, 76, 115, 120
Mystical: ineffability of, 182
Myth(ology), 25–6, 28, 116ff., 120–121, 249

Nadel, Siegfried, 231
Natural sciences, 1, 147, 229
Nature, 186; and culture, 94
Navaho culture, *see* Reichard
Ndembu, 44, 51
Needham, Rodney: *Structure and Sentiment*, 141
Neogrammarians, 12
Network, 153–154, 159–160, 256
Neurath, Otto, 177
Neurophysiology, 2, 106 (see also Brains)
New Criticism, 14, 41, 46, 53
Newton, Isaac 174; Newtonian gravitation, 143
Nietzsche, Friedrich, 4, 160–161, 216, 258
Norris, Christopher, 254
*Nouveaux philosophes*, 21
Nutini, Hugo, 222–223, 231

Oedipus complex, 141
Ogden, C.K., 64–65, 70, 87, 178; *The Meaning of Meaning*, 64
Ontological, 174
Oppenheim, Paul, 223
Opposition, 69, 79, 86; bilateral, 87; equipollent, 88; graduated, 88; isolated, 88; multilateral, 87; privative, 88; proportional, 87–88; (see also de Saussure)
Optimum complexity, 107, 217
Order of law, 51, 227; of nature, 50, 227
Orthogonal, 68–9, 77
Other, 157–158

Paradigm, 77, 152
Parallel, 68–9
*Parole*, 66ff., 80, 85, 94, 101, 110–11, 195, 235
Parsons, Talcott, 126
Pears, David, and Brian McGuinness, 178
Peirce, Charles Sanders, 14, 41, 44–45, 53, 70, 72, 76, 104, 111, 170
Pedersen, Holger, 60
Perception, 17–18
Phaneroscopy, 45
Phenomenology, 45, 152, 160, 169–170, 183, 194, 237ff., 252
Philosopher's stone, 183
Phonemes, 72, 75, 84–85, 92–93
Phonetics/phonology, 83, 85
Physics, 174
Piaget, Jean, 14, 147
Picard, Raymond: *Nouvelle critique ou nouvelle imposture?*, 35
Pike, Kenneth, notion of "emic and "etic," 48, 84, 90, 97, 99; *Language in Relation to*

*a Unified Theory of Structure of Human Behavior*, 48
Plato (Platonic), 63, 161, 177, 195, 203, 206, 209, 251; *Cratylus*, 59–60, 61–62, 72; *see also* Socrates
Politics, 162
Popper, Karl, 61, 247
Porset, Charles, 60
Positivism (positivist) 1, 3, 12, 46, 48, 55, 96, 252
Poststructuralism, 6, 21, 111, 159, 162, 253ff.
Potlatch, 130, 132
Pouillon, Jean, 25, 37, 50n, 65
Power, 154
Practico-inert, 220, 250
Pragmatics, 70
Prague structuralists, 13, 41, 42, 85, 97
Priscianus, 60
Prodicus, 62
Progress, 186
Propp, Vladimir: *Morphology of the Folktale*, 27
Psychoanalysis, 30, 31; psychoanalytic theory, 224
Psychological, 258
Psychologism, 12
Pushkin, Aleksandr: *Eugene Onegin*, 97
Pythagoras, 199

Quine, W.V., 60
Quintilian, 240
*Quinzaine littéraire*, 22

Racine, Jean, 36, 256
Radcliffe-Brown, A. R., 23, 123n, 124–125, 143, 175, 222
Ramsey, Frank P., 179
Reading (and writing), 187
Reference, 77
Reichard, Gladys: study of Navaho culture, 49, 129
Religion, 155ff. (see also Sacred)
Richards, I.A., 64–65, 70; *The Meaning of Meaning*, 64
Ricoeur, Paul, 142, 170, 239, 246
Riffaterre, Michael, 54, 148
Robey, David, 6n
Rome, 156; Romans, 157
Ross, G. R. T., and Elizabeth Haldane, 163
Rostand, Jean, 242
Rousseau, Jean-Jacques, 123–124, 160
Russell, Bertrand, 171ff., 242; *Introduction to Mathematical Philosophy*, 172, 175, 191

Russian Formalists, 41, 42, 85, 97

Sacred, 52
Sade, Marquis de, 38, 151
Sanskrit, 60
Santayana, George: solipsism of the present moment, 245
Sapir, Edward, 95; Sapir-Whorf hypothesis, 46, 96, 146
Sartre, Jean-Paul, 22, 36, 189, 240, 250; *Critique de la raison dialectique*, 131, 187; doctrine of the prereflective cogito, 120, 125; *see also* practico-inert
de Saussure, Ferdinand, 3, 37, 42, 45–47, 59–60, 62, 64–65, 66–67, 74, 78, 82, 85, 94–95, 97, 99, 101, 110–111, 114, 120, 145, 151, 170–171, 180, 212, 235, 248; concept of difference, 86; concept of opposition, 79, 86; *Cours de linguistique générale*, 11, 63, 73, 75, 80, 83, 92: doctrine of the sign, 70–73, 76, 111, 113; doctrine of system, 44, 83, 184; *see also* langue, parole, sign, signified/signifier
Schefer, Jean-Louis: *Scénographie d'un tableau*, 114–115
Scheffler, Harold, 50
Schneider, David, 50; *Marriage, Authority, and Final Causes*, 140–141, 227, 229
Sciences humaines, 32; *see also* human sciences
Self, 29
Self-fulfilling prophecy, 225
Semantics, 70
Semiotics (semiology), 21, 37, 44, 110–111; semiotics-linguistics triad, 113, 121, 170
Sense, 170
Seung, T. K., 3
Shapiro, Harry, 24
Sign, 44, 70–71, 89, 114ff., 135–136, 183, 248
Signiferous (systems/structures), 1, 83, 99, 110–111, 113, 115, 121, 141, 145, 157, 184, 186, 192, 196, 213
Significant other, 146
Signified/signifier, 31, 67, 71, 72–73, 75, 79, 84, 89, 92, 133, 136, 158, 184, 194; linearity of the signifier, 75
Simon, Herbert, 90
Simplicius, 86
Social Darwinists, 126
Social sciences, 1, 34, 147, 229
Socrates, 60, 62, 78
Sound-image, 71–2

Spencer, Herbert, 50, 128
Spinoza, Benedict de, 161, 171
Stalin, Joseph: *On Marxism and Linguistics*, 109
Starobinski, Jean, 81n
Stent, Gunther, 54
Stoics, 44, 60, 213, 240
Structure: derivation, 5; definition, 13
Subject, subjectivity, 29, 30ff., 151, 237ff., 250ff.
Surrealism, surrealist, 22, 33, 213
Swift, Jonathan, 122
Symbolic forms, *see* Cassirer
Synchronicity, 256
Syntax, 70
System, 12–13, 53, 79, 197ff., 220

Tao of physics, 241
Teilhard de Chardin, Pierre, 12
*Les Temps modernes*, 25
Terence: *The Self-Tormentor*, 37
Texts, 159
Thermodynamics, 24
Thompson, D'Arcy Wentworth: *On Growth and Form*, 15
Todorov, Tzvetan, 84
Totemism, 25
Trigg, George, 243
Trobrianders, 228–229
Troubetzkoy, Prince Nicholas, 11, 42, 49, 53, 84–85, 87, 205; *Grundzüge der Phonologie*, 85–88
Trnka, B., 94
Turner, Victor, 51; *The Ritual Process: Structure and Anti-Structure*, 51
Tzara, Tristan, 192

Unconscious, 31, 33, 95, 122, 156ff., 198, 224, 226–227

Vachek, Josef, 13n, 65n, 94n, 97n
Value, 183
Van Gennep, Arnold, 137
Velasquez, Diego, 35
*Verstehen*, 149

Wahl, Francois, 14, 171
Wallon, Henri: *Les Origines de la pensée chez l'enfant*, 93
Warren, Austin, 53–54
Weber, Max, 149
Weisskopf, Victor, 193
Wellek, Rene, 53–54
Wells, Rulon, 47n, 70n
Wisdom, 199
Whitehead, Alfred North: *Principia Mathematica*, 172
Whorf, Benjamin Lee, 95–96; *see* also Sapir
Wittgenstein, Ludwig, 4, 30, 161, 172, 177ff., 195, 248; *Philosophical Investigations*, 189–191, 193; *Tractatus Logico-Philosophicus* 177–182, 190, 237–238, 240–241
*Word*, 42–3
Writing, 159ff., 187, 239

Xenophanes, 155

Zeno, 202
Zukav, Gary: *The Dancing Wu Li Masters*, 242